The Great Debate

A Handbook for Policy Debate & Public Forum Debate

Jonathan A. Wolfson

LightningBolt Press

Naperville, Illinois

The Great Debate!
A Handbook for Policy Debate & Public Forum Debate.
4th ed. Copyright © 2012 by Jonathan A. Wolfson. All rights reserved.

Contributions from Jonathan Krive.
Teacher's Edition by Jonathan A. Wolfson & Diana Wolfson.

Published by LightningBolt Press, Naperville, Illinois.
Cover design by Barry A. Smith

LightningBolt Press
1481 Applegate Dr.
Suite 101
Naperville, IL 60565

More information is available at The Great Debate Website
www.greatdebate.net

Cataloging in Publication Data
Jonathan A. Wolfson
        The Great Debate. Freedom to Communicate.
        Includes index.
        ISBN 0-9746398-2-6
        1. Debates and debating 2. Persuasion (Rhetoric) 3. Public Speaking
        4. Argument

Preface

"Knowledge is of no value unless you put it into practice"
-Heber J. Grant-

You have embarked on a journey into the world of debate. This handbook should be treated as one guide on your path to becoming a great debater. The information in this book is based on experience as both a competitor and coach for a number of years. However, this book is by no means an absolute authority on debate nor should it be treated as such. Debate theory is only theory. There is no complete source explaining what is allowed in debate because debate theory is always evolving.

This book will give you an overview of debate. It provides debate essentials, the information you need to debate in both public forum debate and policy debate, in an easy to read handbook. The Great Debate will give you the basics of debate and offer you solid information to build upon as you grow as a debater. It should not be your sole source of debate knowledge. Use it as a Blue Angels pilot uses his basic flight training – as a launch pad into the fun and excitement of great debate rounds.

Finally, many of the examples used in this book are based on arguments I have heard or read over my years coaching debate. I am not providing them to either support or oppose them, but simply to give the reader an opportunity to see the concepts applied in a practical argument. If you disagree with my example, think critically about the example and do not hesitate to argue with it. Please enjoy this handbook.

Jw

Table of Contents

Introduction: How to Read This Book

*"Yet when genuine debate is lacking, freedom of speech
does not work as it is meant to work"*
-Walter Lippmann-

Textbooks will claim to have the answers no matter what question you might have. Well, every textbook other than *The Great Debate!* This book does not contain everything, but will put you well on your way to becoming a highly proficient debater in both public forum debate and policy debate. Regardless of the type of debate you are planning to pursue, read Contention 1. It covers the basics of debate as an academic exercise including such topics as the components of good arguments and how to support your arguments with evidence. The materials in Contention 1 will serve any competitive debater whether he is learning policy debate, public forum debate, Lincoln-Douglas debate, parliamentary debate, student congress, or model United Nations. Contention 1 discusses some specific note-taking techniques, describes ballots judges use to score debates, and provides tips on preparing to compete in a tournament.

Contentions 2 and 3 delve into the nuances of public forum debate (Contention 2) and policy debate (Contention 3). The unique features of those styles are examined as well as the specific rules, terminology, and techniques of both public forum and policy debate. The book can certainly be read from cover-to-cover, but special attention should be paid to the chapters focused on your chosen debate style.

The chart below offers a suggested order to read the chapters depending on your debate style. *The Great Debate Teacher's Edition* contains a fuller explanation including page-by-page reading assignments as well as a suggested syllabus to coordinate the materials in Contention 1 and the specific Contention for your debate style to go along with the video lectures available on the Great Debate website (www.greatdebate.net).

In addition, key terms are defined in the glossary on page 161.The first time a key term is used it appears in bold type. Look for these bolded terms to ensure you fully understand the debate terminology.

Public Forum Debate	Policy Debate	Other Debate Styles
Observations: 1-2; 13-14; 3-8; 15-17; 9-12	Observations 1-2; 18-19; 3-8; 20-26; 9-12	Observations 1-2; 13; 3-9; 26; 17; 9-12

Figure 1: Suggested Reading Order by Debate Style

Contention 1: Introduction to Debate

Observation 1: What is Debate?

"After last night's debate, the reputation of
Messieurs Lincoln and Douglas is secure"
-Edward R. Murrow-

When you hear the word "**debate**," what comes to mind? Do you think about Presidential candidates standing behind lecterns with a famous newscaster asking questions and the candidates replying? Do you think of a television news program where spokespersons on different sides of a contentious public policy discussion are asked to present their positions and contrast them with the other side? Do you think about a student council meeting where the students disagree about what color to decorate the hall for the next big dance? All of these thoughts are correct. Debate is a type of conversation, formal or informal, where people of different opinions express their ideas in an attempt to have their ideas win the day. In other words, debate is the practice of comparing and contrasting ideas.

The goal of debate is to compare and contrast ideas in order to search for the truth, or the best answer to the question being discussed. What kinds of ideas can you debate about? Literally any idea you can think of may be debated. So long as the idea you are thinking is not a universally-agreed-upon fact, you can debate it. You can debate the best method to train a dog, the most valuable athlete, the best author, the best restaurant, or the most difficult subject. If you find someone who disagrees with you and supports her disagreement with reasons, you have a debate!

At this point it is important to take a closer look at what is actually being debated: ideas. A debate **round** is not about trying to identify which person debating is smarter, or which person is more popular. Instead, the debate is focused on the ideas themselves. When one debater attacks the ideas another debater presents, he is not attacking his opponent, but is contrasting his ideas with hers. This is important because every debate will come down to numerous arguments leveled against the ideas the debaters present in the round, but in the next round it is quite possible those same debaters will stand up and argue for the opposite side of the topic. Because every argument is centered on the ideas being debated, not the people who are making the arguments, everyone can walk out of the debate round knowing that while the ideas were subject to scrutiny, the people who scrutinized those ideas were never the subject of attack.

A. Why Debate?

Debate offers an excellent avenue to learn public speaking, research, writing, critical thinking, and argumentation. Debate also can be a competitive outlet for many students who wish to pursue it. Most debate competitions require oral arguments and so any debater will learn to present ideas through the spoken word. Only a small portion of any society feel adequate standing before an audience and delivering a speech, so debaters who place themselves in that small group prepare themselves to be tomorrow's leaders. A formal debate requires students to have knowledge of a topic prior to beginning the debate. Such knowledge requires research of the major thinkers and writers who have already considered the topic area. Because the world is so rapidly changing, debaters will have to learn to keep up with current events as well as the goings on around the globe to ensure they make timely and relevant arguments.

While impromptu and extemporaneous speaking are certainly important aspects of a debate, many arguments are prepared and written prior to the debate round. Writing and re-writing the arguments, and working with other debaters to make those arguments concise while still persuasive will enhance the writing skills of any debater. No debate is complete without an opponent presenting a contrasting idea. The many contrasting ideas teach debaters to think critically about both opposing arguments and the ideas discussed within the research literature. Throughout the research and writing process the debater also develops a keen eye for logical fallacies and unsupported arguments both in research and in the real world. Finally, a debater will learn the building blocks of an argument as well as how to scrutinize and refute arguments. Learning to present strong arguments will pay off not only in the debate round, but also throughout the debater's life.

B. Pros and Cons

In the real world, people make decision by weighing the costs and benefits of the decision. If you want your parents to purchase Frosted Flakes instead of Corn Flakes, you might try to think about the positive and negative arguments for both types of cereals before you present your request. If your parents are upset that you neglect to eat breakfast each morning, the better taste of Frosted Flakes might be an argument in its favor. The higher costs of dental bills when your teeth decay from the added sugar would be an argument against the Frosted Flakes. The lower cost of the Corn Flakes (without sugar) might weigh in favor of the Corn Flakes, but their bland taste might discourage you from eating breakfast at all and make you less productive in your first few classes of the day.

Decisions small and large are often made based on comparisons of the pros and cons of alternative options. However, there are many times that these calculations are taking place in our minds but are not actually analyzed. Pizza or hamburgers, ice cream or cake, we may not even realize our minds are making comparisons of the pros and cons to help us make these decisions. Debate offers a more formal mechanism for actually comparing and contrasting the costs and benefits of a decision not only for you as an individual, but also for a group.

You can debate anything with anyone. All you need to do is select a topic, pick sides, and list all the pros for your side and cons for your opponent's side. Your opponent will list the pros for her side and the cons for your side. When you add up the pros and cons for both sides, compare them, and find out which side has more pros and fewer cons, you have come to a conclusion about the true answer, or at least the best answer you can reach with the information you already have. Armed with the knowledge that debate is really about deciding which answer is best based on the pros and cons, we can begin to look at a formal structure for this process.

C. How Does Debate Work?

The **resolution** is the focus of every debate round. It tells us what to expect to hear about and what debaters should talk about during the debate. The resolution is the topic of the debate and provides some predictability to everyone in the round. If the resolution says to merge the Central Intelligence Agency (CIA) and National Security Agency (NSA), every conversation in the round will be centered on those two intelligence agencies and whether or not it is a good idea to merge them.

Debate would not be fun if everyone agreed. To ensure disagreement, there are always two sides to a debate. One side is required to argue in favor of the resolution. The other side argues against the resolution. Depending on the style of debate, these sides have different names. In policy debate and Lincoln-Douglas debate, the **affirmative** side or **team** argues for the resolution while the **negative** side or team argues against it. In public forum debate, the **pro** team argues for the resolution while the **con** team argues against it. Finally, in parliamentary debate the *government* team argues for the resolution while the *opposition* team argues against it. No matter the names of the teams, the key to remember is that one team is required to argue in favor of adopting the resolution while the other team argues against adopting the resolution.

Debate rounds consist of one side will making an argument, the other side replying to the argument and making its own new argument, and the first side trying to answer side two's response and reply to side two's arguments. This pattern continues throughout the round for a specific amount of time. Some debate rounds will permit a question and answer period. Other debate rounds will alter the order in which the teams present their arguments. At the end of the round, both sides will attempt to show how weighing the pros and cons should result in their side being declared victorious by a vote to either uphold or reject the resolution.

Formal debate competitions divide a debate round into timed portions in which each side receives fixed amounts of speaking time to present arguments. Generally, each team receives the same amount of speaking time. Depending on the competition, there may be strict rules for when certain types of arguments may be made, whether a debater will speak sitting or standing, how arguments must be structured, or what decorum the speakers and the audience must follow. The formal debate structure provides a context in which the topic may be examined by both sides and offers specific opportunities for the debaters to receive feedback on their argument selection, structure, and their overall persuasiveness.

Observation 2: Resolutions and Competitions

"Free and fair discussion will ever be found the firmest friend to truth"
-George Campbell-

The resolution is the focus of the debate round. Depending on the style of debate, the resolutions may vary. Both the different resolution types and the different debate competitions provide diverse educational opportunities for debaters. Most debate formats employ one resolution style, but some formats use many different types of resolutions. This chapter discusses both resolution types and the competition formats.

A. Types of Resolutions

Competitive debates usually focus on three different resolution styles. There are resolutions of fact, resolutions of value, and resolutions of policy. Most high school debate leagues use value resolutions for Lincoln-Douglas debate and policy resolutions for team policy debate. Public forum debate typically employs fact and policy resolutions which change throughout the competition season.

1. Resolutions of Fact

Resolutions of fact call into question some reality. For example, such a resolution might be "Resolved: The costs of attending college outweigh the benefits." Each side debates the resolution's accuracy or the empirical truth of the statement. By offering **evidence** on each side and refuting the support for an opponent's arguments, the debater of a fact resolution tries to promote the search for truth. Rather than arguing what ought to be done or examining a hierarchy of philosophies, resolutions of fact ask the debater to present proof for one position and to test that evidence with the testimony of the other side. While fact debates may certainly involve normative discussions (discussions about what "ought" to be, whether that is an argument about if freedom is more important than security – a value debate – or about the pros and cons of policies that try to make college more affordable – a policy debate – are all normative in nature), the central question will be descriptive, what position is more accurate right now.

2. Resolutions of Value

Resolutions of value typically question the hierarchy of ideals without the application of these beliefs to actual policy. Value debate merely compares conflicting values or requires a debater to rank a particular value above all other values. Comparative resolutions examine ideas and compare their worth such as: "Human rights ought to be valued over national sovereignty" or "Private property out to be valued over public safety." Absolute resolutions inspect a particular general principle and require one team to prove that it ought to be true most of the time.

All value resolutions call into question the underlying beliefs of a society and consider what "ought" to be done (they are normative). The ramifications of a philosophical viewpoint on the world around us are examined instead of the particular pros and cons of a particular policy or social structure. Value resolutions do not require any discussion of the feasibility of society actually making one value most important, but instead focus on whether that value should or should not influence society. Value debate reduces the debate to the core issues involved in decision making. The value debater presents specific examples (contentions) of a philosophy which results in positive or negative consequences to show the worth of such a value. For example, the team supporting the comparative resolution valuing human rights over national sovereignty might contend that because human life is pre-political (people existed before governments) the first obligation of society is to respect life even if this respect undermines political boundaries.

3. Resolutions of Policy

Policy resolutions ask the debater to change some law or to propose a specific action by the government. Typical policy resolutions include, "Resolved: That the United States should increase assistance to persons living below the poverty line," and "Resolved: That gun control laws ought to be significantly changed." By calling for a change in government action, policy resolutions bring government, law, and the will of the people into question. Questions regarding the workability of a new **plan**, the current problems, the benefits of changing, or the negative consequences of modifications are typical arguments heard in a policy debate round. Both teams research extensively to gain an understanding of the numerous facets involved in the policy being discussed. This prepares them to argue either side of the resolution in a debate round. Policy resolutions call for actions to sustain change. The assumption is that changing the **status quo** will have real-life effects. Many debaters find this practical realm to give the debate more depth.

B. Debate Styles

There are numerous debate styles, each with unique features offering different educational opportunities for debaters. There are four main types of debate which give all sides roughly equal time to make their arguments and where the **judge** evaluates only the words spoken in the round: Policy, Lincoln-Douglas, Public Forum, and Parliamentary.[1] Policy, Public Forum, and Parliamentary debate are team debate with two members; Lincoln-Douglas debate is one-on-one. Each form of debate has its own unique aspects which help debaters develop different skills. Well-rounded debaters seek to become skilled in each form. Let's look at each style of debate in depth.

1. Policy Debate

Policy debate takes many forms. In competitive **forensics leagues**, policy debate is usually team debate with two debaters per team. Some leagues have one-on-one (Lincoln-Douglas) policy debates, but in common **forensics** parlance, "policy debate" means team policy debate. In policy debate each team has four speeches (two per debater) and two **cross-examinations** of the other team. Most policy debate leagues choose one policy resolution for the entire season. Debaters research the topic extensively and prepare arguments to present in the round. Not only is policy debate one of the most prevalent forensics activities, but it is also one of the oldest. The National Forensics League (NFL) began with policy debate for high school students and continues to offer it to students along with other debate styles including speech events.[2]

---

[1] Student Congress and Model United Nations are other forms of forensics competition which include debate components. Because these formats attempt to model after larger governing bodies, there are numerous unique facets of these competitions beyond the scope of this text.

[2] The National Debate Tournament (NDT) for college students has been contested since 1947 using policy debate topics and the longest-running university debate program, Northwestern University, has been debating policy resolutions since 1855.

2. Lincoln-Douglas Debate

Lincoln-Douglas debate (LD) is a one-on-one debate style named after the famous 19th century debates between Abraham Lincoln and Stephen Douglas. LD is typically more focused on philosophical arguments, analysis, and speaking than policy debate. While policy debate still strengthens these skills, research presentation is a greater priority in policy debate. LD uses resolutions of either policy or value depending on the league. Some leagues offer an LD style similar to policy debate with only one debater per side; others use a policy resolution with some adjustments in rules, regulations, and styles. The National Forensics Association (NFA) offers LD policy debate for college students. This style of policy debate is a communication-centered activity which offers policy at the college level spoken at slightly more audience-friendly speeds.[3]

Most high school leagues use a value resolution for LD, although some high school **tournaments** have policy LD. When a value resolution is used, many leagues change resolutions throughout the year to allow debaters to develop their knowledge of numerous values and applications rather than focusing on only one for an entire season. The value format allows debaters opportunities to examine underlying philosophies rather than focusing on the inner workings of policy. Value LD features a contrast between values, not a clash of policy alternatives. While policy may be discussed in a value debate, victory in a value debate is gained by demonstrating the strength of a debater's worldview or philosophy rather than the successful outcome of some policy change. Value LD is another option for students wishing to debate regardless of the size of their **clubs** or teams.

3. Public Forum Debate

Public Forum debate attempts to blend features of policy, value, and parliamentary debate in an audience-friendly debate round. Debaters are not permitted to speak extremely fast, there is less reliance on evidence than policy and LD, and the rounds last only 45 minutes. The two teams argue either in favor of the resolution ("Pro" team) or against it ("Con" team). Resolutions typically change each month to encourage debaters to gain broad knowledge about the world around them. Public forum employs short speeches (4 minutes in length or less) and a **crossfire** period in which both teams ask each other questions in turn. Public forum debaters are required to focus on making their arguments compelling to any lay audience, rather than an audience of debate experts (for more information on the public forum round, see page 75).

The skills public forum develops are similar to those gained in the other debate styles, but public forum requires agility in employing the various styles to the same debate round. Public forum debaters do not present a "plan" to change policy, but instead argue that a particular set of policies or ideas are better than others by presenting contentions. Public forum is a growing debate style at the high school level in part because the resources needed to build a public forum program are less than those needed for other debate forms. See page 71 for further discussion of public forum debate.

4. Parliamentary Debate

Imported from England and modeled after the English Parliament, parliamentary debate is a growing debate form at the junior high and high school levels, and remains quite popular at the collegiate level. This interactive form of debate has two teams of competitors (two per side) who argue as the "government" and the "opposition" rather than affirmative and negative. Parliamentary debate is typically extemporaneous debate. A resolution is announced

---

[3] In contrast, collegiate team policy debate is often delivered at very fast reading speed.

fifteen minutes before the round and teams utilize those fifteen minutes to prepare their arguments and/or cases. During the round, each team gives three speeches and all debaters may ask questions, called points of information during an opposing speaker's speeches. There is no preparation time during the round so the round moves rapidly.

Parliamentary debate resolutions are unique for a variety of reasons. First, the resolutions change every round. Without a set resolution, debaters rely on their knowledge of current events, literature, history, philosophy, social science, and other academic realms to build arguments. Second, outside evidence is generally not allowed. While common knowledge and some specific information may infiltrate the round, the round is focused on argumentation rather than researched evidence. Third, the resolutions may be fact, value, or policy in nature. Resolutions can be worded specifically (This House would cut taxes for America); vaguely, (This House values punishment); or even abstractly, (This House would visit an enchanted island). The government then defines the terms, allowing debaters to find interesting and creative interpretations of the resolution. Finally, parliamentary debate encourages audience participation. Instead of sitting and listening to every argument made, the audience may jeer by saying "For shame!"; offer support by saying "Here, here!"; or applaud by banging the table with their hands during the round. Because the audience is permitted to participate in the round, the entire room becomes lively.

Parliamentary debate is growing in popularity in the United States. Debaters enjoy the opportunity to practice debate skills without all the research required of other debate forms. The National Parliamentary Debate Association (NPDA) and the American Parliamentary Debate Association (APDA) are the two main governing bodies for collegiate parliamentary debate in the United States. Both leagues offer tournaments across the country and national tournaments at the end of the year. Most high school leagues have not fully adopted parliamentary debate, but there are some who have decided to give it a try. Unless you are in a league offering parliamentary debate in high school, this debate style is something to look forward to as you enter college competition. Because it emphasizes impromptu argument more than research skills, parliamentary debate may not be as beneficial an academic tool for the high school student as policy debate, LD, and public forum debate. When a debater enters college, research time may be more limited. So parliamentary debate can offer the opportunity to continue honing debate skills without the time commitment other debate styles require.

This book focuses on team policy debate and public forum debate. If you are interested in applying the skills from this book to other debate styles, the remaining chapters in Contention 1: Introduction to Debate offer the most information to cross-apply to other debate styles. The materials in Contention 2: Introduction to Public Forum Debate are useful in considering how to persuade any audience regardless of whether the context is a debate round or any public setting. Finally, our website, www.greatdebate.net, offers free videos and training materials for Lincoln-Douglas value debate if you are interested in learning more about LD.

Observation 3: Argument Presentation & Structure

"A man finds joy in giving an apt reply - and how good is a timely word"
-King Solomon-

Debate rounds are full of arguments raised by one side, attacked by the other side, and then rebuilt by the original proponent. These arguments go back and forth until one side concedes or time ends. A complete argument entails more than a simple statement of a particular position and should be able to withstand scrutiny. However, even strong arguments can and should be scrutinized. The ability to respond to arguments presented by your opponent is important to the success of your team. Responding to the opponent's arguments, both the arguments they present to support their side and those used to respond to your team's arguments, is called "**refutation**." Refutation points out the inherent flaws of the opposing team's argument while simultaneously turning the argument into a winning issue for your team. Without refutation, debates are simply dueling speeches lacking **clash**. Refutation allows the debate round to delve deep into arguments while simultaneously developing **voting issues** for the judge.

A. What is an Argument?

An argument is a statement backed up with support for the audience to accept the statement and justify adopting the statement for themselves. An argument is more than a simple assertion. For example, the statement "Dogs are better pets than cats" is not, of itself, an argument, but is instead a position. However, "The best reason to have a pet is your own happiness. So dogs are better pets than cats because dogs, unlike cats, want to make their masters happy." is an argument.

We hear statements every day. Whether they are statements made by our parents, siblings, friends, or neighbors; statements we read or hear in the media; or statements we read in a textbook, we are exposed to millions of assertions and declarations each day. In general, we decide, often subconsciously, whether we are willing to accept an assertion as true by applying three tests. First, does the statement correspond with our experience? Second, does the statement have the support of someone whose expertise gives them special credibility on the topic of the statement? Third, does the statement come from someone we particularly trust to be honest and discriminating? If we answer "yes" to each question, we are very likely to accept the assertion. If we cannot answer yes to any of these questions, we are unlikely to accept it. Debaters who use complete arguments guide their audience to answer yes to one or more of these questions. This increases the likelihood your audience will believe the arguments.

A complete argument has three components: a statement of possible truth, support for the statement, and an explanation of why the audience should care about this statement in the first place. In debate, these three elements have special names: "Claim," "Warrant," and "**Impact**."

A *claim* is the statement a debater wants the audience to believe: "Dogs are better pets than cats." Claims tell the audience the exact conclusion you want them to adopt. But the claim, all by itself, does little more than identify what position you are taking. If you stand up and simply say dogs are better pets than cats, you have not made an argument, but simply stated your personal opinion and preference of dogs rather than cats. To enhance your opinion you need support.

The *warrant* tells the audience the claim is meritorious because someone other than speaker agrees with the statement. Consider, "Dogs are better pets than cats. A study by the American Academy of Veterinarians found that two out of three veterinarians chose dogs as their preferred pet rather than cats." The audience is no longer being asked to take your assertion that dogs are preferable on face value. Now you have scientific evidence that experts—veterinarians no less—consider pet dogs preferable to pet cats. At this point the argument could end, but the persuasive power of the argument is severely lacking. Just because you are a nice person, and just because veterinarians believe dogs make better pets than cats, the members of your audience have not yet been persuaded that they should agree with your sentiment. To wrap up your persuasive argument, you need to give your audience ownership of the claim.

An often overlooked, but vital conclusion to every complete argument is the **impact**. The impact tells your audience why they should care about the argument being made. Every good argument not only tells the listener what the arguer thinks (dogs are better than cats), and backs the assertion up with evidence (veterinarians prefer dogs), but good arguments also personalize the claim to make the audience want to adopt the position. After you make a claim and provide a warrant, ask "so what?" or "why does this matter to me?" The answers are your impacts. For example, "Dogs are better pets than cats. A study by the American Academy of Veterinarians found that two out of three veterinarians chose dogs as their preferred pet rather than cats. Therefore, by selecting a dog you are more likely to be a satisfied pet owner who enjoys raising your pet." Now the audience may adopt your position not just because they like you and not even because they think veterinarians are good judges of quality pets, but also because they can identify this decision with their own satisfaction and happiness.[4]

Impacts do not have to be personal to the listener to be effective, but they must explain the gravity of the argument. For example, if you were trying to promote the distribution of mosquito nets you might say: "Mosquito netting is needed to protect against malaria. According to the World Health Organization, mosquito netting reduces the risk of contracting malaria by a factor of ten to twenty. Thus, 500,000 lives could be saved in Africa each year if mosquito bed nets were provided to African families."[5] While most audiences are unlikely to contract malaria, the impact statement expresses the importance of the claim. An impact can be just as effective in persuading your audience to adopt your claim by answering the "so what" question by identifying why the argument matters to the world around them. Impacts are discussed further in Section B4 below.

Complete arguments are the only arguments debaters should use. If a debater only asserts a claim, there is no reason the audience should listen. A claim with supporting evidence is persuasive, but lacks any compelling justification for the audience to believe the statement to be true. A claim supported by credible evidence with a clear explanation of the importance of the assertion forms the complete argument and will provide the audience sufficient justification to accept the claim itself as true. Each debater should practice making complete arguments and identifying arguments which lack any of these vital components.

---

[4] Having grown up with both dogs and cats, and being the current owner of both, I take no position on the preferable pet – both certainly have pros and cons and I leave it up to the reader to come to her own conclusions regarding which pet is better.

[5] Malaria indeed infects millions around the world and the use of bed nets can significantly increase the chance of an entire family's ability to prevent infection and untimely death.

B. Refutation

While refutation can take many forms, a basic structure should include at least four points. Depending upon your style and what speech you are giving in the debate, you may need to add or subtract from the following four points. However, most arguments should consist of a **signpost** or tag line, your argument, comparison of your argument to your opponent's argument, and finally, a conclusion showing how your argument's superiority impacts the round (*I said*, *they said*, compare, and impact). Using these four points to present your argument adds clarity for the judge. Such clarity and ease of understanding are vital to any debate round.

1. Point 1: State Your Opponent's Argument

Mentioning your opponent's argument may seem a bit absurd, after all, why give the other team free air time? By briefly re-stating your opponent's argument, you tell your judge what argument you will be addressing. This "signposting" or "tagging" is crucial to the organization of your refutation in the round. You want your judge to make a note of what you say on the flow (see page 47), but if the judge does not know what argument you are addressing, then your refutation is often forgotten. Signposting is essential to help judges follow arguments in the round.

The length of this point may vary depending on which speech you are refuting. For the first negative **constructive** (see page 105), you should merely state which point you will be addressing (i.e. harm 1, mandate 1, **advantage** 3, etc.). However, if you are the second speaker for your team you should reiterate the point your partner made in his first speech. Then, address the response made by the other team so that the judge knows which response you are addressing. A good debate team will have several responses to each opposing point; therefore, you will have to respond to multiple refutations of your **case** and other arguments.

For example, during debates about immigration policy, some teams argued that the Immigration and Naturalization Service (INS) ought to be reformed and their duties divided among four agencies. Negative teams argued that this would fragment a service which needed to be able to share information. Signposting of the argument looked something like this: (*I said*) "We (the affirmative team) said that the INS needed to be divided to more effectively process visas." (*They said*) "The negative team said dividing the INS would fragment the service and its vital shared information." Depending on what speech you are presenting in the debate round, the length of your signposting may vary, but it should always be brief and ensure everyone is on the same page.

2. Point 2: State Your Argument

The need for this point is obvious; here you state your argument. First you should give a short tag line or a one-sentence summary of your argument so that the judge will have a short phrase to write down on the flow. Stating your argument would look similar to this continuation from the INS example of signposting: (*I say*) "However, I say that information will still be shared and better utilized because the different agencies will be able to perfect their particular responsibilities and better process information they have." After giving your summary, you can expound and explain the details of your argument by making a complete argument as previously discussed.

3. Point 3: Compare The Arguments

When the judge is weighing two competing arguments, there must be something to show which argument is superior. This point gives the judge a reason to accept your argument as better than your opponent's. You can prove your argument is superior by showing how your argument is supported by better logic and reasoning, or by showing that your opponent's argument is based on faulty logic or a logical **fallacy**. Another way to prove superiority is evidence. By quoting qualified sources, you can add credibility to your assertion and show that your argument has better proof than your opponent's. For example, in the INS response, after saying that information-sharing will improve, you can add: "the evidence supports this fact. According to Professor Jones, a restructured INS will be better equipped to achieve its mission without sacrificing information sharing." On the other hand, you can also show how the evidence your opponent used to support his argument is not credible, insufficient, or unqualified. For a fuller discussion of evidence, see page 31.

4. Point 4: State the Impact

This last point is the most important in this structure. If the judge does not know what impact your argument has, then he has no reason to take your argument into account. Just as any complete argument must answer the "so what" question, every refutation must also answer this question. You must show how your argument impacts the round. An impact point should have two facets: impact inside the round and impact on the round. Impact inside the round shows how your argument impacts the hypothetical world that you are dealing with in the debate round. Impact on the round states what point you have won and how winning that point should win the judge's decision. For example: "Because the restructured INS will not only be more efficient in processing visas and will not lose its ability to communicate internally to identify potential criminals, the backlog of immigration applications will be diminished and the nation will be safer. Therefore, the affirmative's plan to restructure the INS is warranted." The impact shows that the affirmative team's case is worth considering both because the argument against it was refuted, but also because it creates concrete benefits for the real world.

Another example: Your claim is that the affirmative team's plan, by abolishing all agricultural subsidies, would cause massive starvation in America. Your impact inside the round would be that countless people would die. Your impact on the round would be a huge **disadvantage** that far outweighs any potential advantages. Your impact on the round should be a voting issue for the judge to decide which team should win. While good arguments may

> During the OJ Simpson trial, attorney Johnny Cochran made the now famous argument: "If the glove does not fit, you must acquit." The argument made impacts both in trial and on the case. His impact in the trial was the glove. The fact was that the glove did not fit. However, this impact was not important if it did not alter the decision at the conclusion of the case. The impact on the case was the link to the vote. Telling the jurors that they "must acquit" Mr. Simpson impacted the argument on the final decision.

Figure 2: Example of Impact In and On Round

neglect impacting back to the **ballot**, impacts make the decision much easier for the judge by helping him prefer your argument at the end of the round when he votes. Both types of impact are used in policy debate disadvantages (see page 133). Good impacts will have the ability to paralyze your opponent's argument by giving the judge a compelling reason to accept your argument. The importance of impacts in refutation is immeasurable.

5. Example of Four-Point Refutation

During income tax policy debates, some teams argued that big government was a direct consequence of the income tax and thus getting rid of big government was a justification for removing the income tax. A full refutation could look something like this: "The affirmative claims big government is a negative result of the current income tax." (stating the opponent's argument) "However, we claim government actually protects those otherwise harmed by uncaring individuals." (state your argument) "According to Arthur Schlesinger Jr. on May 21st 1995, 'Democratic capitalism has not survived and prospered by loyalty to the gospel of laissez-faire and the creed of devil-take-the-hindmost. ... Democratic capitalism has triumphed because of the long campaign mounted by reformers, Franklin Roosevelt foremost among them, to use the national government to humanize the industrial order, to cushion the operations of the economic system, to strengthen the bargaining position of workers and farmers and consumers, to regulate wages and hours, the quality of products and the sale of securities, to insure against recurrent depression by built-in economic stabilizers; above all, to combine individual opportunity with social responsibility...'" (my argument is superior - supported by evidence) "Therefore, a plan which eliminates government, even big government, will harm the unprotected. To protect the helpless, we must maintain the status quo and reject the affirmative's plan." (impacts both in and on the round).

Refutation is important to your success as a debater. If you have wonderful points to support your own arguments, but neglect to respond to the arguments made in contrast, you will find yourself with very little ground on which to claim victory. However, by using refutation you will be able to overcome the arguments against your case while adding strong reasons for the judge to vote for your case. Learning four-point refutation and practicing its application in a debate is important to your success as a debater. This refutation strategy allows you to rebut arguments in a clear, concise, and compelling manner. Continue developing these skills to become a debater who promotes clash and is able to convince the judge of your position.

Observation 4: General Logic and Reasoning

"Rhetoric: a universal art of winning the mind by arguments..."
-Plato-

Austin J. Freeley and David L. Steinberg in their book *Argumentation and Debate*, define *reasoning*: "the process of inferring conclusions from premises." Debaters must be able to formulate and articulate conclusions based on sound premises. Premises must be well thought out in order to support the contention made. Logic and reasoning comprise the foundation upon which a debater may build arguments. The structure of arguments discussed in the previous chapter relies on strong reasoning to support the assertions and make the entire argument persuasive.

This chapter covers the general categories of reasoning. The next chapter discusses specific reasoning techniques as well as their perversion in the form of fallacies. Some general forms of reasoning include *deductive reasoning, inductive reasoning,* and *Aristotle's Syllogism.* A common model of argument is *Toulmin's Model of Argument.* These four reasoning types comprise the general foundation for argumentation in the debate round.

A. Deductive Reasoning

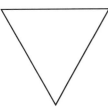 Deductive reasoning proves that a conclusion is true by moving from a general statement to a more specific conclusion. Visually, deductive reasoning is downward-pointing triangle. This category of reasoning argues from broad, overarching premises down to a very specific inference. For example, an argument which points out that current trade policy promotes poverty in South Africa using deductive reasoning could follow a structure such as: *Lack of trade maintains poverty in any nation. America refuses to trade with Africa. The lack of trade by the United States with African nations fosters the continual state of poverty on the African continent. South Africa is extremely dependent on imports and exports, and is directly affected by US trade policies. The US has many trade restrictions with African nations. Without trade, South Africans cannot escape poverty. Therefore the trade restrictions imposed by the US cause poverty in South Africa.* This argument shows a logical flow of ideas that follow a broad premise to a focused contention. The use of deductive reasoning allows the debater to lead the audience from a general statement to a specific conclusion.

B. Inductive Reasoning

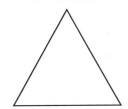 Inductive reasoning shows that a conclusion is true by moving from a specific statement to a general conclusion. Visually, inductive reasoning is an upward-pointing triangle with a wide base. This category of reasoning argues from a specific premise down to a very broad conclusion. The beauty of inductive reasoning is its ability to take an argument which only applies to a specific point and broaden its horizons to encompass numerous other points. When debating tax policy, some debaters argue that the government chronically wastes money. Many use inductive reasoning similar to the following example: *The government spends hundreds of dollars on toilet seat covers for military projects. The government tacks on "pork" amendments to appropriations bills. Pork projects are favors given to other Congresspersons. Pork projects increase the costs of the federal government. Rather than vote against these bills, Congress adds pork to even more bills. Government spends more money than is necessary on many bills. Therefore, the government wastes taxpayer money.* While one may not agree with this argument, the

general conclusion that the government wastes tax money is dependent on the initial fact that tax dollars are wasted in one particular government-funded project. Moving from one specific instance to a broad general statement regarding the system permits the debater to make this conclusion. While inductive reasoning cannot be applied in all situations in a debate, the ability to argue inductively is important in order to persuade the judge of a broad argument.

C. Aristotle's Syllogism

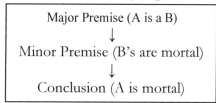

Figure 3: Syllogism

One of the oldest structures for argumentation is Aristotle's Syllogism. Aristotle, one of history's earliest writers about argumentation, believed that a syllogism was a very effective form of argument. It follows a format similar to deductive reasoning, but has only three points. The theory of the syllogism is that if the first two statements are true, the conclusion must also be true.

The statements in a syllogism are called premises. A syllogism consists of a *Major premise*, a *Minor premise*, and a *Conclusion.*

The major premise is a broad statement which can be all encompassing. The minor premise ties the conclusion into the major premise. The conclusion completes the argument. The important factor to note with a syllogism is that each premise is vital to the argument's success. If one agrees with both premises, she will have to agree with the conclusion. However, if either premise is false, the conclusion is not proven. Keeping this in mind will help you effectively use syllogisms.

The syllogism is best demonstrated in the example Aristotle himself used to demonstrate it (though slightly modified as you will see). Major Premise: "All men are mortal." Minor premise: "Jonathan is a man." Conclusion: "Therefore, Jonathan is mortal." There is no question regarding the major premise. The fact is that all people are mortal. The second statement, the minor premise, is also something all would agree with. I am a human (although my parents did tell a story about wolves bringing me to them in the forest one dark and stormy night…). Because the audience agrees with both the major and minor premises, they are obliged to concede to the conclusion. If Jonathan is a man and all men are mortal, then Jonathan must be mortal! Because there is no denying a proper syllogism's conclusion, this type of argument is especially valuable in debate.

Learning to develop and refute a syllogism is important to your proficiency in debate. While the syllogism might often be built simply using deductive reasoning, the importance of the syllogism in formulating arguments cannot be overly stressed. By training yourself to identify the parts of the syllogism, you can become a much stronger debater because the syllogism is highly persuasive and a good way to make the convincing arguments necessary to win the judge's vote!

D. Toulmin's Model of Argument

The Toulmin Model of argument is a helpful method of analyzing argumentation. Toulmin's model is visually represented as a "T" with each end of the T forming the necessary pieces of an argument. The three main pieces, also called the "primary triad" have sub-points which form the "secondary triad." Each triad allows the argument to be dissected and diagramed to examine whether or not the argument is effective. Toulmin's model begins with the primary triad. This triad includes the three basic parts of the argument: *claim, grounds,* and *warrant.*

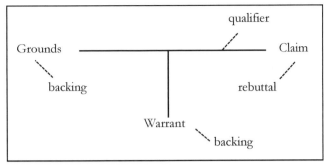

Figure 4: Toulmin's Model

The claim is the argument the speaker is attempting to make. It is a statement advanced for the adherence of others. For example, "Students should have no more than two hours of homework each night." is a claim. The claim will assert a fact, propose a particular value or belief, or advocate for a particular course of action. If these three types of claims sound familiar, they should because they are the three categories of resolutions discussed earlier. The goal of a claim is to present a statement you hope will be accepted by the audience. In order for the claim to legitimately cling to its title, it must be supported. This is the distinction between an argument and an assertion. Assertions have no backing. While they may be true, their lack of support may call into question their merits (see page 13 for a discussion of the difference between an assertion and an argument). Arguments must be supported in order to prove the truth of the matter asserted. Claims are arguments because they are supported by the grounds and warrants. A claim is often made as the conclusion of a complete argument after you have set the stage with the grounds and warrant.

Grounds support both the warrant and claim by providing proof or evidence in support of the claim. Without support, an argument is only an assertion and lacks persuasive power. The grounds provide justification for the assertion and transform it into the argument. Good grounds will cause the reader or listener to agree with the ultimate argument being made. Often, grounds are observations which show parallels between the warrant and the claim, or statements which move the claim closer to the warrant. Using our earlier homework example, you might say "Studies show that teenagers who spend more than ten hours per week on homework are more likely to suffer from vision loss in college." However, without the warrant, the grounds may be shaky.

The warrant provides a bridge between the grounds and the claim. While the warrant may not be explicit, the warrant relies on the attitudes, beliefs, and values of the listener to allow them to make the inferential leap between the evidence they have heard and the claim. For example, the warrant might be "to prevent the loss of vision, homework should be limited." Obviously the evidence does not require this conclusion. There could be multiple reasons for the loss of vision unrelated to the act of doing homework—computer use, the print size of the book, the lighting or the room, etc.—a good debater will employ the warrant to bridge the gap between the grounds she has presented (the study showing a loss of vision) and the claim (homework should be limited to two hours or less). The warrant may use inductive or deductive reasoning to help make the steps between the grounds and the claim. Instead of being a shot in the dark, the warrant shows how the ultimate argument connects with the evidence and all other points made.

After establishing the primary triad, the Toulmin Model further develops the argument by adding a secondary triad. While the primary triad can be an effective means of argument, use of only the primary triad may be less than persuasive. Arguments using only the primary triad that do not prepare for future arguments may be weak. The secondary triad makes the argument stronger than the primary triad working by itself. The secondary triad has three parts: *backing, qualifiers,* and *rebuttals.*

Backing is similar to evidence. Backing supports both the grounds and warrants of the primary triad to give credibility to an argument. When the grounds and warrant have support, the claim is stronger. For example, citing another study showing that students learn better when they have at least three hours of free time at the end of the day before they sleep would further support the arguments that homework time should be limited. Proper use of evidence to verify your argument is an important step in building a complete Toulmin argument.

Qualifiers indicate the force of the claim. If you are not certain of the argument you are making, qualifying it will protect you from some attacks. Further, rather than making absolute statements, the qualifier can make a claim more reasonable. More reasonable claims are easier for an audience to believe. For example, the argument that a single minute over two hours of homework will always destroy a student's vision is difficult to believe. However, the argument that *significantly* more homework time *may reduce* the vision of the student will be more readily accepted. This is even truer if there is evidence which was already presented to support this claim. Qualifiers give your argument more power because they make the argument more believable and make the person arguing sound reasonable.

Rebuttals attempt to predict the response to the argument and cut it off before it is introduced. This is similar to a "spike" in a policy debate affirmative case (see page 126). By predicting that your opponent will argue a specific point and providing a response to that argument in your original argument, your opponent will have to decide whether to make an argument you have already refuted. For example, if you anticipate the argument that students will not learn as much without more than two hours of homework, you can rebut this argument before it even comes up by noting that the additional homework time is directly correlated with students sleeping less and without sleep, their learning is severely hampered. The rebuttal helps to increase the persuasiveness of the argument. If a question seems likely, answering it before it is asked can make it easier for the audience to accept your argument. The rebuttal also offers the opportunity to admit weaknesses in the argument you are making. Proper use of the rebuttal in the Toulmin model is the final piece of your completely modeled argument.

The Toulmin Model of argument helps one find the strengths and weaknesses of arguments. By developing arguments which contain all the necessary components of the model, a debater provides stronger reasoning in support of her case. The properly constructed argument gives your judge more confidence in your ability to substantiate your statements. Using the Toulmin Model enables you to find holes in your opponent's arguments while helping you develop winning arguments for your team.

Gaining the ability to use logic and reasoning is crucial. While these abilities are useful in a debate round, they are also important in life. Being able to formulate a clear and logical argument as well as being able to refute illogical ones will enhance your critical thinking skills. After you learn the skills of deductive reasoning, inductive reasoning, Aristotle's Syllogism, and Toulmin's Model for argumentation, practice is vital to polish your skills. While understanding is important, being able to put your reasoning skills into action is the key aspect of learning to debate. Debate gives you the forum to hone the life skill of reasoning into a tool to make you an excellent thinker.

Observation 5: Specific Reasoning & Logical Fallacies

"The greatest danger in any argument is that real issues are often clouded by superficial ones, that momentary passions may obscure permanent realities"
-Mary Ellen Chase-

With an understanding of the general forms of reasoning, we can now turn to the specific types of reasoning used within each of these forms. Understanding and using these categories of reasoning will enhance arguments. However, misuse or abuse of these specific categories of reasoning, employing fallacies, will hinder your argumentation because fallacies do not stand up when tested by an opponent. After you understand how to use specific arguments, avoid using fallacies yourself, and refute fallacies presented by an opponent, you will be well on your way to developing the best possible arguments.

A. Argument Types

While the forms of reasoning and argument presented in the previous chapter are important, identifying and using specific types of reasoning is crucial to developing your case. One of my college debate coaches, Steve Schroeder, explains six specific argument types useful to debaters. The six categories include arguments by: *principle, authority, sign, analogy, generalization,* and *cause.*

1. Argument by Principle

An argument by principle uses a rule of law or a law of nature to argue. For example, an argument by principle could be that gravity exists. No debater can argue that his plan will eliminate gravity. So, any advantage that would require zero gravity on earth can be defeated. The statement "What goes up, must come down." is an argument by principle. The argument by principle relies primarily on deductive reasoning to support its claim. Because the principle is true, an argument which runs contrary to this principle is false.

2. Argument by Authority

An argument by authority gains its credibility from the person who originally made the argument. For example, if the inventor of the watch were to say that the prime purpose of a watch is to tell time, the argument that watches are intended primarily as jewelry would be undermined. Because of the authority of the quoted person, this argument type claims that arguments in agreement with the authority are correct. Some debaters use this form of argument in debates over theory when they appeal to the authority of a debate theory textbook such as Freeley and Steinberg's *Argumentation and Debate.* By arguing that these authors are authorities in the field of debate theory, debaters claim an argument based upon the writings of these experts is true.

3. Argument by Sign

An argument by sign claims that one thing indicates another. "Where there is smoke there is fire." is an example of an argument by sign. The presence of dark clouds is an indication of rain. Often, these arguments are circumstantial evidence. Because of a certain situation, another situation will also occur. If this situation has occurred numerous times in the past, the argument by sign may be effective. Arguing that one sign will lead to a future action helps debaters develop a problem's ramifications.

4. Argument by Analogy

An argument by analogy compares one thing or idea with another, claiming similarity. This type of reasoning, if used correctly, may be one of the most powerful arguments in persuading a judge. *An analogy used in immigration debates is that immigrants are like chocolate chips in a cookie. While the chocolate chips make the cookie taste good (immigrants are beneficial) too many chocolate chips can alter the cookie and make it a chocolate bar. Thus, a delicate balance of cookie to chocolate chips is important to our nation.* Using such an analogy enables the audience to clearly understand the situation. This analogy made the abstract policy arguments understandable even to judges with little knowledge about the topic.

5. Argument by Generalization

An argument by generalization employs inductive reasoning by introducing multiple examples to prove a general point. Generalization takes many specific examples and then makes a claim which they have proven. For example, a claim that *dogs are good pets* might be made with the following examples: *Petting dogs has been shown to lower blood pressure. Dogs often save their families' lives by warning of danger and even rescuing them. Dogs live well in houses. Dogs are loved by people of all ages. Dogs bring joy to the life of those around them.* After presenting these examples, an argument might be made that dogs are indeed good pets. The argument by generalization allows a debater to present many supporting examples to infer the concluding claim.

6. Argument by Cause

The argument by cause is the application of cause and effect. The argument by cause reasons that if one thing is done, another thing will happen as a result. For example, the principle of physics that "for every action, there is an equal and opposite reaction" is an argument by cause. Because of the reaction, action taken results in either benefits or costs. In a policy debate, the affirmative team would cite the benefits of the plan as arguments by cause while the negative would point to the benefits of the status quo and the costs of the affirmative case. While the argument by sign argues that one observation indicates a situation, the argument by cause states that the results of a situation can be observed. The changes made will have a ripple effect and may affect other areas beyond those intended. An example of the argument by cause is: *"Taking away food stamps from the poor who do not work hurts children because single mothers will be forced to choose between caring for their children and working."* The cause would be taking away food stamps and the effect would be harmed children. Using the cause and effect argument can result in stronger arguments.

B. Fallacies

While using specific reasoning is highly beneficial, misuse of these types of reasoning can result in logical fallacies. Fallacies are false arguments that appear true. Untested, the fallacy may seem to be a strong argument, but once a fallacy is thoroughly examined, it quickly falls apart. Professor Steve Schroeder presents nine fallacies to which debaters may fall prey including: *false analogies, false cause, argument ad hominem, reductio ad absurdum, hasty generalizations, sweeping generalizations, either/or reasoning, straw man,* and *begging the question.* Austin Freeley presents many other fallacies, four of which are explained here: *loaded language, circular reasoning, false authority,* and *appeals to tradition.* Two other fallacies include the fallacies of *composition* and *division.* Good debaters learn to recognize fallacies so they can both avoid using them and counter those who do.

1. False Analogies

False analogies are analogies incorrectly applied to a situation. False analogies seem to apply to the arguments when they are first advanced, but are easily exposed upon further analysis. Here is an example of a false analogy: *Immigrants are like bears. Bears robbed of their young will attack and kill. Immigrants who have their "rights" infringed upon will become vicious and dangerous to the society.* Obviously no link exists in the comparison of bears to immigrants. The lack of any link causes this analogy to be false.

2. False Cause

The fallacy of false cause is a misuse of the argument by cause. Just because two actions occur simultaneously does not imply a causal relationship between the actions. As statisticians stress, correlation is not causation. Even though the American economy was strengthened during the great wave of immigration, it is not necessarily true that this immigration caused the economy to grow. In fact, some argue immigration may have even been exerting downward pressure on the economy. The fact that the two actions occur within a similar time period does not prove their relationship whatsoever. In his campaign for president, former vice president Al Gore used the fallacy of false cause. Gore claimed that the economic boom felt during the time he and President Bill Clinton were in office was a result of his leadership. However, the vice-president cannot claim direct responsibility for an economic situation. Because of the numerous monetary policies of the Federal Reserve, the boom of the technology sector, the president's individual actions, and many other factors unrelated to the vice-president, the economy could rise. Thus, claiming responsibility for an economic boom is an example of the fallacy of false cause.

3. Argument *Ad Hominem*

The third fallacy is the argument *ad hominem* (Latin for an attack "to the man"). *Ad hominem* attacks do not actually attack arguments. Instead, the *ad hominem* attacks the individual or group making the argument. Calling your opponent names or insulting his intelligence does not effectively build your own case. On the contrary, rude behavior harms your own credibility. The *ad hominem* is not a legitimate argument in any situation. Debaters need to guard against taking arguments personally and instead respond to argument with arguments. Remember, debate is not a competition between individuals, but between ideas (see page 5). So keep the focus of the round on the issues and not on one another.

4. *Reductio Ad Absurdum*

A common fallacy in debates, especially when trying to tell the story of a disadvantage in a policy debate, is *Reductio ad Absurdum* (Latin for "reduction to the absurd"). This fallacy exaggerates the argument to absurd proportions. By taking the argument far beyond its fair conclusion, this fallacy tries to reach disastrous consequences from a minor point. Slippery slope arguments are often guilty of this fallacy because they reach bizarre levels. Absurd disadvantages are often comprised of this logical fallacy. For example: *The affirmative case is ending funding for construction of interstate highways. This will force the construction to be slowed. By slowing construction, workers will be laid off. Individuals without jobs are more prone to crime. Criminal activity will increase in areas where construction workers have been laid off. Police will be unable to access these areas because the road construction is too slow. Criminal activity caused by these construction workers will cause some citizens to take matters into their own hands, increasing the criminal activity in the vicinity. Eventually, the police will be unable to control the angry mobs and anarchy will ensue in the area.* As this example shows, reducing an argument to absurd proportions is neither an effective means of arguing nor is it useful in convincing a judge.

5. Hasty Generalization

The hasty generalization is a fallacy which relies on insufficient evidence to make a claim. Arguing that trade between African nations and the United States promotes corruption might be something a debater could prove. However, this argument needs more than one credible piece of evidence to support it. By making a specific statement without being able to support it, a debater is guilty of the hasty generalization fallacy. For example, when debating trade policy some debaters committed this fallacy by arguing that trade with South Africa should be ended. After presenting evidence stating "Africa is a corrupt continent," the debaters would conclude that the United States should stop trading with South Africa. These debaters generalized the situation in Africa, claiming that because Africa as a continent was full of corrupt leaders, all African nations must have been corrupt. By only using one piece of broad evidence to support narrow and specific assertions, they produced a hastily generalized argument. Using more specific evidence and not reading more into evidence than the quotation actually says will help debaters avoid committing this fallacy.

6. Sweeping Generalization

The sweeping generalization takes the hasty generalization one step further. By categorizing objects based on limited evidence and using categorical words such as *always*, *never*, *all*, or *none*, this fallacy falsely links arguments to objects which do not deserve this connection. Several different arguments may be grouped together, however, sweeping generalizations take more arguments than can be justified and clumps them into one group to be attacked. An example of the sweeping generalization in action was visible in many debates about free trade in the Middle East. Many teams argued, "Free trade will always result in an end to terrorism. Free trade, which always helps an economy, will create more jobs and keep people from turning to terrorism. Thus, our policy must be free trade." Though free trade has its merits, these teams neglected to qualify their statements. For example, terrorist activities by Americans against Americans have been committed. If the argument had said *can* result in *less* terrorism, the argument would be qualified and could be accepted. However, because of the use of such terms as *always* and *end*, these arguments are less likely to be accepted. Furthermore, arguments which lack qualifiers are begging to be tested. Pointing out any exception to the unqualified statement brings the entire argument crashing down.

7. Either/Or Reasoning

"This is a dead end. You can only turn left or right. Those are your only choices." By giving the listener only two options, a debater enters the realm of the either/or reasoning fallacy. This fallacy neglects the fact that other options may exist. It attempts to blind the decision-maker into thinking that only two directions can be taken. More often than not, however, there are more than two possible options available. A debater who attempts to lock the argument into a position where it is either one way or the other will be quickly defeated when a third or fourth option is pointed out. An example of the fallacy of either/or reasoning is often debated under funding in policy debates. A typical funding either/or reasoning fallacy might look something like this: The negative team asserts: *The affirmative team needs money to implement their plan. This money will be taken from education spending.* (The affirmative case did not mandate a specific source for funding.) *Either the affirmative will harm education by taking away funds, or the plan will not be implemented and the advantages will not occur.*[6] While this may seem logical

---

[6] This kind of argument can be made in public forum debates where the resolution calls for some specific change and the con argues that in order to make such a change the government would have to provide funds, but those funds would come from a "good" program that cannot afford to lose any funding.

at first, upon further examination this argument begins to crumble. There are other sources of funds which the affirmative might choose to use. Also, there is often little proof that a plan needs a large amount of money to be successful. Finally, the advantages may be able to occur even if the plan were implemented on a very small scale. For any of these reasons, the box in which the negative attempted to place the affirmative case is splintered. Remember, there are usually more than two ways to turn at the dead end, you can always turn around!

8. Straw Man

When an unimportant issue is defeated by one team and that team tries to claim the issue is vital, the team is presenting a fallacy known as the straw man. A straw man fallacy sets up a weak argument on the opposing side of an issue simply to be able to knock it down. These arguments often present a ridiculous caricature of the other team's case or argument. By establishing an argument which seems to be part of the opposition's case and easily refuting it, many debaters feel they have shown a reason to reject that argument and the case as a whole. However, these arguments have done nothing at all. When these arguments are more closely examined, their façade is revealed. An example of a straw man argument is a response to the statement "People would be happiest if every day were sunny" by pointing out that if every day was sunny there would never be rain and we would all die from a drought. Talking about the lack of rain sets up a straw man to knock down rather than engage the real issue. If a straw man is found it is used as a distraction from the real questions involved. Debaters who attempt to use an argument which is a straw man fallacy will see their credibility fall and their ability to win diminish.

9. Begging the Question

Begging the question is a fallacy of unproven backing committed by many inexperienced debaters. Without the support to prove a point, a debater seeks to have the audience accept the argument anyway. In this way, a debater may try to turn the debate away from the lack of backing and toward the claim being made. However, as we have seen before, without necessary support any structure will fall – including arguments. Be sure to back up the arguments you make with evidence and to provide all the parts necessary to create clear, logical arguments.

10. Loaded Language

Politicians frequently appeal to audiences by using terms with emotional meanings. Using loaded language is a fallacy of language which moves an audience, but does not actually make an argument. Such statements as "To protect our democracy," "To defend the Constitution," and "To preserve our rights," all allow a speaker to gain the approval of the audience without necessarily making a legitimate argument. Loaded language can also be used to attack. Calling an idea socialist, liberal, right-wing, prejudice, racist, or unfair may have negative connotations among certain groups. Use of these terms without support is a fallacy and must be exposed in arguments.

11. Circular Reasoning

The fallacy of circular reasoning uses the claim to prove itself. Rather than developing a logically sound argument, circular reasoning makes a claim and uses that claim to support another claim. For example, a student commits this fallacy by making the argument, "Michael Jordan is the greatest basketball player of all time because his autograph is the most prized possession of basketball fans," would commit this fallacy. To show the fallacy, suppose his teacher asks, "Why is his autograph the most prized possession of basketball fans?" The student might respond, "Because Michael Jordan is the greatest basketball player of all time." Rather than actually supporting the two arguments, both assertions are used as support for one another without any proof that either assertion is true. Being able to identify circular reasoning is vital to holding arguments to a fair standard in a round.

12. False Authority

Evidence must be credible. As discussed on page 32, there are many ways to prove the legitimacy of evidence. One fallacy which many debaters commit with evidence is the fallacy of false authority. This fallacy argues that because an individual has authority in one area, that authority ought to be extended to other areas. For example, Nobel Prize winning economist Dr. John Nash is an excellent economist and mathematician. However, he is not an authority on naming the greatest author of English literature. Even though he is a professor at Princeton, his authority does not extend into all areas of life. Instead, his expertise gives him credibility in only limited areas. Using an authority in one area and claiming its credibility in another commits the fallacy of false authority.

13. Appeal to Tradition

Often debaters argue that the status quo ought to be maintained because the world has always been this way. This fallacy, known as the appeal to tradition, maintains that any change would violate tradition. While some traditions may be important, other traditions may be harmful. For example, the United States' tradition in the 19th Century was to prohibit minorities from full membership in society. This tradition was not worth maintaining on the basis that it was the cultural norm. The United States had a moral imperative to end this tradition. Even though change may cause friction, the traditions of the past are not always a legitimate reason to reject change. Being able to point out this fallacy will assist your arguments for a change in policies or beliefs.

14. Fallacy of Composition

The fallacy of composition is a false assumption that the characteristics of the parts make up the characteristics of the whole. For example, if an individual knows ten home school students who have perfect SAT scores, it would be a fallacy of composition to assume all home school students have perfect SAT scores. By assuming the whole is the same as the parts, the fallacy erroneously groups all items that have similar characteristics. Another example would be: "all basketball players lift weights." While many basketball players do in fact lift weights, not all basketball players lift weights. By assuming the behavior of all basketball players match the characteristics of the many players, a debater falls into the trap of the fallacy of composition.

15. Fallacy of Division

The fallacy of division is the opposite of the fallacy of composition. Rather than implying the characteristics of the whole from the many parts, the characteristics of the many parts are assumed from the whole. An example of this fallacy can be seen when looking at an airplane. *Airplanes can fly. The landing gear is part of the airplane. Therefore, the landing gear can fly.* The first statement is true. However, the landing gear of the airplane is not able to fly. Although the landing gear is a part of the plane, it does not have the same abilities as the airplane. Thus, it would be fallacious to assume that the parts can do what the whole does. Keeping the fallacies of composition and division out of your repertoire is important to making cogent arguments.

Reasoning is an important skill in debate rounds as well as in real life. Being able to properly use arguments will give you the ability to persuade others. Also, understanding the different types of arguments, their construction, and their usage will enhance the message you are delivering. While arguments are important, your skills will be severely lacking if you do not take time to learn about fallacies. It is in your best interest to master identifying and refuting fallacies. This will allow you to avoid using fallacies in your own argumentation while you point out the errors of your opponents. Some debaters label fallacies as part of their refutation, but other debaters simply say the argument commits a fallacy without any particular label. The adept debater who knows and understands the skills of argumentation can effectively use these skills to produce arguments which can win the ballot.

Observation 6: Evidence

*"A quotation in a speech, article or book is like a rifle
in the hands of an infantryman. It speaks with authority."*
-Brendan Francis-

Without evidence, you stand before your audience an articulate individual student presenting good ideas. While students certainly have well-reasoned ideas, it is hard to imagine most people taking advice from young students when it comes to making major changes in United States or international policy. Most audience members will even hesitate justifying a change in their own perspectives on serious issues of our day based only on one speaker's opinion. Backed by evidence, however, you are that school student with the support of numerous Ph.D.'s and other policy experts who agree with your ideas! This expert support gives you the credibility you need to persuade the audience and ultimately win the argument.

Evidence is a quotation of any published work. This includes, but is not limited to, books, magazines, professional journals, newspapers, pamphlets, Internet articles, television or radio broadcasts, and other published materials. These quotations are an important part of every round. When you cite evidence, you fulfill your **burden** of proof.

You should obtain the transcripts of any mass media such as television or radio scripts, before quoting it. Also, be sure to cite your quotations. Citations include the title of the article, the author, the name of the source, and the date of publication, and, if available, the page number and web address of the quotation.

Figure 5: Transcripts and Citations

A. Burdens

"Burden of proof" is a phrase meaning that a debater cannot make unsupported assertions and expect to have the audience believe his statement. Instead, he must support each argument. In a debate round, there are two different burdens of proof, one for each side of the resolution: the burden of proof to overcome **presumption** and the burden of rebuttal. In a general sense, all debaters have the burden of proof to prove what they are saying.

First, the proponent of the resolution (the affirmative or pro team) has the burden of proof to back up statements they make and to show that the resolution is needed. If the proponent does not do this, it is assumed or presumed that the views of the resolution's opponents (the negative or con team) are correct and that the resolution is false or unnecessary. Presumption begins the round in favor of the team opposing the resolution because it is assumed that the resolution is not needed (in policy debate, that the status quo does not need change). However, the first speech from the proponent should offer a compelling defense of the resolution (a **prima facie** case) which fulfills the proponent's burden of proof and overcomes the presumption against the resolution.

The team opposed to the resolution (the negative or con team) has its own burden of proof, often called the "burden of rebuttal." Once the proponent has overcome the presumption against the resolution with a prima facie case, the opponent has the burden of rebuttal to disprove the proponent. If the opponent refutes the issues the proponent presents, the opposing team has fulfilled their burden of rebuttal.

After the first two speeches, all debaters have burdens of proof to prove that what they say is true, as well as burdens of rebuttal or rejoinder to prove what the other team says is incorrect (replacing the argument with an argument for their respective side). Evidence is the best way to fulfill burdens of proof and rebuttal in a round.

In policy debate there is an exception to the typical affirmative burden of proof: when the negative team presents a **counterplan**. When the negative presents a counterplan, the negative team has conceded that the status quo is not working and so there is no longer a presumption against change. By supporting a change to the status quo and giving up the presumption against the resolution, the negative team will have to show that its counterplan is preferable to the affirmative's plan. In other words, unless the negative team can prove the superiority of its counterplan over the affirmative's plan, because presumption no longer is in favor of the negative team, a tied round will go to the affirmative. (For more discussion of counterplans in policy debate see page 149).

B. Principles of Strong Evidence

Credibility is important in debate. Credible sources, such as experts in the field, professors, elected officials, authors, and those with personal experiences in the field, make your arguments credible. This expertise is also known as field dependability. A credible source has field dependability. It is important to know what qualifies your source because it is perfectly legitimate for your opponent to challenge the credibility of your sources. However, if you have a good source, you can reject this challenge. Being a credible debater means presenting not only credible authors of the material, but materials your audience will find persuasive.

Professor Steve Schroeder has explained *Seven Principles for Strong Evidence* for debaters. His seven principles are: relevancy, bias, recency, accuracy, applicability, sufficiency, and completeness. Each principle is an important aspect of good evidence. While some evidence may not fulfill each criterion, the more criteria each piece of evidence meets, the stronger the evidence will be in promoting its intended position.

1. Relevance

Relevancy asks whether or not the evidence is closely related to the topic under discussion. If a quotation discusses the price of one product, it is not necessarily applicable to all products. Also, a quotation that does not relate to the resolution is unimportant in the debate round. Relevance may also question the source of the evidence. For example, if the resolution deals with a problem in international trade and all the quotations are from American newspapers, an opponent might argue that there needs to be evidence from international sources because the resolution relates to international issues. An irrelevant quotation or source weakens an argument it attempts to support while relevant evidence maintains its strength.

2. Bias

Bias questions whether the source being quoted is objective or is trying to make a particular argument. Good evidence comes from objective sources whose interest in the issue at hand is limited. If the Congressperson who advocates the affirmative's plan is the only person a team can quote, they are relying on a biased source. If however, the evidence quoted by the pro is from sources who may even oppose the resolution, but who still point out its benefits and strong points, the evidence is much less suspect and strengthens the case the pro is making. While there is no such thing as a perfectly unbiased quotation (everyone who writes has a perspective on the issues at hand) searching for sources with as little prejudice as possible is an important aspect of strong evidence.

Searching for unbiased sources is especially true when looking at empirical studies (studies attempting to identify the causes of a particular phenomenon). An empirical study whose author is looking for and ultimately finds a particular answer to a question is much less persuasive than an empirical study where an author is either unsure of the right answer or hopes to find an answer pointing one way but ultimately concludes the answer points in a different direction. Studies from some think tanks are subject to bias if the think tanks address policy issues from a particular political worldview. When preparing to quote a think tank, be sure the author is not simply parroting the conclusion of her political worldview (or that of her think tank). Instead, ask whether the research actually supports the conclusions presented and only quote honest representations of the underlying research.

3. Recency

Recency questions the age of the quotation at hand. If the piece of evidence cited is ten years old, the entire nation and world may have changed too much to make that quotation useful for a debate round. In a rapidly changing world, old evidence was likely to have been written under different circumstances. Thus the article may support your case only as a result of past events. If you can find evidence within a couple of years of your debate, the current information will usually supersede an older quotation. However, old evidence may still be valid if the world within your debate topic has not changed in many years.

While the age of evidence is important, this importance can be overstated. There are some written sources which, though very old, are still qualified and credible. For example, Thomas Jefferson, George Washington, and other founders of the United States have some ideas which are never outdated. The same is true of many philosophers and great thinkers throughout history. However, on many debate topics, while the principles Washington and Jefferson espoused may still guide current policy, the particular steps in executing current policy will call for a more recent source. Though great thinkers of history may be refuted, the historic nature of their wisdom should not be the sole reason to reject them as a source. Unless the evidence can be refuted by more recent evidence, even old evidence stands in a debate round. When examining a quotation, one must keep in mind that the status quo is not static. Changes in the status quo may alter the relevance of certain quotations. Remember this guideline: more recent evidence that meets the other tests for good evidence is generally preferable.

4. Accuracy

Accuracy asks if the evidence is being correctly presented in the round. First, numbers must truthfully portray the situation. A poll taken of ten friends will not be an accurate representation of all Americans. Good debaters will question statistics and the results of studies to assure the honest presentation of the information. Second, accuracy refers to the context of a statement. Since evidence used in a debate round is only a small sample of the entire article, debaters must be sure to truthfully present quotations which represent the context of the entire article. For example, if an article promotes trade restrictions, but at one point makes an argument for freer trade, utilizing only the portion of the quotation which advocates free trade and implying that the article does the same is a dishonest use of the evidence. By inaccurately representing the context of the article, a team loses credibility in the round. This evidence is also weak because it will be easily refuted by the opposing team.

Third, accuracy must apply to the author. An author who advocates one position in his/her writing but may say something contrary in one instance often still supports the original position. Quoting the one contrary instance is very risky because if the opposing team notes the contradiction of this persons' other statements, your evidence will be disregarded.

Finally, accuracy in quoting an author requires that words are not added to the quotation or removed to change the quotation's meaning. Altering quotations seriously diminishes your own credibility and takes advantage of the trust both your opponent and your audience have placed in you to play fairly. Adding a few words or deleting sections of a quotation to make it say what you want it to say are dishonest and make a good debate impossible. If you are debating against a team that has falsified evidence by altering a quotation or claiming words come from one source when it is actually the speaker's own words, you should carefully point this out to your audience and judge. Such behavior is unacceptable and will typically result in the offending team being disciplined and even disqualified from the tournament.

Accuracy is absolutely essential in evidence. Accurately quoting an article exactly as written, in context, and in line with previous statements, assuring that statistics and figures are correct, and ensuring that every quotation is verbatim will go a long way toward building a precise justification for the position you advocate and will ensure you are not misusing evidence.

5. Applicability

Applicability asks whether the quotation can be applied to the debate itself. First, does this quotation apply to the audience? For example, if the audience is a group of attorneys, using a quotation which states that lawyers are not credible in their interpretation of legal matters is probably not the best idea. On the same note, a quotation from the American Bar Association might have just the opposite effect. Or, if your judge is inexperienced in debate theory, using advanced techniques found in communication journals may confuse your judge rather than strengthen your case.

Second, the applicability of evidence may also question whether or not the evidence applies to the argument it purports to support. It is important to use quotations that discuss the issue at hand directly rather than indirectly. For example, a quotation which argues that protective tariffs ought to be placed on imports to protect new industries in the United States is not effective as an argument for tariffs on agricultural goods which have been in production for centuries. Because this evidence does not actually apply to the argument at hand, it should not be used. Instead, present evidence that agricultural tariffs can protect farms that have been in business for generations and form the foundation for community cohesion. Ensure your evidence is credible and applicable to your audience based on their expertise and that your evidence actually supports the arguments you are making.

6. Sufficiency

Sufficiency asks whether or not there is enough evidence to support a claim. One piece of evidence which supports the argument may not be enough to convince the judge. Thus, sufficient evidence must be provided to persuade an audience. Sufficiency is similar to the stock issue of significance in policy debate (see page 110 for further discussion of significance as a policy debate stock issue), an issue of quantity and quality. Quantitatively, there ought to be many pieces of evidence which support an argument. A case, for example, needs to have as much evidence as possible to build, develop, strengthen, and support the case. However, sheer numbers are not enough. One hundred pieces of poor evidence are not nearly as beneficial as two or three pieces of excellent evidence. Quality is judged based on the variety of sources (good ideas will have multiple advocates) and the credibility of each source. These pieces of evidence will make specific arguments which make your case even stronger. Without sufficient evidence, most arguments will fail, but using sufficient evidence will reinforce the arguments being made.

7. Completeness

Completeness asks whether or not the evidence provided gives a complete picture of the issues at hand. When evidence hides pertinent information it benefits neither the debaters nor the round. Evidence which ignores the facts and continues advocating a position is feeble in the face of the facts. Complete evidence reveals the big picture rather than showing just a corner of the canvass. By bringing complete evidence to the table, a debater promotes clash on the issues. Complete evidence is also much more successful in compelling a judge to agree with the team presenting it.

8. Verifiability

Austin J. Freeley and David L. Steinberg present the additional criterion of verifiability. *Verifiability* asks if the evidence is authentic. First, does the quotation read match the quotation from the source? Falsifying evidence is a serious violation of ethics and is treated as such by forensics leagues. Assuring that the quotation is accurately quoted is a crucial aspect of legitimately quoting material. Second, is the evidence in the public domain? Could other debaters access the material? If the answer to these questions is no, then the evidence is not credible to use in a debate round. Personal interviews of government officials can go a long way in helping debaters increase their understanding of the topic, but they should never be used as evidence in a debate round. Because there is no means of assuring the authenticity of such evidence, it is not ethical to use such evidence in the debate. Debaters should ensure that any evidence they present in a round may be verified by citing the publication, author, and date.

In order to assure verifiability and credibility within a round, every piece of evidence should have a date, a source, a title, and the topic of the article if it has one. The goal is to provide enough information about your evidence for the other team that they have the ability to find that same evidence on their own. Many debaters find it helpful to include the full hyperlink of every article they find online as well as to keep a printed copy of the entire article for every document they plan to quote simply to help others verify their sources if necessary. Furthermore, you should also keep a list of source qualifications on hand. It is not sufficient to simply say, "I quoted a Ph.D." You must be able to show that your source has a Ph.D. in an area that qualifies her to speak on your topic. Many times a team will quote an impressive-sounding organization such as "The Center for Strategic Studies" or "The Policy Research Institute." While the name may sound impressive, you might find that such organizations are not very credible. One organization quoted during immigration debates had little credibility. The organization consisted of an ophthalmologist and other unqualified people with an agenda, but no particular expertise on immigration policy. While they made some compelling arguments, their lack of expertise should prompt caution for a debater. Always have enough information about your evidence so that you can verify its credibility.

These models of good evidence offer debaters eight principles for evaluating their evidence. When selecting evidence to present in a round, the speaker should consider the strength of the quotation with these principles in mind. In the same way, these standards may also be applied to the evidence presented by an opponent. Using compelling evidence which fulfills these criteria will bolster your argument; and pointing out weaknesses in the opposing teams' evidence will diminish the persuasiveness of the opposing argument.

C. Evidence Analysis

While quoting the experts is important, the debater who simply reads a quotation and moves on to another quotation is skipping the most important step. Just as an argument without an impact is less powerful (see pages 13, 101, and 136 for further discussion of impacts), the quotation of evidence is weaker without an explanation of the evidence's importance to the underlying argument. Judges are looking for more than just a statement from experts; judges want an explanation of the evidence, too. For example, if you are attempting to prove that the sales taxes hurt the poor, reading a quotation from an economics journal which says, "The sales tax hurts the poor by making necessary goods cost more" is important and gives credibility to your argument that sales taxes are bad for the poor, but its true benefit comes from combining the quotation with analysis. Analysis not only points out the argument itself, but it also includes an impact or explanation for why the argument should affect your judge's decision. For example, explaining that the rising costs of goods will force the poor to forgo necessities such as food or clothing will influence the judge much more than the abstract idea that sales taxes 'hurt' poor people.

A good method for presenting an argument is to sandwich the evidence in between analysis. (See Figure 6) Leave the judge with a clear conclusion or "impact" after each argument. ("*Therefore* if A happens when B is enacted, and the evidence says A is harmful, we must reject B.") Evidence analysis is important not only because it demonstrates the knowledge you as a debater have, but also because it makes the arguments both easier to understand and more believable.

Opposing Contention: Sales taxes are good for the economy.
Argument: Sales tax is bad because it hurts the poor.
Evidence: Sales taxes hurts the poor by forcing them to pay higher prices for everything.
Analysis: As a share of total income, the poor spend more of their money on basic necessities such as clothing and health care than other individuals. The poor are also most likely to lack available income to pay for anything other than necessities. Because a sales tax will increase the price of everything, the poor will no longer be able to afford the basics they need and will have to forgo basic necessities.

Figure 6: Evidence Analysis Example

D. Evidence Organization

Once you gather your evidence (the next chapter discusses how to find good evidence), you need to organize it for quick access in a round. Evidence organization is imperative. You may have the best quotations in the world, but if you do not know where that evidence is, then it has very little value to you in the debate round. Beyond knowing where you have stored your evidence, you should have a general idea of what evidence you have with you so you can customize your arguments to match the evidence you have as support. You should not go into a debate round wondering if you have any evidence against a certain case or where that evidence is stored. Organization takes two forms: storage, and format.

There are many methods of storing your evidence including file boxes or tubs, note cards, brief cases, folders, binders, and laptops. Depending on the quantity of evidence you will be carrying with you, different storage methods have pros and cons. While a computer can store significant amounts of information, taking a computer up to the podium with you can look bulky and affect your persuasive abilities. A tablet computer may be a better choice. If you have a lot of evidence, file boxes or tubs are probably your best bet. If, on the other hand, you are carrying smaller amounts of evidence, you may find it easier to carry a binder or briefcase full of your few hundred pages of evidence. Most policy debaters use tubs containing multiple file folders inside for each particular topic, while most public forum debaters can use one large pocketed folder with separate tabs for the various topics of evidence they carry into the round. Choose an organized file system that helps you keep evidence well organized and readily available for use.

What you store inside your evidence "box" is entirely up to you, but you should attempt to make the evidence you have gathered as easy to use as possible. This means grouping quotations from different authors on the same topic so you can select which quotation you are going to use to support a particular argument depending on the round. This format of evidence organization is known as "blocking." Each article you read will contain quotations you want to use relating to different arguments. Rather than making a "block" of good quotations from one particular article, a strong block takes quotations from a variety of sources and arranges them by topic. By taking multiple articles and dividing them into smaller parts, the articles become useable evidence.

For example, if you anticipate an argument that free trade exploits workers, you might compile five or six different articles which make the opposite point and put those pieces of evidence, together with short "tags" to highlight the conclusion of the argument, in a single evidence block. Then, when your opponent makes the argument you anticipate, you are prepared with a variety of quotations from different sources to use as support for the arguments you make in response. Often debaters pre-write particular arguments they want to make and place the relevant quotations on those pages. This means you have already written out an argument, complete with claim, warrant, and impact, that can be used to address a particular point you anticipate hearing from the opposition or that you anticipate making in a speech.

Always regard your evidence with this question in mind, "Can I, and will I read it in a round?" If the answer is a definite no, then no matter how interesting the evidence is, you should not print it up and take it with you into the round. Random quotations in your evidence arsenal only clutter your evidence system making it harder to find good evidence. If it is not usable evidence, you do not need it.

Remember, although evidence is important, its purpose is to support your arguments. Do not merely read evidence in your speeches. While evidence helps to substantiate your point, logical thinking and good speaking skills must be employed in your speeches. Speak slowly and clearly enough that the judge(s) will be able to understand your arguments. Evidence gives you credibility to win the debate. Present an argument, use evidence to support the argument, and analyze the evidence in light of the argument to persuade the judge of your position.

Observation 7: Research

"Research is the process of going up alleys to see if they are blind"
-Marston Bates-

Quoting and analyzing evidence is important in the midst of a debate round. Yet to even have evidence to quote and analyze you must find it! Finding evidence is not a quick or easy process, but with some planning and practice, you can be well on your way to developing strong research skills useful to both find debate evidence and to find information for the rest of your life. You will improve your skills each time you dedicate a few hours to searching for evidence, but developing a research strategy and identifying the steps in the research process will make even your early research sessions more productive.

Many debaters complain, "I went to the Internet and searched for one hour and didn't find anything!" With only a few exceptions, most of these debaters have a wrong perspective about how to research. Some are hopeful that the research will simply pop out at them. (Typing in "ocean policy" will NOT produce a case in five minutes. Sorry to disappoint.) Some students cannot find quality information and articles because they are not searching in the right places. Others find interesting articles about the topic but do not fully utilize the information in those articles. Still other students get distracted by emails, instant messages, and the latest sports story. The techniques discussed in this section can help to make anyone a better researcher.

A. Phase 1 – What Does the Resolution Mean?

The research process begins by taking a broad look at the topic. First, examine the resolution for key words. For example, when researching the resolution: "Resolved: That the United States federal government should substantially reform its revenue generation policies" you should begin by making sure you can explain what each word in the resolution means. If you do not know, use a dictionary to look up the words or phrases in the resolution. After you understand the terms in the resolution, circle or highlight the words that seem important to you – words you think will be used by experts who talk about the topic. Examine each of these "key words" from your initial reading of the resolution. It might look something like this (keys words in bold):

> "Resolved: That the United States **federal government** should **substantially** reform its **revenue generation policies**."

Now that you know what the resolution means and have highlighted some key words in the resolution (these are also the words you will probably want to define in your case), you can begin your research.

B. Phase 2 – What Does the Resolution Ask Us to Do?

The goal of this phase is to identify the general landscape of the status quo. In some instances, you will already have a basic level of knowledge about the topic. For example, if the resolution calls for changing transportation policy, a typical lay person will know there are various modes of transportation and that regulation of vehicles, roads, waterways, and the airways is going to be a prominent area of discussion in the debate rounds. Additionally, that same lay person likely knows there are some modes of transportation owned by the government and some private modes of transportation. Although there is obviously much more detailed knowledge and the specific areas under debate will likely delve into that detail, this basic body of knowledge will help any debater prepare to debate such a topic.

> Debaters stay informed. As a debater, you probably keep yourself apprised of current events and other major news topics (especially if you're also competing in extemporaneous speaking). If you don't already read at least one major news source (at least a weekly news magazine if not a daily newspaper), try to get in the habit of keeping yourself informed about the things going on around the world – you'll be a better debater and a better citizen. If the resolution deals with these topics, you'll have the basic level of knowledge to skip this next step. If, on the other hand, the topic relates to some less discussed topic in the current events media, you'll want to do some background reading. Even if you have knowledge, some introductory reading may be helpful as you begin the research process in particular because background knowledge may not identify the major areas of policy disagreement where the debate will typically take place.

Figure 7: Stay Informed

Some topics, however, are not commonly discussed in the mainstream news and only the "experts" spend much time talking about these topics. For example, if the resolution calls for improving fisheries management policy, the average citizen has more limited knowledge and would need significantly more information before in-depth research can even begin. It is useful to identify whether the topic you are going to debate is one about which you already have basic knowledge, or whether it will require some pre-research reading to better understand the topic's landscape.

Your objective is to find one or two articles that provide history, identify the key areas of controversy, and explain the current trends in the policy area. Many think tanks create "backgrounders" which offer exactly this kind of information. For example, the Tax Policy Center produced a short summary of the United States federal government's sources of revenue which would help debaters to understand the current mix of taxes and other revenue sources for debating the revenue generation topic.[7]

To find such background articles, it is usually a good idea to identify one or two think tanks and search for the general topic on their websites.[8] For example, search the website for "tax policy" or "tax reform" and see what articles you can find. You want to find a background article of some length rather than an article seeking to make a particular argument. Recognize that most think tanks have political leanings and bias, but offer detailed examinations of various policy areas. With this knowledge, read the backgrounders from these organizations very carefully. You have two objectives when reading the background articles. First, you are hoping to learn the current state of affairs and the major policy challenges. Second, you are looking for key words and phrases to assist in your next research steps.

Now that you have a background article, real research begins! Print and read the article with pen and notepad nearby.[9] While you read the article you need to identify any and all key

---

[7] The Tax Policy Center, "The Numbers: What are the Federal Government's Sources of Revenue?" available at: http://www.taxpolicycenter.org/briefing-book/background/numbers/revenue.cfm.

[8] Three suggestions: the Heritage Foundation (a conservative think tank), the Brookings Institution (a moderate think tank), and the Center for American Progress (a liberal think tank). Once you identify a couple think tanks you like, you can find your background research through their internal search engines and expand your research to the major search engines after you understand the basic landscape of the topic.

[9] Save an electronic copy of the article in you files as well so that you can find the quotations you want to use when drafting your briefs.

words or phrases you can find in the article. Physically highlight, underline, or circle the words as you read them so you can come back later. These terms will be useful in digging deeper into the topic. For example, in reading about tax policy, you may find discussions of such topics as excise taxes, tariffs, or payroll taxes. Be sure to write down any problems the author identifies. If the author discusses any proposed policy changes, write those down and take a few minutes to think critically about whether those proposals would actually fix any problems.

Finally, look at the references the author cites – are there any article or book titles that look worthwhile to investigate? Make a list of the ones you want to find and read. Do you see any authors cited repeatedly in the other articles? They might be the subject-matter expert you will want to quote to support your positions. Write down any authors whose names come up more than three times, just to keep a running list of "experts" on the topic.

The Internet is expansive. This is both a virtue and a vice. While starting your research on the Internet can be helpful, the Internet's sheer magnitude can lead you down many unsatisfying and less than useful paths in your research process. Also, it is easy to post something on the Internet. There are no credibility checks required before a blog post or article on a personal website are posted. As discussed above, good debaters quote credible evidence from credible sources. The Internet offers many credible sources, but many sources without any credibility as well. If a quotation sounds too useful for your argument, be sure to verify that other credible sources or authorities agree with the quotation's conclusions before you use the quotation in a debate round.

Figure 8: Internet Research Warning

C. Phase 3 – The Big Search

With your notes from reading the background articles in hand, make a list of the key words you have collected. This includes the key words from the resolution itself, i.e. "revenue generation policy," as well as words and phrases you have discovered in the background articles, i.e. "flat tax" and "balanced budget amendment." Go to a search engine such as Google, Bing, or Yahoo, and begin looking up the key words. Look them up individually, collectively, and in different groupings. Additionally, look for phrases both with and without quotation marks – a phrase inside quotation marks requires the search engine to return results only for documents in which the entire phrase is found together; a phrase standing alone without any quotation marks will permit the search engine to return results which contain those individual words spread throughout the discovered page. For example, search for: ["united states", revenue generation policy] ["flat tax" and tax revenue]. Your first search will only return pages where the phrase "United States" is used together. A web article discussing the revenue generation policies of the United Kingdom would not be returned. Each set of search results provides tens of thousands of opportunities to read more about the words and phrases you have searched.

Be discriminating in the websites you actually visit and the articles you read. If the title does not seem relevant, or if the source looks like a random blog, you may end up wasting a large amount of time. Also, do not be afraid to look beyond the first pages of the search. If you only look at the first link or first page you will miss many valuable resources which come up down the page or on later pages. As you find articles of interest, open them in a new tab – making sure to keep your original search page available. Skim the first paragraph of the article online. Ask yourself three questions: "Does this article: **(1)** talk about the topic I'm debating?

(2) identify some particular problem or propose some particular change in policy? and **(3)** come from a reputable source I will be willing to quote in a debate round?"

If the answer to these three questions is "yes," print and save the article in a document. Be sure to include the web address in your saved file and with your printout. If the answer is no, close the window and return to your search. The Internet is expansive, remember? You do not want to waste time reading irrelevant articles or articles from sources you will not be willing to use in a round. And even relevant articles from great sources that simply repeat the background knowledge you have already gained do not help you move toward writing your ultimate debate case (other than possibly providing additional references in their bibliography).

After you have printed five or six articles, step away from the computer. With pen, notepad, printed articles, and your critical thinking cap on, you are now really researching. Read the article, again highlighting/underlining/circling any and all key words you can find in the article. As before, write down any problems or potential "harms" the author of the article identifies. If the author discusses any proposed policy changes, write them down. Then begin thinking about the article critically. Try to identify the underlying assumptions and poke holes in the article's logic.

Ask critical thinking questions such as: "What does the author believe is the cause of the problem?" "What else could be causing this problem?" "What does the author assume will happen if policy changes?" "If the assumption is wrong, will the conclusion be significantly different?" "Does the author cite historical or empirical examples to support her conclusions?" "What harmful consequences does the author ignore?" "Does the author identify opposing arguments and neutralize them?" If you are not satisfied with the answers, or if your answers leave you asking more questions, carefully consider whether you want to stop your research or keep looking for more information. To find more useful sources, look once again at the references your author cites. Finally, as you read, highlight sentences or paragraphs which can support an argument – explanations of why the status quo has failed to serve the needs of the populace or why a particular policy is preferable to the current system. These quotations may be formed into **briefs** (see page 36) and used in a debate round as evidence!

D. Time for Specifics – Tiny Searches for Golden Nuggets

With your articles, your notes, the key quotations and recommendations you have found, sit down with your partner, coach, parents, club, or someone interested in the topic to begin discussing your initial findings and thoughts about the topic. Ask yourself a series of questions: (1) Which side of the resolution do I believe is right? (2) Which side of the resolution will my typical judge prefer? (3) What are the major problems in the current system? (4) What solutions have I found to solve these problems? (5) Are these solutions worthy of further investigation and potential case development? Or are there other problems and solutions in the resolution I would rather spend my time thinking about? (6) What is the best argument for the resolution? and (7) What is the best argument against the resolution? If you cannot answer these questions nor have an informed conversation about the topic, you need to continue your preliminary research. Once you feel comfortable discussing these questions, you are ready to begin researching to develop specific arguments.

Note: After you have developed your case, you will need to gather evidence to respond to every possible case your opponents may run in a debate round and every possible argument you expect against your own case. The techniques discussed below are useful for finding evidence against the arguments you anticipate your opponents making against your case. In order to anticipate these arguments, you must think very carefully about the topic, the current problems, and the myriad options experts have proposed and discussed regarding the topic.

1. Online Research

Return to the search engine and use the same techniques as before. Now that you have identified a particular path to investigate, add key words from that policy proposal or major theme. Search for the new keywords, add them into your old searches, and try them in unique orders. For example, if you think the best method of reforming America's revenue generation policy would be a Value Added Tax, you might want to search ["VAT" and "tax policy" and "United States"]. If, on the other hand, you prefer a flat tax, you would replace "VAT" with "Flat Tax." Another helpful search might include the name of a major proponent of the policy in your search. For a flat tax, you might include "Steve Forbes" who has been a longtime advocate for the flat income tax. All of these steps will produce numerous articles relating to one area of the topic. As before, save and print articles you find from credible sources. Then identify problems and proposed solutions in each article or identify major themes that could support a contention. Highlight key sentences and phrases so that you can return to those documents and copy those quotations onto your evidence briefs or even into your case.

2. Library Research

At the library there are three resources to use. First, go to the library catalog and search for the keywords you have found. Find some books on the topic and skim them. If a book seems to have quality information, look at its bibliography. The bibliography will allow you to glean new sources from the research the author already did! Second, find one of the computers in the library with access to research databases such as EBSCOhost, JSTOR, or LexisNexis. These research databases contain hundreds of thousands of fully-searchable articles from magazines, journals, and newspapers. Again, look at the references and bibliography in these sources. You never know what great article you might overlook if you neglect to read the research someone else already found. Finally, talk with the reference librarian. Ask the librarian to help you find sources which make specific arguments. Many reference librarians will search for articles on your behalf and make your research process more efficient. I suggest approaching a research librarian after the first two steps at the library because they may help you expand the research you already have. While the reference librarians are certainly helpful at all stages of your research, they will probably only give you basic information you could have found by yourself with a little work. If you have already discovered the basic information, the librarian will help you dig deeper.

3. It's Time to Stop Researching

Now you are in for the best part of this whole process. After reading hundreds of articles, skimming many books, and spending a short eternity staring at computer screens and printouts, you will have knowledge about your topic that puts you head and shoulders above your peers. This knowledge forms the basis for your debate topic.[10] Are you finished? Not really. But you now know what you know and can use this knowledge to guide your future research.

The time you spend learning about the topic in your first month of research will go a long way toward helping you prepare for the entire debate year. Often you will find policy analysis from a think tank which discusses a few key problems in a particular policy area, explains how those problems were caused by the current policies, and proposes specific changes in policy to

---

[10] In Public Forum and Lincoln-Douglas debate where the topics change frequently, the amount of time you take to become familiar with the topic should necessarily be shortened compared to policy debaters. See the section "Public Forum Research" for a brief discussion of the unique features of researching for that debate style.

remedy the situation. These policy analysis articles are a debater's best friend – they form the foundation of a fully researched case and a springboard as you prepare to identify a viable solution to several harms in the status quo (see page 122 for a discussion of a policy debate case).

After you have a substantial amount of research begin outlining the case or other arguments you want to make. This should take a couple hours or one afternoon. Outlining arguments will help you identify the gaps in your research you need to fill. For example, if you have evidence that says nuclear weapons threaten the environment, but no evidence to support your claim that a treaty can reduce the proliferation of nuclear weapons, you can identify such gaps as part of your outlining process. Outlining arguments and entire cases also provide a great opportunity to use the research you have accumulated and increase your familiarity with the evidence you already have gathered.

4. Future Researching

Later in the season when you need to find specific information or evidence, you know what to do. First, determine what you need it to say. Second, identify and use key words for your online search query in search engines and academic research databases. Third, rearrange the key words and read articles from think tanks which hold a **paradigm** friendly to the argument you are trying to make. Finally, if you still cannot find the evidence you need, or if you want even stronger arguments, seek out the reference librarian.

E. Public Forum Research

The combination of shorter debate rounds and frequently changing topics requires public forum debaters to research in a slightly different manner from policy debaters. While a policy debater may have months to become fully immersed in a topic in order to identify the very best arguments both in favor of the resolution and opposed to it, public forum debaters generally have only two or three months between the time a resolution is announced and the end of debates on that topic that debate season. Public forum debaters must quickly identify the major arguments within the resolution. They cannot dedicate months to fully understanding the resolution before writing cases.

Even though there is less time to dedicate to researching a given topic, public forum debaters cannot become lazy and ignore the necessity of developing significant knowledge of the underlying topic. A good public forum debater will develop a strategy to ensure she knows all the major arguments she could face within the topic area and that she has sufficient general knowledge about the topic that she can engage in intelligent discussion on numerous facets of the topic. This means recognizing the limited time to research and seeking a couple comprehensive overview articles of the topic early in the research process. It also means working together with a partner or a number of other debaters who can help to share the burden of becoming well-versed in the major researchers and major arguments debates under the resolution will encompass. Teamwork can certainly help all debaters to find significantly more information than they could individually, but the value of teamwork is highlighted because public forum debate topics change throughout the debate season and so complete knowledge of the entire topic is impossible.

Debaters should read two or three overview articles, identify a couple additional articles from the bibliography, and then begin brainstorming possible case ideas. These articles should be written by topic experts, academics and researchers who have dedicated thousands of hours to the topic, not debate coaches or fellow debaters. While articles focused specifically on how a debate topic may be debated can certainly help prepare you for the arguments you might hear in a debate round, they are often too focused on the debate round and miss important aspects of the topic area known to the experts. All the while, debaters can and should focus on becoming well-versed in the basics of the topic area. Often public forum debate cases will address an aspect of the resolution you and your partner have not anticipated. To be prepared to debate in such a scenario, it is important to understanding the major arguments about the resolution and the general arguments both in favor of and against the resolution.

After brainstorming potential contentions and case ideas, public forum debaters should try to find one or two major proponents who support the ideas under consideration. For example, if you and your partner want to write a case supporting an international peacekeeping mission in Sudan, find two political leaders or academics who have proposed such an idea and read what they have to say. The writings of experts who advocate for your case will serve as excellent evidence to support your case. Do this for both the pro and con case, and then try to identify experts who disagree with the experts that support your case. This will prepare you to defend your case against attacks and will also prepare you to attack other teams who make arguments similar to your own.

Public forum debate does not require debaters to ignore the general principals of research discussed earlier in this observation, but it does require debaters to more carefully manage their research time and quickly move from initial research into case writing. By recognizing the unique challenges of public forum debate research, debaters can develop their own strategy for research success: coupling sufficient general knowledge with more specific support for the contentions you and your partner intend to raise in your pro and con cases. Research is no less important in public forum debate, but debaters must ensure they understand the unique challenges they face to develop the knowledge they need to compete and win.

Research Questions to Ask

Does this article:
(1) talk about the topic I'm debating? (2) identify some particular problem or propose some particular change in policy? and (3) come from a reputable source I will be willing to quote in a debate round?

After you find articles ask:
(1) which side of the resolution do I believe is right? (2) which side of the resolution will my typical judge prefer? (3) what are the major problems in the current system? (4) what solutions have I found to solve these problems? (5) are these solutions worthy of further investigation and potential case development? Or are there other problems and solutions in the resolution I would rather spend my time thinking about? (6) what is the best argument for the resolution? and (7) what is the best argument against the resolution?

Figure 9: Research Questions

Research can be a difficult part of any academic project. While debaters should know how to research, many are better at making arguments than finding the evidence they need to support those arguments. Following these research techniques is one way to develop a strong foundation on which to build excellent research skills. If debaters will take the time to learn the skills of research they will not dread the research process because they will be able to produce quality evidence to support their winning arguments without wasting time wading through useless information.

Observation 8: Flowing

"He listens well who takes notes"
-Dante Alighieri-

Good debaters not only present their own positions, but they also identify the positions of their opponents before specifically refuting those positions. Over the course of a debate round, there may be twenty or more major arguments (complete with quoted evidence and statistics) made by each team to support the contentions and responses to the arguments made by opponents. Because it is impossible to remember every statement opponents make in the round, debaters have developed a note taking method to use during the debate round which is called "**flowing**." While this method may take a little getting used to, with practice, it will start to flow naturally (pun entirely intended).

Flowing is important because ignoring an argument made by your opponent is considered conceding that point to your opponent. Debaters must make sure they remember both what an opponent is arguing and their team's responses are to avoid conceding arguments. However, there is not enough time to actually record and review every word of every argument to ensure you do not ignore any arguments. Flowing is a middle ground which allows you to note the most significant arguments made by debaters on both sides, identify how you have addressed those arguments, and ensure that you point out issues your opponent has conceded by ignoring or dropping.

The flow gives a visual representation of the round so that you can observe arguments which need to be addressed or that have been **dropped**. By dividing the page into separate sections for each speech (eight sections for public forum and policy debate, five sections for Lincoln-Douglas debate, and six for parliamentary debate), notes can be taken from each speech across the page and every argument can be traced throughout the round. For each speech, debaters take short-hand notes for the arguments presented. The counter argument made in reply is noted next to it. Each argument made on a given subject should be connected by arrows or noted near the other related arguments. This helps the debater quickly see both what has been said and what remains to be addressed. Flowing will help you keep the round organized. Practice noting as much information from each argument in a fashion which assists you in following the arguments in the round. For an example of a blank flow sheet see page 177. Flowing allows you to keep your debate organized.

A. Basics

To flow, it is best to have at least two different colored pens and note paper (many debaters use a legal pad, but any paper will work). Divide the pages into eight columns (one column for each of the eight speeches). Next, as each speaker presents arguments, take notes in consecutive columns. The first speech for the affirmative or pro team (First Affirmative Constructive, 1AC, or First Pro Constructive, 1PC) is "flowed" in the first column, and the second speech for the negative or con team (First Negative Constructive, 1NC, or First Con Constructive, 1CC) is "flowed" in the second column, and so forth…. (These speeches and their shorthand abbreviations are discussed in more detail on pages 75 and 105). Use one color pen for each team's speeches (i.e. blue for affirmative or pro and red for negative or con). The key is to take your notes in reply to each particular argument directly next to the argument in the prior box. I like to use arrows between the original argument and the response just to be sure I'm following along. As long as the arguments are flowed next to one another you can follow the responses across the entire page.

Flow all the vital information: the argument's tag, the source of the quoted evidence, and the proper location of where it "flows" in relationship to prior arguments. Some debaters also try to include valuable, but not vital, secondary information such as: the impacts, a brief summary of the evidence, and missing links between the evidence and the ultimate conclusion your opponent is raising. If you can think of your response and get it written down without losing track of the arguments being made, jot a few notes to yourself in the space where your speech will be on the flow sheet.

B. Examples

Below is an example of a very basic flow of two arguments in the constructive speeches in a policy debate round (see page 105 for a fuller discussion of the components of the policy debate round). The first speaker (the first affirmative or 1A) makes two arguments: (1) Though many things are subject to debate, we can all agree that the sky is blue; (2) We support the proposition that A is true. The opposing speaker (the first negative or 1N) replies to those arguments: (1) We cannot agree that the sky is blue all the time, in fact right now the sky is gray; (2) The fact of the matter is that A is not always true. The first speaker's teammate (2A) answers: (1) While the sky may appear gray right now, a gray sky actually requires that it have a blue background; (2) Even if A is not always true, A is true more often than A is false. The second speaker's teammate (2N) replies: (1) No one defines the color of something by its background, but the foreground, thus a gray sky is gray and not blue; (2) There are numerous instances where A is false, it is only sometime true, thus we continue to hold that A is not always true.

1AC	1NC	2AC	2NC
Sky is blue	Sky is gray	Gray skies require blue background	Background is not how we define a color, the foreground is
A	Not always A	A more often than not	A only sometimes

Figure 10: Example Policy Debate Flow

The following is an example of a very basic flow of two arguments made beginning with the second speech in the round and flowing through the summary speeches in a public forum debate round (see page 75 for a fuller discussion of the components of the public forum debate round). The first speaker (the first con or the 1C) makes two arguments: (1) When comparing colors, red is preferable to blue; (2) We support the proposition that A is true. The opposing speaker (the second pro or 2P) replies to those arguments: (1) Red cannot be better than blue because blue is associated with fun and fun colors are better; (2) The fact of the matter is that A is not always true. The first speaker's teammate (2C) answers: (1) Comparing colors on the basis of fun is ridiculous, colors should be judged based on whether they are useful to artists and society; (2) Even if A is not always true, A is true more often than A is false. The second speaker's teammate (1P) replies: (1) Celebrations employ blue more than red and blue prompts excitement among crowds and so it is clear blue is a more fun color; (2) There are numerous instances where A is false, it is only sometime true, thus we continue to hold that A is not always true. The first speaker rises again and answers: (1) Artists and fashion designers use red more than blue, and thus because red is more useful, it is better than blue; (2) We have shown that A is true most often which is all we have to do to show that A is deserving of support.

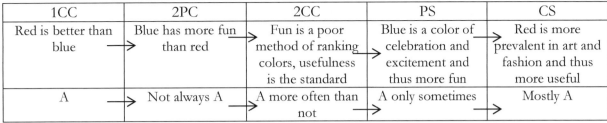

1CC	2PC	2CC	PS	CS
Red is better than blue	Blue has more fun than red	Fun is a poor method of ranking colors, usefulness is the standard	Blue is a color of celebration and excitement and thus more fun	Red is more prevalent in art and fashion and thus more useful
A	Not always A	A more often than not	A only sometimes	Mostly A

Figure 11: Example Public Forum Debate Flow

The flow does not capture every word used in forming the argument, but provides enough notes to remind the note-taker what was said in the speech. Notice how the argument about the sky does not simply repeat itself, but develops over the speeches. Also notice that the arrows connect the arguments so it is easy to see which point is made in response to another point (i.e. "Not always A" is in response to "A" and not in response to "Sky is blue"). Recognize that non-speech interactions (cross-examination, crossfire, preparation time) are not included on the flowsheet. While these interactions are certainly important parts of the debate round, in general the only arguments which judges ultimately use to make their decisions are those made in the speeches themselves.[11]

C. Flowing Special Arguments

Every debate style has special arguments which may arise only in particular speeches. For example, counterplans (discussed on page 149) and disadvantages (discussed on page 133) in policy debate and the second speaking team's case in public forum debate (discussed on page 83) are not presented in the very first speech in the round. These arguments can be flowed in a variety of ways. The best method of preparing to flow such arguments is to set aside one or two flow pages at the beginning of the round for these special arguments. Because counterplans are usually presented in the first negative constructive, the page is divided into seven sections. The same is true for the second team's case in a public forum round. Rather than trying to fit these arguments into other parts of the flow, it is easier to follow along by saving separate pages of your flow for the arguments. That way you will be sure to address these arguments in the round.

Another concern many debaters have is trying to flow their own speeches. While it may be helpful to have these notes, this is where having a good partner comes in handy. Rather than trying to pre-flow the arguments you are going to make (other than for your case—you already know what you are going to say so type up a prepared flow page with the major arguments and paperclip it to your flow pad), your partner should keep track of the arguments you make to ensure you are not missing anything. If you and your partner work together, you can be sure you are noting every argument that comes up in the round.

D. Flowing Practice

Flowing, just like taking notes in school when listening to a lecture or reading a textbook, takes practice. There are thousands of words being spoken in a round. You must identify only the most important words to write down so you can remember what your opponent said and know how to reply. All the while, you will be thinking about how you plan to respond and listening to the next argument! Develop your own shorthand (i.e. "USFG = United States Federal Government") so you do not have to write long words or phrases. Practice writing small enough that you can have plenty of information on each page, but not so small you have

---

[11] This does not mean cross-examination or crossfire are unimportant. As pages 89 and 131 discuss, the questioning periods are important to establish yourself as a credible advocate.

trouble reading what you wrote. Also, practice writing quickly while maintaining the clarity and legibility of your writing. Some debaters have found that flowing on their laptops using a spreadsheet program works well. Depending on your league, this may be an alternative option you could consider if you have trouble reading your handwriting or if you can type faster than you can write. Flowing will not be great without practice. With many rounds of practice, you will become a master at flowing. Then you will be able to keep track of the numerous arguments flying around in the debate round with ease.

One useful method of practicing flowing is to take notes everywhere you hear someone speaking. This includes television news, classroom lectures, educational web clips, and speeches to groups on any topic. By learning to write quickly and absorb as much information as possible whenever you listen, you will improve your flowing as well as improve your listening skills. Another practice tip to try with your team is to watch debaters who read evidence and their cases at a very brisk pace while trying to flow the arguments they make. Then review your flow with teammates or other debaters who have watched the same speech to see what other arguments you missed. Watching a video of a debate round with more experienced debaters who can flow the round themselves and then review your flow will also improve the quality of your flow. Re-watching the same debate after discussing your flow with your coach or teammate will give you a chance to put your new-found strategies into practice.

The flow is a vital part of keeping the debate round organized. Even if you have strong arguments, if you make it difficult for the judge to follow the debate round, the judge is more likely to lose focus or miss arguments you are trying to make. By flowing the debate round, you can tell the judge exactly which argument you are addressing and help the judge know where the round is going at all times. Though not the most exciting aspect of debate, the flow will help you keep track of the many arguments in the debate round. Flowing is also a valuable tool to lend structure to your arguments. A strong flow will enhance the organization of the round so the judge can spend her time focusing on the reasons you have won the argument rather than trying to figure out how your arguments fit into the round.

Observation 9: Strategy

"Strategy without tactics is the slowest route to victory.
Tactics without strategy is the noise before defeat."
-Sun Tzu-

Competitive debate offers more than the opportunity to test ideas against one another. Debate, like every "sport," requires strategic planning as well as in-round adjustment to identify and execute a plan for victory. Choosing which arguments to make, the timing of arguments, the method of presenting an argument, and identifying what matters to your audience are debate strategies. Because debate is mainly focused on how to persuade your audience, debaters must consider more than just the arguments they make. Judges will consider how persuasive each speaker is, the strength of the arguments each speaker makes, how comfortable the speakers are in making those arguments, and whether those arguments are appealing to the audience. Debaters do more than make arguments; they must strategize about the likely responses their opponents will make and the likelihood the arguments will win the judge's vote.

A. Judges

Talk to the judge when you make arguments in the round. You only have to win his vote. Be as persuasive as possible. Do not rely on good lines of argumentation alone. Clear, persuasive speeches can go a long way in persuading the judge. Presenting structured arguments (see page 13) and following the order of arguments from the flow (see page 47) make a debater more persuasive.

Another tactic is to cater your presentation to your judge. If you know your judge likes economics, talk about economics. If he likes ethics, talk about ethics. If your judge likes unique debate theory, try out your latest alternative method of argument. Catering your arguments to your judge is most useful if you know something about your judge's prior experience or his judging philosophy. If you know this information, you can debate in a manner which will best communicate with him. Even if your judge does not provide his philosophy or tell you what he is looking for in the round, you can learn to read his preferences by watching his reactions to the arguments made in the round. If he seems particularly interested in one topic or especially persuaded by a particular argument, focus your energy and speech time there. If, on the other hand, one argument seems to annoy the judge, move on to something else. Keep in mind that if the judge votes against you, you did not persuade him that you should have won. The judge is always right. The judge may make a decision you disagree with, but his vote is all that matters in the end. It is your job to make the reasons to vote for you clear enough for the judge to make a decision in your favor.

B. Speech Presentation

Presentation is very important to your success as a debater. You may have the strongest arguments on paper, but if they are not presented in an organized and convincing fashion, you will find it difficult to persuade your audience. Most good debaters are also good speakers. Although the case, refutation, evidence, and logic used in a round are what the judge is supposed to vote on, your presentation of the various components of the debate, the case, refutation, evidence, and logic are equally important. If you speak well, use good arguments, and remain poised throughout the round, your ideas will be better understood. If you have an inexperienced judge, your speaking skills are even more important to persuade the judge that you are credible and the arguments that you are making deserve his vote. However, even in a round with experienced judges, better speakers will usually win close rounds. If you are overly aggressive you will lose credibility and possibly the round. Your effectiveness as a debater will be closely connected to the quality of your speeches.

The pace of your speech will vary by debate league and debate format. Some leagues require "conversational" speaking in policy debate, while others permit "spreading" meaning reading as fast as possible. In public forum debate, you must speak slowly enough that judges who are not former debaters can still follow your arguments. Because public forum's purpose is to persuade any audience, no matter their background, the rules explicitly limit your speaking speed. No matter what rules your league follows, you should make sure your words are understandable and you appear persuasive to your audience. This means making eye contact with the audience, providing a clear **roadmap** and organization of your points and subpoints in the speech, and identifying which issues the judge should focus on as the round comes to a close.

Quality speaking goes hand in hand with winning debate. Good debaters are effective speakers. While good debaters will spend significant time practicing the various skills needed for a debate round (see page 55 for practice drills to improve debate skills), they also spend time honing their public speaking skills. Giving speeches, even those unrelated to debate, will help you better communicate a message. By altering your rate, tone, and pitch, you will be more interesting to the audience. Practicing articulation, working on non-verbal communication, and establishing rapport with an audience will cultivate your skills of communication. There are numerous resources to help you become a better speaker, but the skills of strong verbal communication should not be overlooked when learning the unique skills of formal debate. A debater who strengthens his speaking skills will be more likely to win rounds.

C. Roadmap

Setting a strategy before the round begins is important for both teams. If you support the resolution, your goal is to convince the judge and the audience that it should be adopted by developing and strengthening your case. Your goal is to develop and strengthen your case in order to convince your judge and audience that your positions should be adopted. If you oppose the resolution, you should use every chance you have to undermine the resolution whether that is by opposing the other team's case or presenting your own case against the resolution. Translating your strategy to your words in a round is a hallmark of good debaters. The ability to adjust the strategy throughout the debate round depending on the arguments made against you separates the great debaters from the good debaters.

One way to translate your strategy into practical steps in the round is to look at a debate round as three roadmaps. First, the team supporting the resolution has a roadmap of where they want to take the round. Second, the negative has their roadmap as well. Third, the other roadmap is the one being drawn during the round by all the debaters. As debaters spend time talking about the strong points on their own side of the debate round, they attempt to make the third roadmap look more and more like their own roadmap. Conversely, the more time a debater spends talking about his opponents' strong points, the more the third roadmap will look like the planned roadmap of his opponents. Each team's goal should be to move as far along its own roadmap as possible by spending more time talking about the points they are winning rather than defending losing points or trying to undermine the opponent. Most often, the team which better achieves this goal will win the round.

A good check for partners during the round is to ask, "Are we moving along our roadmap?" If the majority of each speech is spent defending your position against the attacks of the opposition, you are not following your roadmap. Simply defending your position against attacks is not going to be enough to persuade the judge that your arguments are strong. The more you argue for your position and the longer you remain on your roadmap, the better you "draw" the map you desire for your judge. Spend time selling your case so the judge is persuaded to cast a ballot in your favor rather than trying to persuade the judge to cast a ballot *against* your opponents. Keep the roadmap idea in mind as you debate and use it as a tool to keep you on track.

D. Turnarounds

The turnaround uses opposing arguments against the opponent. Through inductive reasoning, the turnaround can help the audience see a bigger picture than the original argument revealed, showing that what was thought to be a strong attack against you is actually a point in your favor. For example, a disadvantage can be turned around and shown to be an advantage. All debaters can utilize the turnaround. Arguments may seem to support one position, but when scrutinized, support an opposing view. For example, if your opponent argues that cutting subsidies to college bookstores will cause hundreds of students to go without their textbooks, a turnaround might point out that cutting the subsidies will actually reduce tuition costs by more than the average student pays for books so students will actually save money in a world without the bookstore subsidy. (See page 137 for discussion of the turnaround in responding to a policy debate disadvantage).

Turning an opposing argument into an argument supporting your cause is highly effective because your opponent cannot argue that the underlying premise is faulty without undermining his own credibility. Why, your judge would ask herself, would he argue that an argument he originally made was no longer correct? An effective turn will leave your opponent to concede the issue and hope the judge gives it little consideration in her final analysis. For example, if your opponent argues that treating juveniles as adults in the criminal justice system results in safer streets because the juvenile offenders are in prison for longer terms, you could turn this argument by noting that long prison terms result in hardened criminals who will make the streets significantly more dangerous when they are ultimately released. Your opponent cannot question your argument because his entire argument is premised on safety today, but you are pointing out the long-term loss of safety.

A specific type of turnaround is the linguistic turnaround. While communication theory research has devoted time to this topic, its explanation is warranted here as well.[12] The basic premise of the linguistic turnaround is the use of the exact words, actions, or visuals of an opponent to identify the argument's underlying weakness. By quoting an opponent directly, a debater uses the linguistic turnaround. For example, if one debater states: "placing innocent individuals in prison is an acceptable risk to reduce crime," his opponent might attack this argument by pointing out how the position is well outside the mainstream. When politicians quote their opponents making outrageous statements, they are employing the linguistic turnaround.

The turnaround can also take the form of redefining terminology. If an opponent keeps using a term such as "liberal" with a negative connotation, you can turn around this argument by showing times when liberalism was beneficial (i.e. America's founding fathers were "liberals" because that they did not want to conserve the current system). The use of the

---

[12] The linguistic turnaround is discussed in great detail in Palczewski and Madsen's 1993 article "The Divisiveness of Diversity: President Bush's University of Michigan Commencement Speech as an Example of the Linguistic Turnaround" published in *Argumentation and Advocacy*, Vol. 30.

linguistic turnaround is a valuable debater's tool. The ability to recognize opposing arguments which actually support your case will make you more successful.

E. Concede Issues

Often debaters feel they must argue every issue which arises in a round. If an opponent says rain is cold, the debater believes she must contest the point. Even if the statement about the temperature of the rain is made in passing, some eager debaters think they have an obligation to contradict it. Not only does the limited time in a debate round make contesting every argument impossible, wasting time discussing the unimportant statements leaves debaters with less time to develop the truly important arguments (for a discussion of how to identify important issues in the debate round, see pages 97 and 155). Arguing against every point can also make the debate round hard to follow because minor points are discussed at length. It is not bad, and even advisable, to concede some issues. It is in your best interest to debate the issues you have the best chance to win, rather than simply being argumentative on every point.

Identify which arguments actually matter to winning the round and focus on those. If you do not intend to spend significant time debating a particular matter, do not bring it up. Once you highlight an issue, the judge believes that issue matters in the round. Ignoring issues, just like ignoring petty comments in the real world, minimizes their importance to the audience. If you are planning to wrestle with your opponent over one issue, spending time explaining why your position is better will be much more beneficial than quickly noting your disagreement with every minor issue along the way. Even though you are debating, there is nothing wrong with admitting the other team is right on some issues. Admitting your opponent is right makes you appear more reasonable. By arguing everything, you seem to be arguing for the sake of arguing instead of trying to give the judge a clear picture. If you concede issues, the judge will see those which you do contest as more important and be more willing to give ear to your arguments. Focusing on important issues shows the audience you are reasonable and focuses their attention on your strongest issues, thus giving you the edge.

Observation 10: Practice Drills

"Practice is the best of all instructors"
-Publilius Syrus-

Debaters gain proficiency in the various facets of debate through drills which develop the entire debater. Some of these drills require a club or a few people knowledgeable about the topic, others can be done alone, and still others can be done with any group of people even if they are non-debaters. Drills give debaters opportunities to practice specific aspects of a debate round without all the pressures of keeping the entire debate in perspective.

A. Cross-Examination / Crossfire Practice

Cross-examination practice can be done in many different ways.[13] Depending on the size of the group, one debater reads his case and the other debaters flow. Immediately following the case, each student is allowed a two minute cross-examination of the speaker. This usually works best with 6-8 students. The rules are simple: no question may be repeated; each questioner must use the entire two minutes; both speakers must take the questions seriously; and someone must write down every question asked. The questioner must maintain control of the questions, move on to new questions and attempt to trap the speaker into admitting a weakness or conceding an argument.

This practice is a wonderful learning experience for both the cross-examiners and cross-examinee. All students learn that cross-examination is not a time for bullying, being rude, overbearing, or aggressive. Instead, cross-examination is a time of questioning which, when properly utilized, strengthens your case without personally tearing down the opposing debater. Learning to strike the balance between taking charge without being aggressive and being confident without being cocky, are two more lessons learned and refined through cross-examination practice.

The student being cross-examined will learn many skills during this period. If there are seven students cross-examining her, the questioning will last nearly twenty minutes. Since during this time no questions are repeated, the case will be thoroughly attacked. During this exercise the debater will gain insight into areas of weakness in her case. The list of questions will help the student to recognize areas of weakness which will guide her research to fill the holes. She will also gain endurance by standing up and remaining focused for the long questioning period which will prepare her to stay poised for the much shorter seven to eleven minute periods of real rounds. Finally, the student being cross-examined will build confidence in being cross-examined. Rather than dreading the period of cross-examination, students will begin to see cross-examination as a time to use refined skills and strengthen the case. This perspective of cross-examination will better prepare students for the competition. They will begin to look forward to the privilege of turning questions into springboards to strengthen their case.

Cross-examination practice also gives the other students greater time to think about a good cross-examination. Rather than using the first questions which come to mind, some students will be able to thoroughly examine the case and ask questions they ordinarily would not have the time to develop. This gives all the debaters an opportunity to function at a higher level and set their own goals of reaching that level on a regular basis. By not allowing students to repeat questions they are forced to come up with questions of increasing difficulty

---

[13] This drill can be equally beneficial in practicing public forum debate's crossfire or parliamentary debate's points of information.

for the speaker. The in-depth questioning expands the horizons of all debaters involved in the practice by requiring them to dig deep to find new questions to ask. This also encourages students to volunteer to ask cross-examination questions quickly rather than try to avoid participation.

By limiting the round to just the cross-examinations, the students learn the value of building a line of questioning which can trap the speaker in a contradiction. Sometimes it takes just one extra question to get there. The value of one more question should be pointed out by observers after a questioner has finished. The art of asking questions will begin to become more apparent to the debaters. Rather than simply asking questions about quotations read, cross-examination will become a tool in building a case against your opponent. The confidence from practicing lines of questioning and asking other questions cannot be matched. Because there are no speeches after the cross-examination, the debaters focus on the questions. This teaches debaters to use the cross-examination period to build arguments rather than as a transition between the speeches of the two sides.

A few notes: One temptation is to alter the time for questioners. At first, students may not have enough questions to fill two minutes and they may complain that two minutes is too long. However, after one or two questioners rise, there will be plenty of requests for extra time because students will want to ask more questions than two minutes permit. By forcing the debaters to limit their time, they begin to realize the importance of managing their cross-examination time. Rather than seeing it as a limitless frontier, cross-examination becomes a precious time to fully utilize. Another consideration is coaching during the questioning. It is good to coach the students regarding how to stand, where to stand, where to look, etc., during the cross-examination practice. However, the students should formulate their own questions without assistance from a parent/coach. Even if a question does not seem to apply, there is time for coaching question formulation at a later time. Coaches or leaders should take notes about which questions could have been better asked, but the coaching during the cross-examination practice should be kept to a minimum. Finally, let parents and other observers get involved in this drill. If they understand the topic, allow them to get up and ask questions as well. Everyone who asks questions should do so as if it were a round. It is recommended that every student practice being cross-examined using this type of drill at least once before a tournament.

B. Generic Negative Drill

The purpose of the generic negative drill is to prepare you for a case presented by your opponent you were not prepared to debate before the round began. It is best suited to help develop proficiency in arguments which undermine the foundation of a case, the major premises of the case, or the underlying foundation of the resolution rather than the specific aspects of the case. The generic negative drill helps debaters develop a repertoire of negative arguments which can be run in nearly every situation.

Read a "squirrelly" case the debaters have not heard before (a case not typically run under the topic) and give one minute to prepare a two minute speech using evidence against the case. This drill teaches debaters to use generic evidence to build arguments against all sorts of cases. Similar to evidence-less debating (see page 60), this negative drill forces quick thinking about a case they have never heard and stretches debaters thinking to utilize analytical skills to identify weak arguments and arguments which employ logical fallacies (see page 23).

An alternative method is to write down four to five assertions on the top of a page and require each debater to prepare two full arguments in response to each of the assertions. After writing out the arguments, the debaters stand up and present their arguments by clearly articulating which assertion they are addressing and providing clear impacts to every point made. For example, write down the assertions: low taxes will help the poor, regulations increase safety in children's toys, and subsidies punish consumers by forcing them to pay higher prices. Each debater should use three-point refutation (see page 15) to make two responses to each assertion.

This drill gives debaters a chance to test their negative philosophies (see page 127). Arguing that change is harmful and then applying that argument to a "squirrelly" case can be great practice in using the philosophy. Rather than having a long speech to argue against each and every point of the case, the negative drill constrains debaters to one, two, or three arguments which undermine the entire case. Even if an unfamiliar case is presented, this drill gives you practice to successfully argue the merits of the status quo as well as the harms of changing it.

C. Refutation Drill

Three and four-point refutation are the most effective ways to address arguments in a debate round. They provide a structure upon which a strong response can be built (see page 13 for a discussion of how to present arguments). The refutation drill will begin to make three and four-point refutation (see page 15) natural parts of any debater's responsive repertoire.

Divide into groups of two or three students. Pull out a list of arguments about one case and focus on one main topic. The first student presents two arguments in support of her contention or advantage. The next student uses 3-point refutation (Do not forget the impact) to reply to the statements. Switch. Continue until you have made at least ten arguments and your opponent has replied to ten arguments. If the refutation does not include an impact, be sure to point this out and have the debater repeat the argument with a clear impact. Then switch sides of the debate. First, make at least ten arguments. Then refute at least ten arguments.

An example can clarify how this drill should look. The first student argues that wind energy should be subsidized because (1) it is currently too expensive to compete with fossil fuels and (2) promoting renewable energy will protect the environment. The opposing student replies to both arguments: (1) my opponent argues wind energy needs a subsidy to compete with fossil fuels, I say even with a subsidy wind energy is too expensive to compete, therefore subsidizing still-uncompetitive wind energy will simply waste money in already tight government budgets; (2) my opponent also argues that renewable energy protects the environment, but I say wind energy actually endangers migratory birds which are vital to our ecosystem, therefore there is little environmental benefit from renewable energy and this minimal benefit is not worthy of a government subsidy with tight government budgets.

This drill is most beneficial when the debaters are unwilling to let their teammate make an argument leaving out one of the points in the refutation. If a debater neglects signposting, the other debater should point this out and make him re-start the argument. The same if the debater forgets to include an impact. The more repetition of the three and four-point refutation style of argumentation a debater performs, the more likely he is to use this format in every round and in response to every argument.

To increase the level of difficulty, try to refute your teammate's refutation (Argument; Refutation of the argument; Refutation of the refutation of the argument). When the whole team comes back together, everyone should try to present and refute one argument for the whole group. The debaters should be sure to follow the structure in each repetition of the argument and every debater should help ensure that each refutation ends with a clear impact to explain to the judge why the argument matters and why she should vote for your team.

D. Piranha Pack

The purpose of the piranha pack is to find every possible hole or weakness in a debate case, while also identifying the remedy to these problems. A piranha pack is similar to cross-examination practice, but the debaters do not have to take two-minute turns. Piranha packs begin much like cross-examination practice. Both partners should be present for this exercise to be most effective. A case is read and everyone flows (for discussion of the components of a debate case for public forum debate see page 83 and for policy debate see page 115). After the debater reads the case, everyone may ask any questions they might have as well as point out arguments against the case. For example, if someone asks, "Can the current system provide the people of America with a good national defense?," the team defending the case would write down the question and provide their answer. Another person could then point out that this plan will eliminate an important means of military intelligence. Both partners should have a piece of paper and alternate writing down the questions, comments, and arguments given against their case. Unlike cross-examination practice, piranha packs do not require questions from only persons knowledgeable about the topic. Instead, allowing people who are unfamiliar with the topic to ask questions, comment on unclear areas, and make their own arguments and observations will give the case additional strength.

1. Guidelines

Here are some important guidelines for a piranha pack: (1) Only one person can talk at a time. If everyone starts talking at once, no one will gain anything from the experience. (2) Because there is no set time for each person to speak, a few people may begin to dominate the conversation, so a facilitator might need to ask debaters who are dominating the conversation to allow others to speak. (3) Limit the size of the group to roughly eight debaters and a few others who will be providing comments and feedback. (4) Select someone to serve as the moderator or facilitator. He keeps the conversation from becoming bogged down so that all participants are involved without one speaker dominating. If one speaker begins dominating the conversation, call on other participants to ask questions and engage with the material. (5) It is a privilege to have your case critiqued in a piranha pack. Do not take offense if your case is under attack. The students having their case attacked need to capitalize on the opportunity to have other people identify new weaknesses in their case. (6) Unlike cross-examination practice, the team presenting their case should only answer questions. They should not try to respond to arguments. When arguments are introduced, the team should simply write them down for later analysis. (7) Involve everyone. The more voices and the more unique arguments raised in the session, the stronger the case will become. (8) Set a time limit and stick to it. Since piranha packs tend to get lively, you may be tempted to keep working even past the time limit. Do your best to set a time limit (30-45 minutes) and stick to it. This drill will allow enough time to delve deeply into the case without becoming either too exciting or boring for any of the participants.

2. Next Steps

After the piranha pack is over, the team who presented the case should take every argument, comment, question, and point into consideration. After writing them down, they should make certain that they have evidence and a complete argument to answer each and every point brought up in the piranha pack. This will prepare the case for competition. Later, the team should decide who will work on what portions of the case the next week and divide their responsibilities to assure that the piranha pack was not in vain.

3. Benefits

The benefits of piranha packs are many. First, the team having their case piranha packed will be shown numerous new shortcomings or holes in their case. By finding these holes, the team can spend the next week working out the kinks in the case so that they will be prepared for tournament arguments. Second, piranha packs allow all students who participate in questioning to hear numerous arguments. While cross-examination practice gives debaters a chance to understand lines of questioning in action, piranha packs show the numerous arguments which can be made on just one case. Rather than the surface arguments, piranha packs (because they last for a long period of time) tend to bring out the deeper arguments about the foundation of the case. This type of argumentation may be foreign to some students, but it will soon become a part of their debate repertoire. Third, this activity gets everyone involved. Unlike cross-examination practice where knowledge of the topic is imperative, the insight of people without topic or debate knowledge is helpful in a piranha pack.

Piranha packs are a great way to strengthen a case, build group camaraderie, teach argumentation, and have fun in the process. Students who use the piranha pack see the benefits in their argumentation as well as in their own cases. While the piranha pack is no sure fire way to build an impenetrable case, it does help to fortify the case and the team involved by giving them greater confidence in their ability to defend their own arguments in a round.

E. Evidence Find

The evidence find is a basic drill which helps you practicing quick retrieval of your evidence. The drill can take place alone, with your partner, or even as a large group. Someone calls out a topic (trying to be somewhat specific), for example "flat taxes help the rich" and the debaters see how long it takes to find evidence on that topic in their evidence box. Later, the difficulty of the drill can be increased by moving on to specific quotations or briefs. Knowing where your evidence is in your files prepares you to use it in a round. The worst part of debate is wasting time digging through your files for the evidence you know will win the round. This drill tests your organizational skills as well as your ability to quickly access what you have organized.

While this drill may seem elementary, it is often neglected by debaters. The ability to find evidence at a moment's notice may sometimes be the difference between using prep time to strategize with your partner and simply stacking up pieces of evidence to use in a speech. The debater who can find her evidence with ease can manage prep time and the time during the other speeches much more effectively.

This drill can be varied in a few ways. One method is to practice accessing evidence without looking at your files. This helps you keep your eyes on your flow, the speaker, or your partner while you find your evidence. If you can find your evidence by simply reaching into your box, book, or card file, without looking, you will have no problem accessing files when you can actually look! Another variation is to switch boxes with your partner. Try finding evidence in his/her box and assure that you both have the same evidence. This way you will both be able to find files in each other's boxes in the rare case that you misplace your own evidence.

F. Mini-Debate Rounds

The mini-round cuts a policy debate into a shorter period. With the purpose of limiting the arguments and making the round move more quickly, mini-rounds give debaters some in-round experience without taking the nearly two hours a full policy round requires. Rather than debating the case in depth, mini rounds force debaters to focus on the key arguments from the onset. Superfluous arguments are ignored because they waste precious time. Debaters make clear, concise arguments and then move on to more arguments.

Mini rounds can be tailored to your needs regarding time, number of students, and goals. A typical mini round cuts most speeches in the round in half. For policy debate the first speech (1AC) is still eight minutes, but the cross-examinations are one and a half minutes, the other constructive speeches are four minutes, and the rebuttals are two and a half minutes (the first rebuttal, the 1AR, is given three minutes). Each team is given three minutes of prep time. These rounds last about 45 minutes leaving time for some comments by a judge at the end of the round. Another option is to use the public forum time structures—diminishing the speaking time from four minute constructive speeches to only one or two minute **final focus** speeches—as it requires the end of the debate to focus on only one or two key arguments.

One precaution should be taken in mini rounds: do not allow the round to suddenly become a race. Debaters must continue to speak at the same pace as a normal debate round. If debaters move too quickly, they will lose the judge and therefore lose the round. These speeches should look just like any debate speech except that they simply address fewer arguments.

Mini rounds are valuable especially at the beginning of the debate season. After a case is built, mini rounds can help all the debaters to get back into debate mode. These rounds can also fit into much shorter periods of time which saves time for other items of importance at debate meetings. The mini round gives debaters a chance to focus on only a few arguments. This gives them greater reason to directly attack arguments rather than approach them slowly. It also trains debaters to make clear, convincing, and concise arguments in longer rounds. By concentrating on only the key issues, debaters will learn to select important arguments and to concede or ignore unimportant arguments. Shorter time limits help time management in full rounds. Rather than burying the good arguments in a mound of unimportant issues, the shorter time forces the debaters to focus on the most important (see page 155) issues that build a stronger case. These skills, when transferred into full rounds, will help the debater be the best she can be.

G. Evidence-Less Debate

Debaters may find themselves in the state of deficiency when it comes to evidence. There will be rounds where debaters do not have evidence to refute a specific argument or an entire case. When this situation arises, argumentation skills are tested to the fullest. In preparation for this precarious situation, debaters can practice debating without evidence. These debates could be full rounds, mini-rounds, or any other type of round. The only rule is simple: no evidence is to be used by either side and neither team may argue about evidence.

Evidence-less debating is unique. Being able to find holes in a case without relying on the "experts" is an important aspect of becoming a good debater. There will often be times when you lack evidence to defeat an opponent's argument. At such times you must rely on logic, common knowledge, and specialized topic knowledge you have developed in order to win. By debating without evidence, you learn that arguments are the foundation for a debate round. Evidence simply supports the arguments you are already making. Rather than centering the debate on the evidence you have, arguments become the central theme of the round.

Each team has weaknesses in their arguments. Often debaters rely on the "experts" to point these out. Other times, these weaknesses are ignored because debaters do not have a piece of evidence to point out the weakness. Instead of focusing on the evidence a debater has in his box, evidence-less debating forces debaters to examine each argument on its own merits. Often arguments begin to come "out of thin air" and the debaters realize their own grasp of the topic. Overall, evidence-less debating makes the debaters stronger in their skills.

Evidence-less debating is a skill which capable debaters develop. Because the round is based on arguments rather than evidence, debating without evidence helps the student learn to utilize arguments alone. When evidence is once again permitted, the arguments become much more clear and convincing. The evidence simply adds support to the already convincing argument. Debating without evidence builds more confident debaters.

H. Critiqued Rounds

The critiqued round (also known as a stop-start round) brings all aspects of coaching into the debate round. It allows the coach/parent/captain to see the students in action and give tips and other pointers during the round. Critiqued rounds are valuable for all students involved as well as for those who observe.

Critiqued rounds follow a few general guidelines. First, the debaters have extra note paper to write down the comments given to their partners. Second, each team must be prepared to stop at a moment's notice during a speech or cross-examination/crossfire. Third, the timer must stop the time during each comment from the judge.

The judge who critiques has a unique responsibility in a critiqued round. Instead of simply taking notes and giving written comments to the debaters on the ballot or verbal feedback as the debaters pack up their materials, the judge stops the debaters during their speeches to point out ways to improve. For example, during the speeches, if an argument is not clear, the judge will stop the speaker and ask, "What are you trying to say?" When the student answers, the judge will attempt to help the student formulate a clearer argument. The immediate feedback will not only make the argument clearer in that speech, but it will also help the debater construct stronger arguments in the future. Judge comments may encompass critiques regarding speaking style, argument construction, evidence use, poise, non-verbals, and logic. Often debaters make unnecessary arguments. Asking the debater why he made the argument helps the debater consider his contention and find better arguments in the future. The critique will point out as many aspects of the speech as possible in order to give the speaker additional help in becoming a better debater.

Depending on the experience level of the debaters, the judge can decide how picky to be. Often some debaters will have many more aspects of their speech which need to be scrutinized than others. Some debaters will need assistance in formulating questions and arguments in the round. Other debaters only need to polish their arguments. The judge should give critiques at the level the student can assimilate. As a judge, it is important to allow the student time to speak. Critiquing every little item may not allow the speaker more than a sentence at a time. Depending on the experience of the students, this may be beneficial, but it will not be encouraging for beginning debaters. Taking into consideration the skills and experience of the debaters will help them gain the most from the experience.

Students need to be aware of a few key aspects when being critiqued. First and foremost, being critiqued is a great privilege. While the judge or judges who critique you may not always seem to make perfect sense or to understand your reasoning for making an argument, they are giving you their time and energy in an effort to help you to become a better debater. Be grateful that you have been selected to be critiqued. Do not take offense at the comments given for your betterment, they are not meant to demean you in any way. Respect the judge and any other person who might be critiquing your speeches as someone who can equip you to present successful arguments in real rounds.

Second, debaters need to take notes during the round. It is imperative that the critiqued round not end with a few comments tucked away in your brain. Taking note of every comment made to your partner will provide a long list of helpful hints to consider after the round. Finally, treat the round as a real round. Pretend that the critiqued round is just like any other round so that you will make the mistakes you are in the habit of making. Then, these can be pointed out and eliminated during the critiqued round so they will not reappear in a real round.

Critiqued rounds are wonderful practice for real rounds. By exposing yourself to the critique of a judge in the midst of a debate you will discover areas you can change to make you a more proficient debater. The debater who makes the changes prescribed will find herself becoming stronger in all areas of the debate round. Rather than simply bringing a few comments to light at the end of the round, instant comments allow you to remedy the situation at that moment. At the end of the critiqued round you will be exhausted, but when you look back on the experience, you will be very glad that you did it because your debating will be better for it.

While the debate round is the ultimate challenge for a debater, the drills he uses to prepare for rounds are often the difference between a strong and weak round. Drills, like those used in athletics or music, can help develop fundamental skills in controlled settings. These drills hone in on portions of debate which can be overlooked in full debate rounds. The debater who uses drills and practices debate basics will be more confident in the round. These drills develop skills as they simultaneously prepare debaters for debate rounds and build the fundamental skills into good habits for real rounds. Then, a natural part of the debater's routine focuses on the arguments of the round without worrying about the specific mechanics.

Observation 11: The Debate Ballot

"The best way I know to win an argument is to start by being in the right"
-Lord Hailsham-

The winner of a formal debate round is decided when the judge records her decision on a ballot. While debaters often care little for anything other than the vote in the round, there are many other aspects of this ballot which are beneficial for debaters, parents, teachers, and coaches. The ballot has many sections which can be used to assist debaters in strengthening their debate skills. There are speaker points (sometimes including specific categories to rate), speaker rankings, speaker comments, and an area for an explanation of the reason for decision. Depending on the ballot, each portion can offer a debater specific feedback. Each section of the ballot has unique purposes which help debaters gain greater proficiency in their skill. An example ballot is available in Figure 12 below and also in Appendix 2 on page 178.

A. Speaker Points

Speaker points are awarded to debaters during the debate round based on their performance in several aspects of their debating. The points awarded in each category range from 1 point (poor) to 5 points (excellent). Awarding points is quite subjective. Judges often have diverse criteria for their ratings. Many judges try to rate 3 as the average in the round. Debaters who impress them in an area receive a 4, and those who are superior receive a 5. In the same way, the ratings fall with poorer than average performance. As judges gain more experience, they begin to have clear criteria for their own methods of rating speakers. But because of their subjectivity, speaker points often vary every round.

Some ballots simply require the judge to assign a total score, but other ballots divide the scores into six different categories. The six categories on many ballots for which the judges assign points include: *persuasiveness, organization, delivery, evidence, cross-examination,* and *refutation.*

1. Persuasiveness

Persuasiveness refers to a speaker's ability to convince the judge. A persuasive speaker makes logical arguments which lead to the ultimate conclusion the debater advocates. Debaters who receive high marks for persuasion are those who not only make structured arguments which support their ultimate conclusions (see page 13), but also identify the weaknesses of an opponent's argument by explaining the logical holes in the arguments (see page 23). Passionate speakers who clearly explain the justification for their position will earn high persuasiveness points (see pages 97 and 155).

2. Organization

Organization takes into consideration two areas: speaking and appearance. First, the organization of speeches needs to be clear and logical. Preview what you are going to say, say it, and tell the judge what you said. Use clear signposts to organize the arguments for the judge and ensure you have enough time to make the arguments you tell the judge you will make (see page 13). Second, organization refers to the way you present yourself. Shuffling through pages of evidence while standing at the podium instead of smoothly moving from one page to another makes you appear disorganized. Having your papers neatly stacked instead of crumpled and falling off the podium will make you appear more prepared and orderly (see pages 36 and 67). Debaters whose arguments are clearly structured and who appear organized will obtain higher scores for organization.

3. Delivery

Delivery incorporates both verbal and non-verbal delivery (see page 51). In verbal delivery, proper word use, articulation, rate, tone, and other audible expressions are evaluated. A poised and polished speaker will earn higher marks in delivery. Non-verbal delivery includes all visual stimuli during a speech such as gestures, facial expression, and poise behind the podium during both speeches and cross-examination. Too many gestures, distracting habits, or lack of poise may be reasons to reduce the delivery score. Proper use of both verbal and non-verbal communication will enhance the score a speaker receives for delivery.

4. Evidence

The speaker point category of evidence refers to the quality and quantity of evidence, the ethical use of the evidence, and the proper incorporation of evidence into the arguments presented. If a debater uses better evidence than her opponent, then the evidence score will reflect that superiority. Conversely, if the evidence is lacking in credibility, the score will fall. Debaters should also strive to provide the proper amount of evidence. Providing so many quotations that there is no argumentation, only evidence, in a speech will reduce the score. Presenting too few quotations to support the arguments made is equally problematic. Using evidence which meets the tests for good evidence will enhance the rating given for evidence (see page 32 for these tests). Finally, the evidence needs to support the arguments made – quoting evidence that does not make an argument more persuasive harms a debater's overall credibility and will undermine the evidence speaker rating score. Using evidence ethically to support the arguments made will result in high evidence scores.

5. Cross-Examination/Crossfire

Cross-examination scores are based on the questions asked, the answers given, and the poise shown during cross-examination (see page 89 for more information about crossfire and page 131 for more information about cross-examination). Good questions penetrate the opposing arguments, in order to set up future arguments. Good answers turn the questions meant to harm arguments into springboards for strengthening your own case. Poise during cross-examination means being confident, standing in a position which neither portrays dominance nor submission, and maintaining your position at the podium when you are being questioned. Probing, insightful, and polite cross-examination will gain speaker points while poor questions, poor answers, or poor poise will reduce the score. Rude debaters who are abusive in cross-examination or crossfire will have their scores reduced. Practicing cross-examination is important to developing the skills which will produce higher ratings in this category (See page 55 for a drill to improve skill in cross-examination or crossfire).

6. Refutation

Refutation is the ability to respond to arguments brought up by your opponent. Using three and four-point refutation can increase your points in this category (See page 15 for a discussion of refutation and page 57 for a refutation drill). Good refutation points out the flaws of the other team's argumentation and augments the strength of your own arguments. A speaker who does not actually respond to his opponents' arguments, but instead only argues a pre-set group of arguments will not receive high points in refutation and is unlikely to win the round. Directly clashing arguments will not only help debaters win rounds, but it will also increase the refutation points.

AFFIRMATIVE/PRO	NEGATIVE/CON
First Affirmative Speaker:	**First Negative Speaker:**
Speaker Points (1-5 for each category) • Persuasiveness _____ • Organization _____ • Delivery _____ Total: • Evidence _____ • Cross-Examination _____ • Refutation _____	Speaker Points (1-5 for each category) • Persuasiveness _____ • Organization _____ • Delivery _____ Total: • Evidence _____ • Cross-Examination _____ • Refutation _____
Speaker Comments:	Speaker Comments:
Second Affirmative Speaker:	**Second Negative Speaker:**
Speaker Points (1-5 for each category) • Persuasiveness _____ • Organization _____ • Delivery _____ Total: • Evidence _____ • Cross-Examination _____ • Refutation _____	Speaker Points (1-5 for each category) • Persuasiveness _____ • Organization _____ • Delivery _____ Total: • Evidence _____ • Cross-Examination _____ • Refutation _____
Speaker Comments:	Speaker Comments:

I voted for (circle one):   Affirmative/Pro   Negative/Con

Reason for Decision:

Figure 12: Sample Debate Ballot

B. Speaker Rank

Once speaker points are compiled, speakers are ranked against each another. If there are no ties in speaker points, the speaker with the most points is ranked the top speaker in the round (1st) and the speaker with the least points is ranked last (4th). While there may be ties in speaker points, there can be no ties in speaker ranks. Ranks compare the debaters in the round rather than simply making a judgment based on the judge's subjective standard of what is excellent or average.

C. Comments

After rating and ranking debaters, the ballot has space for comments to each speaker and both teams. These comments may encompass any area of the debate round and often give the speaker reasons for the ratings, complement positive aspects of the performance, and provide the debater with areas to improve. Debaters should view comments as a great way to improve their skills. Although some comments may not seem warranted, comments help to build better debate fundamentals and encourage continued growth. The judge should also use this area as a mouthpiece for reprimanding any inappropriate behavior which any debater displayed in the round. Every comment helps the debaters grow and become stronger.

D. Voting

At the bottom of the ballot there is a section for voting for the team that has won the debate round. The judge may select to vote for or against the resolution (affirmative or negative in policy and Lincoln-Douglas debate, pro or con in public forum debate, or government or opposition in parliamentary debate).[14] A vote for the resolution is a vote for the team supporting the resolution, in favor of the resolution itself, and the case the team has presented. A vote against the resolution is a vote for the team opposing the resolution, against the resolution itself, and for the case presented against the resolution. While the vote is not the only important part of the ballot (the comments and speaker points/ranks are beneficial), the vote is a significant part of the ballot which debaters always anticipate.

After voting, the judge writes the reason for decision (RFD). This portion of the ballot explains the voting issues which the judge felt were important enough to warrant his decision. The judge often points out the key arguments which affected these voting issues. Some judges will list all the voting issues given and will explain which team won each issue and how it affected the decision (see pages 97 and 156). This section also gives the judge an opportunity to congratulate all debaters or to give comments to all debaters in the round.

The ballot is an important tool judges use to help debaters improve their skills. Debaters should soak up as much information as possible from their ballots. Parents and coaches should note the character qualities exposed on the ballot and assist their students in developing proper character while becoming better debaters. Rather than just looking at the ballot to see if your team won, debaters should use the ballots as a mirror to identify areas to improve. If you use the ballot effectively you will become a better debater who sees higher ratings, better ranks, and eventually more wins because you have strengthened your communication skills.

---

[14] Some debate leagues permit judges to select a "double loss" if both teams are extremely abusive and do not participate in any meaningful clash. A double loss is a severe vote. It does not signify a tie. While there are justifications for a double loss, it should only be used if the debaters on both teams become physically violent, extremely verbally abusive, or do not argue in a manner which allows debate to continue (moving so quickly that the judge cannot follow either team). Remember, this vote is a disciplinary action against both teams. Most tab rooms will question a judge extensively before allowing a double loss ballot to be accepted.

Observation 12: Preparing for a Tournament

"It usually takes more than three weeks to prepare a good impromptu speech"
-Mark Twain-

After spending hours learning debate theory, studying and researching the topic, and practicing debate, you are ready to debate in a full-scale debate tournament. Tournaments will be some of the best parts of your debate experience. Tournaments test your preparation, topic knowledge, case strength, ability to formulate arguments, and stamina to debate multiple times in a single day or weekend. A few key aspects of preparing for the tournament include: organization, timing, dress, and supplies.

A. Organization

Prepared debaters know where their evidence is stored and anticipate which arguments they will make in a debate round depending on the arguments an opponent raises. Organization means sorting the evidence you have so you can find it during the debate round. Keeping all your information in an accessible location is important. You do not want to waste time looking through your evidence or trying to find an argument against your opponent. Figure out a method of keeping your evidence organized (see page 36 for tips on evidence organization) and be sure you know where everything is before you get to the tournament.

Not only is having your evidence organized in a logical and clear manner important, but good debaters also organize the ideas they want to raise before they walk into a round. While preparation time can be used to select specific lines of argumentation, prior to attending a tournament you and your partner should create an organized plan of attack on both sides of the resolution and against any cases you anticipate hearing at the tournament. This means outlining the arguments you want to make both to attack particular arguments and to back up the key points of your own case. Coupling this outline with evidence will allow you to spend less time thinking about how to say something and more time deciding whether that line of attack is best suited to your particular round.

Being organized will permit better time management in debate rounds and allow you to focus on strategy. Confident debaters are able to take charge of each facet of the round. Being able to easily access your evidence will allow you to back up arguments without wasting time looking through your files while preparing the arguments you want to make before the tournament will give you greater confidence the argument you are making is the strongest one you have. Organization before a tournament will make the debate rounds less daunting and more enjoyable.

B. Timing

Every part of the debate round is timed. While most "rules" in debate are themselves debatable (there are, by the way, few official "rules" in most debate leagues), the time limits of a debate round are not negotiable (see page 75 for public forum debate speech times and page 105 for policy debate speech times). Knowing this, debaters ought to make certain their arguments will fit within the allocated time. This begins by looking at the case you plan to present. If the case does not fit within the time limit, important arguments will be left on the sidelines. If an entire section of the case remains unread there may be no justification for supporting the resolution in that round. Also, if your pre-written speech goes over the time limit, you will lose credibility because you appear unprepared. For all speeches, going over the time limit makes a debater sound frantic to get in another argument rather than confident the arguments she chose to make were persuasive.

To keep yourself within time, practice reading evidence and making a corresponding argument to see how long it will take to make the complete argument. Some debaters find it helpful to write down how long it takes to read a piece of evidence or how long it takes to present a complete argument at the top of the page containing the argument or next to the quotation. Then when you stack up the arguments you want to make during prep time, you can be sure you will not run out of time to make them. Another way to keep yourself in time is to set up short time limits for each section you are debating. For example, the first negative speaker in a policy debate round might set aside three minutes for **topicality**, one minute for the criterion, two minutes for the harms, and two minutes for the advantages (see page 128 for more discussion of the **negative block** and strategy for division of the negative team's labor). No matter how many arguments a debater makes, once the allotted time passes he moves on to the next topic. This prevents the debater from getting caught up arguing one point for too long. Practice giving speeches and moving along with the time.

Depending on the debate league, you may be required to time yourself. Even if the league provides timers, it is always worthwhile to bring a stop watch with you to a tournament. You should know the time limits for each speech and the number of minutes of preparation time each team receives. If you are required to time yourself, take the time piece with you to the podium or wherever you are standing when you deliver your speech. Use the count-down feature if possible so that everyone in the room will know when your time has expired. Practice debating using your own timer and having someone in the audience give you time signals so that no matter what style of time keeping occurs at the tournament you attend, you will be prepared.

Stay within your time limits in every speech and in each cross-examination. Not using more time than you have been given shows respect for the time of your judge and your opponent. And remaining poised by refusing to rush through arguments just to stay within the time limit will also enhance your credibility. Practice using the time you have been given to develop a strong case and be prepared to articulate each point you want to make within your time to persuade in an efficient and effective manner.

C. Dress

Some leagues have strict dress codes for their debaters while other leagues do not have any particular requirements. No matter the league, you should show your audience respect by dressing appropriately. Your clothes should be well kept and should not distract. Your appearance can communicate that you are confident and can give your judge a positive first impression. Remember, a judge is going to judge you based on how you look as well as how you debate. Dressing in a distracting manner does not help you to gain credibility.

Most forensics leagues require some sort of professional dress, although there are policy debate leagues in which anything goes. For example, STOA and NCFCA have dress codes for debaters premised on modest professionalism. If you are expected to wear professional attire for the debate tournament, that means a suit or blazer with a necktie for the men and a suit or dress with a jacket for the ladies. Regardless of the requirements, make sure your clothes are clean, ironed, and worn properly. Do not wear distracting accessories (such as large earrings, oversized watches, large bracelets, large or brightly-colored necklaces, or neckties with wild patterns). No matter the dress requirements, wear professional colors: neutral and not too bright (black, brown, gray, or navy suits are usually best). If the judge is focusing on the things you are wearing instead of on the arguments you are making, you are losing credibility and may lose the round.

The shoes you wear need to be comfortable. During a debate tournament you will be standing up for many arguments, walking across the campus where the tournament is being held, and carrying lots of evidence with you all the time. Make sure the shoes you wear are broken in so your feet will not hurt after the first day of the tournament. Also, your shoes should have sufficient traction so you will not fall if floors are slippery or wet. The shoes should also be shined and well maintained – learn to maintain your shoes to look their best.

Even if you are not required to wear professional attire, select comfortable clothing that still shows respect to your audience. Debaters who look like they did not shower and are wearing their pajamas into the debate round may lose credibility. As a speaker, you have been given the platform and should show the respect to your audience they deserve. Take pride in the clothing you choose to wear when you debate and this pride will come through in the debate round. Looking professional or at least well put together will go a long way toward helping the judge see you and your arguments as credible.

D. Supplies

A debater cannot debate without some basic supplies. Two different colors of pens are useful in flowing. Using one color for each team makes the flow much easier to read during the round. These pens will not be helpful without paper to write on. The paper of choice for many debaters is the 8½" x 14" legal pad for its extra space, its binding which keeps all notes in one location for the entire round, and its hard back so that it may be held during cross-examination or crossfire without "wilting" while you ask questions. Your evidence, flow paper, pens, and stop watch are all the basics you need to debate.

Beyond the basics, many debaters find it helpful to bring other supplies into a debate round. Debaters could whisper to one another, but doing so often causes them to miss something said by the speaker. Talking to your partner while an opponent is speaking is seen as rude by some judges. To avoid missing arguments or appearing rude, many debaters write notes to each other during the round. Some teams use small notepads, others use full flow pads, and still others find post-it notes their medium of choice. Post-it notes and the post-it flags are also helpful in writing down your own arguments. Because post-it notes can be placed on your flow or on your evidence briefs in appropriate places, they remind you of when and where to make the arguments you have written down for yourself. Most debaters find post-it notes to be valuable tools and as my brother Benjamin Wolfson noted in his national finalist expository speech in 2003, "Post-it notes never stop sticking for you!"

Some debaters like to have a highlighter or additional pen colors to make notes or to call out particular words on their flows or on evidence. Others find it helpful to keep a stapler in their evidence box in case briefs or cases come unstapled. Extra paper clips or tape can also be useful. Many debaters like to keep a copy of a dictionary or some key book cited by many debaters under the topic for reference in the middle of the debate round. And some more superstitious debaters keep a little trinket in their debate box for good luck. Debaters often keep snack items such as peanuts, granola bars, or trail mix in their boxes to eat between rounds just in case the tournament does not provide meal breaks. Finally, many debaters appreciate having a bottle of water available during the round. While the round may not seem long, speaking for any length of time without water can leave you with cotton mouth and make your words less understandable to your audience. As you go to more tournaments, identify the supplies you think you cannot live without and be sure to pack plenty of them in your debate box when you head to a tournament.

Tournaments are your chance to test your preparation in a competitive setting. Your attitude at tournaments is extremely important. If you attend tournaments willing to learn as much as possible, you will come out of every tournament a better debater. Watching experienced debaters and talking with other competitors will give you incentives to keep improving your skills. Often, making friends and hanging out with the other students between rounds and at meals is the most enjoyable part of a tournament. If your tournament experience is weighed by wins and losses, you are setting yourself up for disappointment. However, once you learn to take wins and losses in stride, you will become a better debater and the wins will come as fringe benefits. Your attitude will affect your level of enjoyment at a tournament. Treating tournaments as icing on the cake of learning good argumentation skills and remembering that the ultimate purpose of tournaments is to groom your skills will give you a positive tournament experience.

Contention 2: Introduction to Public Forum Debate

Observation 13: Public Forum Debate

"Freedom is hammered out on the anvil of discussion, dissent, and debate"
-Hubert Humphrey-

Public forum debate is one of the newest additions to the competitive forensics circuit, although it has a long and illustrious legacy in the real world. The goal of a public forum debate, just like other debate styles, is to persuade the audience to vote for or against a particular resolution. Unlike many debate formats, however, public forum does not require special debate vocabulary or knowledge of detailed theory from either participants or judges. Public forum debate focuses on developing debaters who can persuade any audience to support a particular position through a series of short back and forth speeches which mimic the real world debates on television between pundits and politicians.

Public forum debate is a communication focused debate on the pros and cons of a particular position of fact or policy. For example, a public forum resolution might be "Resolved: Failed nations are a greater threat to the United States than stable nations." The debaters spend the entire debate round attempting to persuade the audience of one side of the resolution or the other. They must speak at a conversational pace, make strong, logical arguments, and support their arguments with credible evidence. The resolutions in public forum debate change frequently, often every month, which gives debaters the opportunity to study multiple topics throughout the year and become more well-rounded thinkers about the pressing issues of the day.

One of the goals of public forum debate is that any audience be able to follow the arguments and have the opportunity to be both enlightened and persuaded during the round. For this reason, public forum rounds are judged not only by "debate experts" who may score a debate round based on technical arguments related to debate theory, but also by lay people or "community judges" who bring a different set of standards to evaluate quality persuasive arguments. Because the goal is audience-centric "public" debate, debaters must demonstrate solid logic, reasoning, and analysis of the issues they raise. The debater is required to support the arguments she makes using credible evidence, but the evidence plays a more limited supporting role than policy debate and does not dictate the arguments the debaters will make (as opposed to most policy debates in which the evidence will dictate the major issues discussed in the round). Both teams will identify the arguments of the opposing side and clash their own arguments with the opposing arguments to provide a clear picture of the two sides in the round. Ultimately, a public forum round will communicate the pros and cons of the topic in a manner which gives audience members the opportunity to make a well-reasoned decision regarding which team was more persuasive and which side of the resolution is best.

The two teams in a public forum debate round are called the pro and con. The pro argues for the resolution while the con argues against it. The teams are comprised of two speakers who give two speeches each and attempt to speak with one voice through the entire debate round. Unlike most debate formats, the debaters begin the round with a coin toss to determine speaking order and which side of the topic both teams will take. Once the round is underway, the two sides have an opportunity to confront each other's arguments both indirectly through speeches and directly in the crossfire period where the debaters take turns asking and answering each other's questions. The speeches allow both teams to press their strongest points and refute the points of the other side. The crossfire gives each team the chance to ask and answer questions which tests the arguments both teams are making.

The speeches themselves are not as long as most other debate formats. The entire round is only thirty-seven minutes including the preparation time reserved for both teams. The longest speeches are four minutes long, while the shortest speech lasts only one or two minutes. With a limited time many debaters from other genres will be tempted to speak excessively quickly, but public forum rules require speaking at a reasonable pace so that audience members without any technical proficiency in debate will be able to follow along.

By limiting the time debaters spend on one topic and in the round, public forum debate offers many debaters the opportunity to hone their debate skills without the significant time commitment necessary to become fully immersed in a topic for policy debate. Couple the shorter time period in each round to present information with the required slower pace of presenting the information in the round and public forum debaters should not expect to spend the quantity of time researching and preparing for their debate rounds. However, because the topics change frequently, debaters must quickly switch gears between topics during the debate season. While public forum debaters cannot claim to possess the depth of research knowledge a policy debater might have on a particular topic, public forum debaters possess significant knowledge on as many as ten topics per season. Public forum is growing in popularity due to the somewhat lighter workload, the practical application of debate to the real world, and the opportunity to begin debating with much less initial training on the technical details of a debate round.

Observation 14: Public Forum Debate Rounds

"Honest differences of views and honest debate are not disunity.
They are the vital process of policy making among free men."
-Herbert Hoover -

The public forum debate round offers competitors an opportunity to test their mettle against opponents by giving speeches, presenting arguments, and asking questions. Rounds are only thirty-seven minutes long which means there is limited time to develop a position, refute attacks, and identify the weaknesses in an opponent's arguments before the judge will make her final decision. The pro team is attempting to uphold the resolution in every argument while the con team is focused on rejecting the resolution. Each team has four speeches and there are three crossfires. Each debater gives two speeches, participates in one crossfire against an opponent and participates in the "**Grand Crossfire**" with all four debaters in the round. Let's take a closer look at each portion of the public forum debate round.

A. Preliminary Matters

Many debate formats set the sides each team will be arguing and the speaker order before the teams enter the room. Public forum, however, gives the debaters the opportunity to begin strategizing even before the first argument is made. The first action to take place in a public forum round is a coin toss. The winner may decide either which side (pro or con) they wish to advocate or whether to speak first or second. Depending on the type of resolution, some teams prefer to be able to advocate for one side as often as possible. If, however, the debaters believe setting the initial groundwork for the debate by speaking first is more important, the team could select to speak first and allow the team that loses the coin toss to select which side of the topic to advance.[15]

Here are five tips for making your decision after the coin toss in a public forum debate round. First, if you believe your judge and audience are very likely to agree with one side of the resolution, select that side. It will be much harder to persuade the judge to vote for an idea he disagrees with than to overcome being the second or first speaker. Second, if you believe one of your cases is stronger or more persuasive, select that side. Your first goal should be to have equally strong cases for both pro and con, but it is not uncommon to have one case you and your partner find easier to advocate. If one case is stronger, or if you and your partner just enjoy arguing for that side of the debate, you will be more persuasive in selecting that side for the round.

Third, if your second speaker always leaves a great final impression with the audience and you want her to be able to give the last speech in the round, pick second speaker. We know that people tend to remember the first and last things they hear more than those in the middle. If your second speaker knows how to deliver an amazing final focus every time (see page 97), taking advantage of being the final speaker may be the best strategy. Fourth, if you want to be able to frame the debate from the beginning and have the first chance to offer extensive criticism of your opponents' case, choose first speaker. Speaking first allows your case to set the worldview for the round. For example, if you explain that the round is all about whether education is improved through promoting human rights, your opponent will have to not only make his case, but also attempt to frame the issues in terms of your

---

[15] Some debate tournaments pre-select the speaking order (pro first, then con) and other tournaments will set speaking sides as well, but the coin toss is an integral part of many public forum debate rounds.

education argument. If your theme or perspective can change the course of the debate round, speaking first is to your advantage.

Finally, if you believe your opponents' case on one side (say pro) is stronger than their case on the other side (say con), and you are confident that your pro case is at least as strong as your con case, choosing to go pro will force your opponent to argue from their weaker position. Your primary goal in every debate round is to advance the arguments in favor of your own case (see page 52 for a discussion of the strategy of a roadmap), but facing a weaker case will give you additional time to spend building up your own case rather than tearing town your opponents' case. Identifying a weak opposing case should not be your primary reason for selecting a side in a public forum round, but it should be a consideration if the first four strategies are not determinative for you and your partner. While the side you pick is secondary to the arguments you are making in the round, it is valuable to feel confident that you are debating from your strongest position at the onset of the round.

For purposes of this chapter, we will assume the team on the pro side will speak first.

B. First Pro Constructive [1PC – 4 Minutes]

The first pro speaker presents the pro team's case in a 4-minute speech called the first pro constructive (1PC). Unlike all other pro speeches in the debate round, this one is completely pre-written (the structure of a good case is discussed in the next chapter on page 83). The 1PC begins by telling the pro team's story that explains why the resolution ought to be accepted. Generally, the pro team presents contentions to justify the resolution and provides structure to the arguments in favor of the resolution. The con team will generally address the pro's arguments in this order. Without a strong first pro constructive, the pro team's case will be easily defeated.

C. First Con Constructive [1CC – 4 Minutes]

The first con constructive (1CC) is used to present the con team's case. As with the first pro constructive, this speech is pre-written (see page 83). The 1CC tells the con team's story and may contrast some of that story with the pro team's story in an extemporaneous fashion. The goal is to present contentions which justify rejecting the resolution. As with the 1PC, the order of the arguments in this speech will generally form the contours of the arguments for and against the con case through the remainder of the round. Because the pro team has already presented its case, the first con constructive may also level a few attacks against the pro case if there is any time to do so, but this is a secondary priority when presenting the 1CC. While nearly all of these arguments against the pro case will need further development in the later speeches (and nothing prevents an argument from being introduced in the second con constructive for the first time in the round), providing some direct attacks against the pro case can prevent the second pro constructive speaker from simply attacking the con case and strengthening the pro case. The first con constructive offers an excellent opportunity to make an early impression in opposition to the resolution.

If the first con speaker were to speak first, he would not be able to anticipate the arguments made by the pro team and so the speech only presents the con team's case. Similarly, if the pro team speaks second, the first pro speaker would have an opportunity to include a minimal amount of refutation against the con team's case in the first constructive speech. Because you will not know whether you will be speaking first or second in a round, it is advisable either to write all cases with up to thirty seconds of time for responsive argument against the opposing case or to write slightly shorter cases for times when you find yourself speaking second.

Refutation in the second speech in the round (1CC if pro team speaks first, 1PC if con team speaks first) is generally limited to the arguments directly addressed by points within the pre-written speech. For example, assume the pro team speaks first and argues that taxes on businesses should be lower by presenting three contentions: (1) high corporate taxes increase the price of all products for consumers; (2) lower corporate taxes result in more job creation by companies; and (3) low corporate taxes prevent companies from moving their businesses overseas which prevents the jobs from being outsourced overseas and keeps the tax revenue for the government. Then assume the con team argues that business taxes should not be changed using three contentions: (1) corporate taxes are at historic lows; (2) corporate taxes provide more money for the government to spend to benefit all citizens; and (3) current corporate tax rates do not discourage business hiring. When presenting the pre-written arguments under the third contention, the first con speaker could most certainly identify how this contention is in direct conflict with the pro's second contention. With a few sentences, the con speaker can explain why her arguments ought to be preferred and quickly dismiss an entire contention of the pro's case.

D. **Crossfire between the 1P and 1C [3 Minutes]**

The purpose of this crossfire is for clarification of the arguments your opponent has made. Crossfire also offers a chance to strengthen your case by leading the other debater to agree with your positions (for tips on crossfire, see page 89). For example, if the resolution calls for the pro team to advocate obtaining energy even if it places the environment at risk, asking a question to have the con debater admit that the environmental risks of energy production are overblown could significantly strengthen the pro team's argument. Use all crossfires wisely. Do not be overbearing or too aggressive. Ask your question, allow your opponent to answer it, permit your opponent to ask a question, and give a clear and concise answer. Be polite as you develop logical conclusions about the arguments in the round for the judge.[16]

E. **Second Pro Constructive [2PC – 4 Minutes]**

The second pro constructive (2PC) delivered by the second pro debater offers the pro team its first opportunity to defend its case against the arguments presented in the previous speech and to attack the con team's case. The first priority of the 2PC is to rebuild any weakened parts of the pro case from arguments made in the 1CC or in the crossfire. Any significant challenges need to be addressed and the audience should be led to believe those challenges are not important enough to undermine their support for the pro case. While being positive is always nice, the 2PC must also go on the offense by attacking the con team's case. Identifying weak areas of the con case will shake the audience's confidence in arguments which claim that the resolution is not needed. This is also the last time the pro may introduce a new argument because the summary speech and final focus speeches are limited to explaining why your side should win. They must not be used to introduce or develop any entirely new ideas. Clarity is of great importance in the 2PC because the remaining speeches are too short to sufficiently develop every argument. You must decide which issues truly matter to your audience and the judge. Be concise. Give the judge a good reason to vote for the resolution.

---

[16] Debaters should be sure to remind the judge of any points admitted in crossfire by pointing out the admissions in later speeches. These admissions should also be impacted to the voting issues in the final focus if possible.

F. Second Con Constructive [2CC – 4 Minutes]

While the 1CC offered limited opportunity to undermine the pro case, the second con constructive (2CC) speech offers the second con speaker the opportunity to devote significant time to attacking the pro team's arguments while also reserving time to answer the criticisms of the pro from the 2PC and crossfire. As with the 2PC, the first priority is to rebuild any weakened pieces of your own case. In addition, the most important points of the pro team's case need to be addressed and refuted. The goal of this speech is to both rebuild the con case and tear down the pro case. If these dual goals are met, the 2CC was effectively used. Make sure you cover every argument you think is important because this is the last time the con may introduce a new argument. Remember, in the summary speech and the final focus speech, you are limited to explaining why your side should win. You may not develop an entirely new idea during those final two speeches. Again, it is important to be clear because at this point in the round there will be insufficient time to dig deeply into arguments. Once the round passes the halfway point, it speeds to the finish. Make concise and persuasive arguments to give the judge a good reason to cast a con ballot.

G. Crossfire between 2P and 2C [3 Minutes]

This crossfire is often more argumentative than the first because there is less need for clarification and because the lines separating the two sides have been clearly articulated. As a result, both debaters will attempt to attack the areas of their opponent's case they believe are weakest and will attempt to make convincing arguments supporting their own case. If possible, both debaters will try to turn arguments against their team's case into arguments that support their team's case instead. Again, crossfire offers a chance to strengthen your side by leading your opponent to agree either that your side is correct or that their side is incorrect. For this reason, you should carefully think through your answers before you respond to questions. Otherwise, you might give your opponent a great advantage by conceding a strong argument for your team. As with all crossfires, be polite as you prod your opponent or answer questions and be sure to permit your opponent to ask and answer questions during the crossfire period. A strong second crossfire will help your team maintain its persuasive powers for the remainder of the round.

H. Pro Summary [PS – 2 Minutes]

Now that all the arguments are on the table, the first pro speaker must provide a concise summary of where the round stands to set up the decision the judge or audience must make at the conclusion of the round in the pro summary (PS). This two minute speech cannot be used to develop any new lines of argument. Instead it should be used to identify the issues on which the round will hinge — the key disagreements between both sides. In this speech, the pro speaker should reinforce the pro constructive arguments. Do not just say it again! Take this opportunity to strengthen arguments by supplying more evidence and expanding on previous strong arguments while refuting the con's arguments. The PS is about reviewing the various impact arguments as persuasively as possible (see pages 97 and 155). A good summary speech will identify one key point from each contention and explain how the pro's contentions are stronger and the con's contentions do not justify rejecting the resolution. If there remain any factual disagreements between the teams, this speech should be used to quickly explain why the pro is more in line with the facts.

I. Con Summary [CS – 2 Minutes]

With only nine minutes of debate remaining, the first con speaker's con summary (CS) must articulate the con team's version of where the round stands to set up a clear decision for the judge or audience to make at the conclusion of the round. As with the PS speech, this two minute speech cannot be used to develop any new lines of argument. Instead it should be used to identify the issues on which the round will hinge — the key disagreements between both sides. In this speech, the con speaker should reinforce the arguments he and his partner made in the constructive speeches. Reinforcing does not mean simply repeating the arguments. To reinforce or strengthen an argument, the CS speaker should supply more evidence and expand previous strong arguments. At the same time, the CS must refute the pro's arguments. Because you know the issues the pro believes are the most important in the round, many CS speakers choose to follow the PS structure by simply refuting each argument made by the pro team in their summary. When doing so, the con must be sure to do more than reject the pro's arguments. The CS must actually advance the con team's position as a positive alternative for the judge to consider. This summary should review the various impact arguments made by both teams, identify one key point from each contention, and explain how the con's contentions are stronger and the pro's contentions do not justify rejecting the resolution. If there remain any factual disagreements between the teams, this speech should be used to quickly explain why the con position is more in line with the facts.

J. Grand Crossfire [3 Minutes]

The grand crossfire is the most exciting three minutes of the debate round! Unlike one-on-one question and answer segments from cross-examinations in policy and Lincoln-Douglas debate or "points of information" in parliamentary debate, the grand crossfire invites all debaters to question one another while being simultaneously subjected to questions. Take the difficulty of sharing a crossfire period with your opponent and double the fun by adding in your partner and your opponent's partner. Now you have the grand time known as the grand crossfire.

As with all crossfires, you have the chance to clarify arguments, strengthen your own side, and identify weaknesses in your opponents' side. Now that both teams have identified the key issues in the round in their summary speeches, this crossfire should hone in on those areas of disagreement and attempt to identify a winning position. This crossfire offers a final chance to strengthen your side by leading your opponent to agree either that your side is correct or that their side is incorrect. Since there is almost no speaking time remaining to save a lost argument, careful thought before asking and answering questions is vital.

The hardest part of this crossfire is sharing the short three minutes with three other debaters. Generally, you should assume you will only be able to ask one question because you have to give both your partner and your opponents time to ask questions. It is all the more important since four debaters are asking each other questions at the same time to maintain calm. This bears repeating: as with all crossfires, do not be overbearing or aggressive. It is too late in the round to let your emotions take control. Ask your question and allow an opponent to answer it. Then permit your opponents to ask a question and give them a clear, concise answer. Decide in advance whether you or your partner will ask the first question. Work out some kind of signal or agreement so you do not talk over one another in answering the other team's questions. Only one debater from each side should ask or answer a question. This enables the judge and audience to follow the arguments and helps you keep the crossfire flowing. As with all crossfires, be polite as you prod concessions from your opponents or answer questions to strengthen your case in order to maintain your persuasive powers for the remainder of the round.

K. Pro Final Focus [PFF – 1-2 Minutes]

In the final pro speech, the pro final focus (PFF) the second pro speaker gives the judge a <u>few</u> reasons to vote for the resolution and for the pro team (see page 97). Although you may want to cover most of the issues discussed in the summary speeches and the grand crossfire, the most important goal in this speech is to convince the judge that *your team* should win the round. In the very limited time you have (some leagues only give you one minute for the final focus), your best option is to give the judge voting issues. In this final speech, select and promote a few strong issues that will motivate the judge to vote pro. Most debaters give the judge two or three strong reasons to vote pro. The voting issues should compare and contrast the summary arguments to show the judge how the pro side is preferable and should win the judge's vote. Do not be afraid of explicitly telling the judge to cast a pro ballot; just be sure you are giving her good reasons to do so. If possible, try to tell a story in this speech that the judge will remember when she makes her decision. To win a pro ballot, you must show that the resolution is worth upholding by giving the judge good reasons for her decision. This is your last chance to speak, so make it count.

L. Con Final Focus [CFF – 1-2 Minutes]

The con final focus (CFF) is the final speech of the round. In this final con speech the second con speaker must refute the pro team's arguments, strengthen the con arguments, and convince the judge that the con has won the round. In this short speech (only one minute in some leagues and at some tournaments) debaters must hone in on a couple overarching reasons for the judge to vote against the resolution and for the con team (see page 97). As with the pro's final focus, your goal is to convince the judge to cast a con ballot. The CFF must address the issues discussed in the summary speeches and the grand crossfire only in ways that directly relate to your chosen voting issues. The voting issues should be a two or three strong reasons that motivate the judge to vote con. It is also important to compare and contrast your voting issues with the pro team's voting issues to show that the con side is preferable and should win the judge's vote. If possible, try to tell a story in this speech that the judge will remember when she makes her decision. To win a con ballot, you must show that the resolution is worth upholding and give the judge good reasons for her decision. Do not be afraid to actually tell the judge she should to cast a con ballot, but make sure you are giving her good reasons to do so. Conclude your speech by making some small but memorable persuasive arguments. The final focus is your last chance to speak, so make it count.

M. Preparation Time [2 Minutes Per Team, Per Round]

Preparation time is given to each team at the beginning of the round. Each team begins the round with two minutes which may be divided any way they see fit throughout the round. This includes before a team's own speeches and before crossfires. However, no prep time is used before the first speech in the round (1PC or 1CC depending on which team elected to speak first). Prep time is useful to formulate strategies with your partner, collect evidence, and ensure strong organization before you rise to present. It is also useful in deciding which arguments will become the winning voting issues in the final focus. Prep time gives partners a chance to solidify their "debate roadmap" for the round (see page 52). It allows teams time to formulate a cohesive strategy for attacking the other team's arguments or for defending their own. Be careful to manage your prep time wisely in order to maximize your effectiveness.

While prep time may be used at many times throughout the round, some times are better than others. Good debaters maximize their use of prep. Because the pro cannot prepare for what will be argued, it is better strategy for the con to use prep time prior to the 1PC. This gives the con an advantage because the pro will have to use prep later. Both teams must be sure to save enough prep time for the final focus speech in order to ensure that the most important voting issues do not fall through the cracks. Because of crossfires, each speaker will have three minutes of non-speech time which should also be utilized in preparing speeches. If this time is effectively used, the majority of prep time can be used strategically.

Many debaters feel the necessity to talk with their partners during the round. Often an opponent will make an argument that can be refuted with a piece of evidence. In the moment, it seems important to pass this information along to your partner. However, it is not advisable to whisper during your opponent's speeches. Instead, write down comments and pass a note to your partner during the speech so you can both remain attentive to the speaker, flow, and simultaneously communicate without appearing rude. Save your comments which you must voice to your partner for preparation time. This assures that you do not miss arguments and keeps you from being viewed as disrespectful to the speaker.

After the round, thank your judges, congratulate the other team and put away your supplies. Use this time to prepare for future rounds and to note skills to improve. Work with your partner to come up with answers to questions or arguments you did not anticipate. And take time to get to know your fellow competitors. If you build friendships and spend time developing your debate skills, debate will be an enjoyable and rewarding experience.

> First Pro Constructive (1PC)
> First Con Constructive (1CC)
    > Crossfire Between First Speakers
> Second Pro Constructive (2PC)
> Second Con Constructive (2CC)
    > Crossfire Between Second Speakers
> Pro Summary (PS)
> Con Summary (CS)
    > Grand Crossfire Between All Speakers
> Pro Final Focus (PFF)
> Con Final Focus (CFF)

Figure 13: Public Forum Speeches and Abbreviations

Observation 15: Public Forum Cases

"There are always three speeches, for every one you actually gave.
The one you practiced, the one you gave, and the one you wish you gave."
-Dale Carnegie-

This chapter discusses the typical method of presenting a public forum debate case. The first constructive speech for both the pro and con teams will typically present a case either supporting (for the pro) the resolution or opposing (for the con) the resolution. The case will introduce the arguments both teams will support and refute throughout the round. They must be well written, clear, concise, and persuasive all at the same time. Cases are generally pre-written and short enough to fit within the four-minutes allotted for the first pro or con constructive. Also, it is not uncommon to have shorter versions of the case in the event that you will be speaking after the other team's first constructive. A shortened version of your case allows you extra time if you want to attack one or two opposing arguments in the first constructive speech (i.e. if your league has a coin toss and either side can be the second team to speak, both pro and con will have shorter versions of their cases. Otherwise only the con case will be short enough to read in roughly three to three-and-a-half minutes).

Public forum debate is focused on communicating to any audience member regardless of his experience as a debater or knowledge of the specifics of a given policy area. Therefore, the public forum case must be clearly written, well-researched, and easy to understand for all audiences. This also means the four minute time limit is much more constraining because the pace of speaking must be slow enough for a non-debate audience to follow what you are saying. By remaining aware that your case must persuade the lay audience, you will ensure your case, and the pace at which you deliver it, can successfully win a public forum debate round. (A sample public forum case is available in Appendix 3.)

A. Goals
The primary goal of a debate case, or any persuasive paper or speech, is to compel the audience to agree with its conclusion. To obtain this overarching goal, there are four sub-goals to reach when writing and delivering a persuasive debate case. First, make sure your audience wants to listen to you and what you are talking about by grabbing their attention. Second, make sure the key controversy in the round is clear by clarifying any potential areas of confusion. Third, identify strong reasons for your audience to accept your position. Finally, summarize the arguments you have made by wrapping up the speech with a compelling conclusion.

Do these steps sound familiar? They should. Any basic five-paragraph essay follows a similar format; even paragraphs follow this format. Speaking and writing have some significant differences, but the structure of a good persuasive speech and the structure of a good persuasive essay are not so different that you need to learn an entirely new method of writing only for debate. In debate you use some alternative language to describe what is going on inside the speech in contrast to the description of the various pieces of a paragraph, but your final product should read on paper as well as it sounds to an audience when spoken.

Just as every basic essay starts with an introductory paragraph to both identify the main point of the essay and provide a roadmap for what arguments will be made in the paper, your speech should introduce the key conclusion and preview the arguments to come. The main body paragraphs are an opportunity to expound on specific points which support your ultimate conclusion. There is no rule about how closely related to one another your body paragraphs must be, but they all must support the essay's main thesis. So too your case should provide clear arguments in support of your side of the resolution. Finally, a good essay concludes by reminding the audience of the thesis, repeating the main sub-points, and leaving the audience with a sentence that asks them to support the thesis. Your conclusion should remind the audience of the resolution, summarize the main points to support or reject the resolution, and ask the audience to vote for your side of the resolution.

B. Attention Step

A debate case offers both teams the opportunity to tell their story. Every speech and every debate case should begin with an **"attention step"** to draw the audience into the story. Highlighting a real world problem that the resolution addresses by using a quotation, story, or compelling statistic is a time-tested method of grabbing an audience's attention. For example, under the resolution that government should permit financial incentives for organ donation, the pro team might cite a statistic for the number of people whose lives are on hold waiting for an organ transplant followed by a quotation from an economist stating that prohibiting any financial incentives for organ donation results in thousands of unnecessary deaths as people wait for donated organs. The pro case would then transition into the resolution, quoted exactly, by saying "and this is why we support the resolution: Resolved: …"

No one wakes up in the morning and thinks: I would love to go hear forty minutes of speeches and arguments on a random topic. In fact, even people who love debate are prone to become glossy-eyed at the end of a long debate tournament. The attention step is your chance to wake your audience from their slumber and motivate the next forty minutes of their day. Your audience is giving you the privilege of their time so you need to show that you appreciate that gift by respecting the audience. You can show them respect by making sure they understand what will be discussed, ensuring you are polite and pleasant to your opponents and everyone else in the room, and providing interesting arguments to help educate your audience. If someone is going to spend forty minutes listening to you debate, you should show them the respect they deserve and make the debate enlightening and interesting to them.

The attention step is not a requirement, but will make a case more persuasive as well as show your audience that you respect their interests and time. Rather than starting off by simply quoting the resolution and explaining why you support it, the attention step allows you to give your audience some sense of the motivation behind the resolution. The attention step should answer three questions: (1) why should we (the audience) care about this topic? (2) why should we agree with your position on the topic? and (3) what difference do your arguments make in the real world? The attention step should also set the stage for the round in a manner that benefits your side of the debate.

1. Why Should We Care?

Debaters and the audience should care about the debate topic not just because the league or tournament director set the topic, but because that topic is actually of importance to those individuals inside the room and to society at large. For example, the resolution "red is better than blue" could be debated in an academic sense for hours on end (I'm sure many artists have strong feelings and arguments to make on such a topic), but beyond the debate round itself, such a discussion might not offer the audience a justification to spend the next forty minutes of their lives listening. However, if the topic is whether private or public investment in space exploration is preferable, such a discussion has far-reaching impacts which can serve as a much greater incentive for the audience to pay attention because their own pocketbook is at stake, as well as the proper role for the government in the space race and technological advancement. Your attention step should give the audience a sense of the scope of the issue—Does the issue have implications in our daily lives? Will the discussion make a big difference in the lives of people our society deeply cares about? Will the discussion make us feel safer? or Does our society have some obligation to address a specific need?—before shifting into the specific argumentative points you seek to make.

2. Why Should We Agree? Why Does This Matter?

The attention-getter should not only tell your audience why the topic is relevant and worth considering, but it also should give the listener the opportunity to identify with your side of the resolution. Do the overwhelming majority of experts agree with a particular position or has new research revealed that a particular position is correct? Is there some moral obligation to take a particular position or is some societal ideal violated by staking out particular ground? If your introduction can identify some reason your audience should actually want to agree with your position you have stepped beyond simply informing them that something interesting is about to be discussed and have placed them on notice that their own worldview ought to conform to a particular pattern.

To actually gain your audience's agreement, it is often necessary to more fully develop your contentions. However, giving a brief preview of what is in store – a short quotation from an expert the audience is prone to respect, or a compelling story of someone whose life is actually affected by the topic – will go a long way toward helping your audience identify with the topic. When your audience identifies with the topic, they are more likely to identify that your argument is not only worthwhile to think about, but worthy of their agreement too.

Audiences are also more interested in accepting a position if they understand how the real world, the world they see every day, is influenced by the outcome of a debate round. For example, debates about criminalizing cyber bullying offered numerous real-world implications for debaters to evaluate. Schools have duties of protecting students, shaping their beliefs, and yet still offering avenues for students to express themselves. Further, schools are not intended to replace the role of parents in monitoring the behavior of students when they are outside the school. Reminding the judge and audience that any debate round does not occur in a vacuum but has implications for real people in a real world can help move the debate out of the theoretical and into reality. When judges think their decision matters, they are more likely to vote in favor of your position because they are considering the much broader societal concerns which debaters must address if they are to persuade the audience.

3. Set The Stage in Your Favor

The introduction also allows you to begin the conversation on your strongest ground. The audience may have some level of skepticism, but a strong case that draws them in will also provide a paradigm from which your audience can look at the entire round. If the topic is income disparities, a pro arguing that disparities harm democracy will be able to focus on the inability of poor people to move into higher-paying jobs (a lack of socio-economic mobility) with the implication that those without disposable income cannot afford to participate in politics, then the future arguments from the con arguing that income inequality is not harmful will have a higher hurdle to surpass. The opportunity to make the debate focus on the strongest arguments in your favor should never be taken for granted. Many debates in the real world are won or lost based on how the issues are framed. The original terms used to set the language and underlying assumptions often may determine the most final conclusion. This is equally true in academic debate rounds. If you can make the audience believe your side of the resolution is preferable before your opponent even has a chance to respond, you have gone a long way toward winning the final ballot. One great way to do so is to quote someone who says the problem with the world is the absence of today's resolution. For example, "In his recent best-selling book, Professor Smith said: 'I have found that income disparities leave poor people unable to participate in the democratic process and so politicians ignore their needs. If income inequality were eliminated, the political system would better address the needs of everyone in society.'" Such a quotation is a great way to get your audience's attention and bring them in line with your way of thinking all at the same time.

C. Clarification

With your audience convinced and now eager to listen to the debate, you need to provide them a clear picture of what to expect in the next forty minutes. And all the more important, you need to tell them what to expect in the remaining minutes of your first constructive speech. The case should quote the resolution, clarify what this resolution is asking you to do, define any terms which may cause confusion or be contentious, and identify which positions you will be taking in the round. This section should be short enough to leave plenty of time to present your main contentions.

The first thing you need to do is to tell the audience what the focus of the debate round will be: the resolution. Even though you have talked about the topic in your initial attention step, you need to provide the exact wording of the resolution so everyone knows you are not simply talking about the cost of college education, but you are actually comparing the costs of obtaining a college education to the benefits. Most teams will say something like "We support (or oppose) the resolution 'Resolved that … .'" After you have quoted the resolution, tell the judge and audience what the resolution is about. This may mean providing very brief background of the topic or identifying the key disagreements on the issue so the judge is aware of the views on both sides of the resolution. Obviously you do not need to make the arguments of your opponent, but it can be helpful to put your spin on opposing arguments before they are presented.

There are often terms in a resolution which should be clarified. Unlike policy debate with its myriad arguments about definitions in terms of topicality, the definitions in public forum are intended to ensure that terms which may be confusing or might be twisted by an opponent are clear from the round's onset. Many words do not need to be defined, but definitions are helpful in outlining the nuances of some key phrases. For example, the term "income tax" may seem straight-forward, but tax policy experts have argued for years whether a consumption tax (such as a national sales tax) is an income tax. If a term is important to the debate round and may not be clear to the audience, or if you are attempting to only address a narrow aspect of the resolution with your case, definitions are important. If, however, you are debating a topic your audience is likely to already know (such as the electoral voting process for selecting Presidents in the United States) there is nothing wrong with using the commonly understood terms and neglecting to define them. For a discussion of the types of definitions used in a debate round, see page 140.

Remember the analogy to an essay? Now is the time to present your overarching thesis for the case. The thesis should be a simple statement that ties your contentions together in support of the resolution (or in opposition to the resolution). Your thesis should be something you and your partner are planning to say multiple times during the round and something you are hoping the judge remembers when he casts his ballot. A thesis should be applicable to each contention you will present and should support your side of the resolution. Finally, preview your two or three contentions, just using their short tags so everyone knows where you are going. For example, consider the following thesis and preview: "We believe that private funding of spaceflight is preferable because it will be less costly and will lead to greater innovations than public funding could ever hope to accomplish. We will show this in three points: 1, government space funding has significant waste, 2, private funding saves tax dollars for other priorities, and 3, multiple private researchers will be more innovative than a government-controlled process." The thesis and preview clearly articulate what the pro hopes to prove and preview the main arguments they will use to support the thesis for the public v. private funding of human space exploration topic.

D. Contentions

The contentions form the body paragraphs of your essay or the meat of your debate case. Your audience is listening for you to give them clear reasons in favor of (or opposed to) the resolution. Each contention should independently point out the correctness of the resolution or the benefit of a ballot in your favor. Do not rely on all your contentions standing strong at the end of the round. You should be able to win and uphold your thesis and the resolution if just one contention remains intact at the conclusion of the round. Each contention should contain three parts – a claim, warrant, and impact – just as all good arguments should. Every case should have at least two and no more than three contentions. A contention can contain more than one claim, warrant, or impact, but it is important to be mindful of time constraints. Do not try to say more than you have time to say.

The claim is a statement made which must be proven. For example, the argument "Gun control laws increase crime" is simply a claim. Good debaters will carefully word claims to make them easy for a judge to write down. This is called a "flow tag" and simply means using word economy to limit the number of words that summarize the argument.

The claim is supported with evidence, called a warrant. The warrant is some kind of expert or other credible individual stating an argument in line with the claim. For example, a quotation from the Department of Justice noting that states with the most strict gun control laws have the highest rates of violent crime could be used as the warrant to support the claim.

Finally, an argument needs more than a claim and warrant to be successful. It needs an impact statement. The impact asks the all-important "so what?" question. Assume the claim and warrant are correct and gun control laws do increase crime. Why should anyone care and further, why should this matter in the debate at hand? The impact answers both questions. The impact explains that more lives will be saved without strict gun laws than with those laws. Saving lives, as it is often the stated goal of gun laws, ought to weigh in our minds when deciding whether to have the gun laws in the first place. In this hypothetical argument, saving lives should prevail. (For more discussion of the parts of a complete argument, see page 13.)

E. Conclusion

Just as any good five-paragraph essay does not stop after making its third point, a good debate case will not abruptly end after presenting the final contention. Instead, a short conclusion helps to make the entire speech more persuasive and offers another opportunity to advocate for or against the resolution. The conclusion should briefly repeat the main contentions, the thesis, and the resolution. Many debaters finish the speech by tying everything back to the opening attention grabbing quotation or statistic to remind the audience of the need to vote for their side of the resolution. For example, reminding the audience of the thousands of people dying waiting for organ transplants and your expert's belief that providing financial incentives would save their lives is a compelling way to bring the speech full-circle and help persuade the audience of your position. This is your last chance to make a first impression – don't waste it!

After you write your case and begin working to perfect it, you may realize that it needs to change. Do Not Fear! Continual improvement and revision will help you develop a better case. Read your case to your teammates, your parents, your coaches, and anyone else who will listen. If they think something is unclear, reword or reorder the case to address your miscommunication. The key is to ensure your case is persuasive to any audience. After you hear a strong response to your case you may also decide it is worth replacing one contention you have with a newly researched and written contention. This entire process will strengthen your case while also helping you to become more familiar with the topic area. Finally, the process of writing and re-writing your case, just as with writing and re-writing an essay, will make you a better writer and will make you a stronger thinker and debater.

Observation 16: Crossfire

"Successful people ask better questions, and as a result, they get better answers."
-Tony Robbins -

Crossfire, the most exciting part of the public forum debate round, is very important to success for a debate team. Every debater must ask and answer questions for three minutes, recall specific arguments already made, and anticipate the traps being set for him, all while trying to identify the gaping holes in his opponents' arguments. Crossfire offers the judge an unfiltered perspective of both teams' arguments under scrutiny and a glimpse of how strongly both sides actually believe in the arguments they are making. The questions may reveal weaknesses in arguments or identify how confident a team is in the argument they are making. Crossfire also may help clarify exactly how various arguments ought to be weighed by the judge in making her decision.

Because crossfire is unlikely to be scripted and is impromptu, it offers the judge a unique opportunity to evaluate both teams and their arguments. For this reason, crossfire offers every debater the opportunity to gain (or lose) credibility. Whether a debater is asking or answering a question during crossfire, he must recognize that the judge is observing not only the questions he asks and the answers he gives, but the judge is also observing the poise with which he asks and answers questions. Be assertive, relaxed, and calm when you are asking and answering questions during crossfire. Stand strong and speak in a confident tone.

A. What is Crossfire?

Crossfires are three-minute question and answer periods that take place between either two or four debaters following the first three pairs of speeches. The diagram below visually represents when the crossfires take place and who crossfires whom (for a description of the pieces of a public forum round, see page 75). The first two crossfires occur following each pair of constructive speeches (crossfire one takes place after both the pro and con have presented their cases in the first constructive speeches; crossfire two takes place after the second pro and con constructive speeches) and feature the two most recent speakers (the first pro and first con speakers crossfire one another in crossfire one; the second pro and con speakers crossfire one another in crossfire two). The third crossfire, the "Grand Crossfire" takes place after the summary speeches and features all four debaters.[17] During crossfire, both debaters take turns asking and answering questions. During the grand crossfire, all four debaters take turns asking and answering questions. Customarily, debaters will stand during the crossfire, although many judges prefer to have all four debaters remain seated during the grand crossfire so the judge can see all four debaters.

Unlike cross-examinations which take place in many debate formats, crossfire requires a debater to bounce back and forth between asking and answering questions and rewards concise, stand-alone questions which do not require significant follow-up to make a point. Both sides in a crossfire will ask questions of the other side and receive an answer. Immediately after receiving the answer, the debater will listen to and answer a question from the opposing debater. While a debater in cross-examination is similar to a baseball player who is either on offense or defense at any given point in time, the debaters in the midst of a

---

[17] Because the pro and con teams do not always speak first or second in the round depending on the results of the coin toss, it is often easiest to remember that the crossfires take place after the second, fourth, and sixth speeches in the round. If the pro speaks first, this will be after the first con constructive, the second con constructive, and the con summary (and vice-versa if the con speaks first).

crossfire are more like basketball players who must play offense and defense switching between the two in a matter of seconds. To excel, a debater cannot try to ask a series of questions designed to reach a final damaging conclusion. Instead, the questions must be designed to quickly obtain answers which will later be employed in attacking the opponent's position.

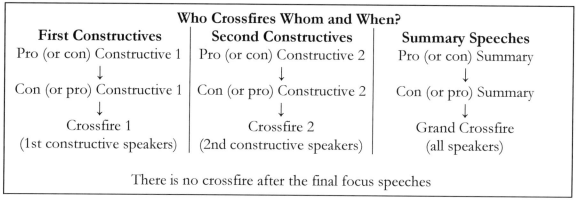

Who Crossfires Whom and When?		
First Constructives	**Second Constructives**	**Summary Speeches**
Pro (or con) Constructive 1	Pro (or con) Constructive 2	Pro (or con) Summary
↓	↓	↓
Con (or pro) Constructive 1	Con (or pro) Constructive 2	Con (or pro) Summary
↓	↓	↓
Crossfire 1	Crossfire 2	Grand Crossfire
(1st constructive speakers)	(2nd constructive speakers)	(all speakers)
There is no crossfire after the final focus speeches		

Figure 14: Crossfire Speaker Order

Another unique feature of crossfire is that neither side is actually in charge of the three minutes. Generally debaters will ask a question, receive an answer, and then concede the floor to the other debater to ask a question. At most, a debater will ask one brief follow-up question after receiving an initial answer before turning over the floor to the other debater to ask a question. If the person answering does not have any more questions to ask, the questioner may use the remaining time, but this seldom occurs. Both debaters are attempting to control the time through both the questions they ask and the answers they give. An easy question will leave your opponent with more time to ask her questions while a long-winded answer will prevent you from asking another question. Further, if a debater is trying to save a "zinger" question to make a compelling conclusion, he cannot be certain how early in the crossfire to bring it up in order to avoid the expiration of time.

B. Purpose of Crossfire

Crossfire has five main purposes: to clarify, to identify weakness, to attack weakness, to defend yourself, and to gain credibility. No one purpose should dominate a strong crossfire, but the final purpose is often the most important because judges may decide close rounds based on which debater they are more prone to actually believe. Careful preparation before a round will enable a debater to effectively employ crossfire to accomplish each purpose.

1. Clarify

If you are unsure of any major points your opponent is making, you should begin your crossfire by clarifying these points. Your first goal is to make sure you know what positions your opponent believes so that your other questions will be relevant. For example, asking "Is it your contention that a ten percent excise tax on gasoline will reduce demand for gasoline?" clarifies exactly what your opponent is claiming. If your opponent is actually saying an excise tax will reduce demand for gasoline by ten percent, and you thought you heard ten percent tax, clarifying will prevent you from making an irrelevant argument. Do not, however, clarify arguments you are planning to ignore; only clarify arguments that you are going to attack to ensure that you know what your opponent said before you begin to argue against it. Another purpose of clarifying is to get your opponent to repeat outrageous claims or assertions just to point out to the judge how unpersuasive the arguments are. If you primarily use crossfire to clarify arguments, you should work on flowing (see page 47) so your limited crossfire time may be used more effectively.

2. Identify Weakness

Next, you should attempt to point out weaknesses in your opponent's positions. If your opponent argues that higher fuel prices could have many effects including increasing demand for fuel efficiency, asking such questions as "Does your Brookings Institution quotation actually say that people will demand more fuel efficient vehicles if the gas tax rises?" probes whether the evidence or other support (warrant) can actually be used to support the particular argument that the gas tax would increase fuel efficiency demand. If an argument is missing a warrant or lacks a necessary link, probing questions can identify those holes in the argument and provide you an opportunity to undermine both the argument itself and your opponent's credibility. Another way to find weakness through questions is to compare the sources behind your evidence and the evidence quoted by your opponent. If you read a quotation from an energy economist saying a 10% tax will increase demand for fuel efficient vehicles by less than one percent, and your opponent read a quotation from an environmental activist saying that a ten percent tax will increase demand for fuel efficient cars by fifty percent, a question to identify a weakness might ask whether energy economists are better at predicting the effects of energy taxes on demand than environmental activists.

3. Attack Weakness

Some debaters choose to identify weaknesses in opposing arguments, but leave the actual exploitation of such weakness to the next speech. An alternative method is to actually attack the weaknesses in the crossfire. To attack a weakness generally requires two questions, but a simple follow-up from the earlier question may be sufficient. Rather than stopping the questioning after asking if the Brookings quotation supports the argument, an attack question would ask: "You said the Brookings quotation did not actually say a gas tax would increase demand for fuel efficiency, so you don't actually have any evidence to support your assertion that a gas tax would lead to greater fuel efficiency do you?" The same follow-up question could be asked when comparing experts: "If the experts predict a ten percent gas tax would only increase demand for fuel efficiency by one percent, aren't there better methods than a gas tax to achieve more fuel efficiency?" An alternative method of attack is to trap your opponent with his own words or otherwise put him on defense by asking such questions as "Won't raising the price of gasoline make it more expensive for the poor and elderly to heat their homes?" When your opponent is defensive, the positions he articulates appear less credible. The risk you take by attacking the point during crossfire is that your opponent will have the opportunity to respond and clarify his earlier argument in an effort to avoid your ultimate conclusion. Given the limited crossfire time, you will generally have limited opportunity for attacking questions during a single crossfire.

4. Play Defense

Crossfire offers you a chance to defend the arguments you and your partner are making by both the answers you give to attacking questions and by pointing out shortcomings in the refutation against your case. A weak argument against you is just as ripe to be identified (and often more important) as a weak argument in support of your opposition. You can use crossfire to defend your positions by undermining arguments raised against your team's claims. For example, if you have argued that increasing the gasoline tax harms the poor and your opponent replied that the poor are less likely to own cars and thus are only minimally harmed, you could ask a question such as "If the gasoline tax increased the price to transport food, clothing, and other necessities — products the poor obviously need — won't higher prices for those necessities harm the poor?" Asking probing questions to note the internal contradictions your opponent makes in attacking your case or the lack of evidence used against your case will go a long way toward strengthening your own case.

5. Build Credibility

A final purpose of the entire crossfire period is to maintain and build credibility for you and your partner. The judge is constantly looking to see if you are confident in the arguments you are making and whether you are comfortable under attack. She will ask herself whether your questions are worded to obtain a helpful answer, whether you are being polite and sharing the crossfire time, whether you refrain from interrupting the other speaker until he has given his concise answer, and whether your responses to probing questions are weak or strong. If you ask probing questions without sounding petty (do not ask a question just to score a cheap point, ask a question to make an impactful argument for your team) and remain poised while answering questions regardless of whether they seem reasonable, the judge will be more prone to believe the arguments you are making and vote for your team at the end of the round.

C. Asking Questions

Crossfires begin by one team asking the other team a question. When it is your turn to ask a question, what should you do? First, you should plan ahead and try to identify two or three weaknesses in your opponent's argument to attack. Second, your questions should be precise. A short question which calls for a direct answer is always preferable to a long-winded question that could be answered in a number of ways. Finally, your demeanor when asking a question should be polite, but firm. You should ask a direct question, receive a direct, concise answer, insert a quick follow-up question if necessary, thank your opponent, and then allow your opponent to ask you a question.

1. Plan Ahead

Once you know what your opponents stand for, think about what arguments you will make in response. For example, if they are claiming that taxing junk food will make Americans more healthy, consider whether you want to attack this claim for its assumption that a tax will reduce demand for junk food, its assumption that people will reduce their consumption of food instead of their other purchases, or its assumption that junk food is the cause of unhealthy Americans. Depending on which angle you wish to attack, you will want to ask questions to probe the assumption. If you want to attack the assumption that a tax will actually result in less consumption of food, you might ask: "when the price of food rises, aren't people more likely to put less money in savings rather than stop buying food?" If the answer is people will simply save less money, the argument in your next speech will be that a tax on junk food will not make people healthier, it will just deplete their savings and put them at risk of financial ruin if they do become seriously ill. If you have prepared this argument in advance, turn the argument into a question to ask during crossfire.

Be sure to ask about seemingly amazing claims that just sound too helpful to your opponents' arguments. If you hear an argument that sounds too good to be true, it probably is. If your opponent says that a ten cent tax on fast food would eliminate obesity, you can bet there must have been some sort of misunderstanding between the evidence and the conclusion. Do not allow these kinds of claims to go unopposed during crossfire. Pointing out the likely error will not only undermine the argument your opponent is making, but will give you additional credibility in the judge's mind.

2. Precise Questions

Your questions should ask for a specific answer. Avoid open-ended questions which allow long-winded speeches instead of direct answers to the question. Asking "why would a tax on fast food reduce obesity?" gives your opponent too many opportunities to make a speech in support of his case. Instead, ask "can you quantify exactly how high a tax on fast food would have to be in order to reduce the rate of obesity by ten percent?" Your opponent cannot answer this question by providing an explanation of why a tax is good or why obesity is bad, but must instead answer with precise figures which are more informative, but less prone to strengthen his case.

Further, your question should be short and to the point. Do not ask a question that takes more than ten to fifteen seconds. It is not uncommon for a debater to forget where a question even started if it goes on for more than a short sentence, and your audience will be less prone to listen for an answer to an unclear question. Precision is even more important with follow-up questions. Even though debaters generally take turns, it is acceptable to ask a short follow-up question after your opponent answers your question. These questions should quickly contrast the point of the answer your opponent just gave with his own side of the resolution or with another point his team has already made.

3. Poise

No matter whether asking or answering questions, you must remain poised, polite, and kind during crossfire. Interrupting your opponent to ask your question, or refusing to let her answer will not endear you to an audience and will not strengthen your arguments. Instead, focus on winning the hearts and minds of your audience by politely pointing out the weakness of your opponent's case and their individual arguments. Stand tall. Remind yourself that you have a great depth of knowledge about the topic and that you have the privilege of standing before an audience, be it one judge or a room of thousands, to explain your position on specific arguments. Just as with any speech, it is important not to make too many gestures or get too animated—you are making important points and your demeanor should reflect the respect you want your audience to give you as a credible advocate.

D. Answering Questions

If asking questions and coming up with arguments is not enough to do, crossfire also requires you to answer nearly as many questions as you ask. As with asking questions, you should be certain that your answers help to make the round clear both for the other debaters and for the audience. Your answers should be concise and responsive to the question. You should also find ways to champion your positions by going on the offense when answering crossfire questions.

Your first goal when answering a crossfire question is to ensure everyone in the room is clear about your position. If your opponent asks a question and it is clear he does not understand a key fact in your argument, begin your answer by clarifying that point. Make yourself as clear as possible so everyone who hears you knows what position you are taking. When everyone in the room knows what is going on, you are in a better position to explain how your arguments should prevail. A confused judge or audience will result in a disappointing ballot. Disorganized or confusing debates also will not provide the enjoyable, educational debate you hope to have.

When you are asked a question, give a concise answer. You may then expand your answer if your opponent allows you to do so, but be sure to leave yourself time to ask the questions you want to before time expires. Avoid rambling answers by focusing on your basic argument and returning to its main premise again and again. And be careful about answering more than you were asked. For example, if your opponent asks whether a gas tax will make it more expensive for families to take their children to school, discussing the increased expense of food transportation will only give your opponent another target to attack. A concise answer which makes the attack appear frivolous will go a long way toward increasing your credibility in the round.

Your answers should also seek to advance your side of the resolution. Every question is an attempt to undermine your arguments. However, with each answer you have the chance not only to prevent your arguments from being undermined, but also to strengthen your arguments. Every second you can talk about the strengths of your points during crossfire is effectively free speech time for your team to advance your position. If your opponent lets you give an endorsement of your argument, do it, but make it short and sweet.

Find ways to connect your answers to other strong points in your case. If you can turn a question attacking one contention into a sales pitch for not only that contention, but your other contentions as well, the judge will be more likely to believe each contention is worthy of support. By tying every question back to your strongest arguments, you are showing the judge a path to cast a ballot in your favor.

When you are being asked questions in crossfire, be calm. Be careful not to get excited, and avoid sounding rude. Even if the question your opponent asks is irrelevant, your response should be gracious and calm. Do not be afraid to answer questions, even if the questions harm your case. If you attempt to avoid answering questions, you will do yourself more harm than good because the judge will note your avoidance of the issue and give it additional weight in the round. Finally, if you are unsure about the answer, do not be afraid to say so. It is better not to give an answer than to give an incorrect answer which will hurt your credibility when you either correct or concede that point later in the round.

E. Grand Crossfire

The grand crossfire gives all four debaters the opportunity to join the fray before the final focus speeches. While the techniques for asking and answering questions already discussed still apply, this crossfire is of great importance because both teams have already summarized the key issues on which the round will hinge. The grand crossfire allows the teams one more chance to challenge those issues before the judge casts her ballot.

Because all four debaters speak during the grand crossfire, cooperation and teamwork between partners is very important. Decide in advance which partner will ask the first question and divide up issues from your case so you both know who will answer particular questions. You do not want to interrupt your partner or give the judge any reason to believe the two of you are not on the same page. Most debaters will also develop some kind of signal so they know when their partner wants to make a point. It is also important to remember that your questions and answers should be concise. Only one partner should ask a question and only one partner should give an answer.

With twice as many debaters participating in the grand crossfire, each debater may ask and answer fewer questions. For this reason you must be careful to select only the very best questions possible and make your answers mini-sales pitches for your side of the resolution. This limited time may also increase the pressure to become rude or speed up, but this temptation must be resisted if you are to maintain your credibility. Polite persuasion is the recipe for a successful grand crossfire.

The questions you ask in the grand crossfire should still matter in the debate round. If the issue was not part of the summary speeches, it is irrelevant to the judge's ballot and should be ignored. Also, your questions should attempt to identify the clear lines between the pro and con in the round. If you can help the judge see exactly where both teams stand on important issues, the final focus speeches can attempt to explain why the side on which your team stands is deserving of the judge's ballot. Your questions should reveal your opponents' weak voting issues and your answers should point to the strength of your key winning arguments. Be sure to impact your answers to reasons the judge should cast a ballot in your team's favor. In this way, you will find success in the grand crossfire.

Conclusion

The crossfire offers an exciting challenge to every public forum debater and should be recognized as a great opportunity to test the claims of an opponent and build the credibility of your own arguments. The judge will consider not only the arguments you make, but also the way in which you make them. Remain poised and be polite. Do not be overly aggressive. If you are overbearing or rude, the judge may not want to vote for you. Additionally, you will lose credibility. Without credibility, your arguments will be much less persuasive and you will likely lose the round. Focus on maximizing the three minute crossfires to build your credibility and refer to those crossfire questions and answers in your speeches so that the judge will find your arguments more convincing.

Observation 17: The Final Focus

"Be sincere; be brief; be seated"
-Franklin D. Roosevelt-

Making a good first impression, the purview of the first constructive, must be your priority if you are to appear credible for the duration of the debate round. Leaving a lasting final impression will be equally important as you and your partner attempt to gain a ballot in your team's favor. After the grand crossfire, each team has one very short speech (one to two minutes) in which to leave a lasting impression for the judge as she leaves the room to cast her vote. How these precious seconds are used will often make the difference between victory and defeat.

A. Important Arguments

Every debate round is full of arguments, both strong and weak. Despite their short length compared with many other debate styles, public forum debate rounds still have their fair share of weak or less than persuasive arguments. Good debaters minimize the number of bad arguments they present and make as many good arguments as possible in the limited time they have. The challenge for a debater is to think through the many arguments made and refuted in the round in order to repackage the best ones in a persuasive manner for the judge in the final focus.

1. Identify Important Arguments

The first goal is to identify which arguments are important. To identify which arguments are important, ask yourself three questions: (1) does this argument address the resolution? (2) does this argument help or hurt my side? and (3) if the judge agrees with this point, could he still vote for me? Arguments unrelated to the resolution are usually not the most persuasive in the round and will not be the reason the judge votes for or against you. Your final focus should center on the resolution. You should spend your time talking about why the judge should vote for or against the resolution. Arguments about something other than the resolution are irrelevant and not worth presenting in your final focus.

The final focus should also pivot between the issues that help your side of the resolution and those which hurt your side. The arguments that help your side should be your primary target unless your opponents' attacks seem most persuasive. Do not neglect to answer strong attacks that actually hurt your position. Identify the key arguments from the entire round, those arguments that may shift the balance between your side and the other side in the round. Once you identify the key arguments, spend the bulk of your final focus time discussing how you have won these arguments.

The important arguments will not only focus on the resolution, but they will also attempt to predict and address whatever the judge considers important. This is most vital when deciding which opposing arguments to discuss. If your opponent makes a far-fetched argument that permitting plea bargains will result in no criminals being fully punished for their crimes, the judge is likely to ignore it because it is a categorical statement unlikely to persuade anyone because some criminals will reject the plea agreement. Spending time talking about this superfluous argument is a waste of precious final focus time.

If the judge is not going to vote for or against the resolution because of an argument, the final focus should ignore it. It is never a certain bet which arguments judges consider when they cast their ballots. Taking time to watch the judge's reactions during the speeches to see if any arguments appear more persuasive to the judge or whether the judge is waving some arguments off as unbelievable will enable you to identify which issues matter to her ballot. This is especially true when deciding which opposing arguments to attack in the final focus. Asking yourself whether the judge could still justify voting for you even if she believes a particular argument will help you make sure you are only refuting the most important opposing arguments in your limited final focus time. If your arguments focus on the resolution, strengthen your side, and focus on issues that are at risk of persuading the judge to vote against you, your final focus can persuade the judge to cast a ballot in your favor.

2. Impact

Your second goal in the final focus is to show the judge how you have won the important arguments. Impacting the arguments is the best way to show how you have won the arguments. Impacts take on four key roles in your final focus. They show how you win a particular point, how that point affects the resolution, compares that winning point to your opponents' winning points, and justifies a ballot in your favor. By providing clear impacts, the judge does not have to connect the fragments of your argument. Instead, she can focus on why your entire argument is already persuasive when she decides to vote for you.

At the end of every fully-structured argument a good debater will provide an impact, a statement explaining why the argument matters in the round. The impact's initial role is to convince the audience that they ought to believe the argument. In the final focus, you should refer back to any major impact statements of your important arguments to remind the judge how you have already won those arguments in the round.

Just as important arguments are intertwined with the resolution, a strong impact in the final focus will tie the argument back to the resolution. For example, if the topic is whether the cost of college outweighs the benefits, an argument that earning potential only rises by a few thousand dollars for young college graduates could be tied back to the resolution as proof that taking on one hundred thousand dollars in debt for a small increase in short-term earning potential is not worth the cost. If a debater has already won this point, she should tie it back to the resolution by reminding the judge that the focal point of the round is weighing the costs and benefits of college and that in this particular case the benefits do not outweigh the costs.

The next part of the impact is comparing and contrasting your winning arguments with your opponents' strongest arguments. Explaining how the magnitude of the impacts on your side outweighs the magnitude of the impacts on the other side will be your most effective tool. For example, if your opponent has explained that for Ivy League graduates, earning potential rises by $25,000 per year, this impact can be outweighed by the small increase in earning potential for non-Ivy League graduates because only a small handful of college students attend Ivy League schools. By articulating that the power of the impact against you is much weaker than the impact on your side, you compare and contrast the strength of the underlying arguments and persuade the judge to your position.

Finally, because the focus of the round is not simply winning arguments, but supporting or rejecting the resolution, the last part of any impact is tying the arguments back to the judge's vote for or against the resolution as it was argued in the round. By providing impacts which both support your position and then show how your positions are stronger than those of your opponent, you give the judge good reasons to vote for you. The key is to remind the judge that each of these impacts not only has shown that your individual arguments are stronger than those of your opponent, but also that the cumulative weight of your arguments leave the audience with no choice but to vote for your side of the resolution. For example, arguing that despite the increase in potential income for some college graduates, the vast majority of college graduates end up with significant debt and only marginal increased earning potential means there is, for the majority of the population, a high cost and low benefit to attending college. The value of a college education does not, in general, outweigh the high costs of debt and lost years of earning while attending college and so the resolution ought to be rejected. Tie each impact back to the resolution to use the final focus to persuade the judge to cast a ballot in your favor.

B. Voting Issues

Rather than repeating the arguments that have taken up the first 30 minutes of the round, the Final Focus should be true to its name and focus the audience on the key reasons to cast a ballot for one side or another. These key reasons are commonly referred to as voting issues. While weighing the impacts provides the judge with reasons you have won a particular point, voting issues synthesize the entire round into a few main points for the judge to consider when casting her ballot.

The first question the voting issues should answer is why one team should win this round. Do you win because your case has not been challenged by the other team, because the evidence supporting your case is the most credible and persuasive, or because your opponent's case has been completely undermined? Depending on which reason you should win, you will want to focus on specific examples that support the reason. For example, if you win because you have demolished the opposing case, you will need to identify the main premise of the case and how your arguments have triumphed. If you cannot determine two or three reasons you should win the round, it is a safe assumption the judge will not either and will most likely vote against you. Voting issues give you a concise way to provide the judge with reasons to vote for you.

Debaters often believe they have won every issue in the round and every point they make is stronger than the points made by their opponents. While this confidence is admirable, the judge will be much more likely to believe that one team has won the round if they rest their justification for a vote on the strongest points in that team's favor. Voting issues should be the strongest issues which support your side and should be very specific. There is nothing judges dislike more than hearing vague voting issues. Unclear voting issues require the judge to take a long time to review the round, think about the various arguments to figure out what issues were important, and why one side won those issues.

Take a few moments before your final focus speech to decide which two or three points you have made that are broad enough to incorporate the entire round and justify voting for or against the resolution. For example, when debating whether NATO improves the lives of the Afghan citizens, the argument that NATO has helped a small tribe in the Eastern Mountains to improve public safety in their community is probably not substantial enough to be a voting issue. While this improvement certainly supports the resolution, it is small relative to the entire debate about whether NATO helped an entire nation. Such small justifications should not serve as an independent reason to cast a ballot for the resolution. Instead, look for a voting issue such as "Public safety and police forces now protect citizens while upholding the rule of law." Such a voting issue provides a substantial, nation-wide impact and allows the judge to focus on a much bigger issue when he votes. The focus on your strongest two or three overarching points which prove that the resolution should be supported (or opposed) is the goal in selecting your voting issues.

The last question to consider is which conflict between the two sides gets to the heart of the topic. Under the NATO in Afghanistan resolution, it would be easy for the two teams to make numerous disconnected points about the pros and cons of NATO's involvement in Afghanistan. However, a good debater will not only focus on the strongest issues he has raised during his speeches, but he will identify the greatest conflict between the two teams to show how he and his partner have emerged victorious. For example, while both teams may discuss various measures of quality of life in Afghanistan which may include women's rights, public safety, infrastructure, the legal system, and education, the debate will likely discuss one of these areas with the most clarity and depth. Strong debaters identify this issue, maybe the plight of women for example, and show that even though Afghan women still face less than perfect situations, the newfound rights are significantly greater than anything those women received prior to NATO's presence. By making the improved status of women a voting issue, the pro team is able to focus the judge on a conflict between the sides where the pro side is strongest. At least one voting issue should try to identify the key disagreement and explain why the disagreement should be resolved in favor of your team.

C. Presenting Voting Issues

The final focus is a short speech. Even in leagues where the speech is two minutes long, there is no time to waste talking about something that will not matter to the judge's ballot. Every word you say in the final focus should be spoken with the intent to persuade the audience to vote for your team. While this is true of every speech in the round, the final focus offers a very brief opportunity to persuade which must not be squandered. The voting issues should take up the bulk of your final focus. When presenting your voting issues, you should follow the rule of three, identify the key conflicts arising under those voting issues, weigh both sides, and impact the voting issues – reminding the judge to cast a ballot in your favor. Presenting clear voting issues will make your final focus more persuasive and the round easier to judge.

1. The Rule of Three

The rule of three is relatively straightforward: because people tend to more easily remember lists of three items, you should provide no more than three things for your audience to remember after you finish speaking. In a final focus, the rule of three means identifying no more than three reasons to vote for your team. Offering any more reasons will be both difficult to fit into the short speech and will make the voting issues less memorable. The rule of three does not mean you must identify three reasons to vote pro (or con). It just means that you should limit the number of reasons to cast a ballot for you to three or less.

The three reasons you select should not build on one another, but should be able to stand alone as "independent" voting issues. If your voting issues build on each other and the judge disagrees with one, she will have to vote against you. If, however, your three voting issues are truly independent, she can vote for you on any one of the issues with which she agrees. Another important key when selecting your voting issues is to attempt to make them equally strong. You are better off having two strong voting issues than two strong voting issues coupled with a weaker third one. If the voting issues are not worthy of being independent justifications to cast a ballot for your team, you are wasting time talking about them in your final focus.

2. Weighing Key Conflicts

Each voting issue will hinge on one or two main portions of clash in the debate round. The actual arguments made in the round will dictate who will win these issues, but the most typical conflicts will be over which side has correctly stated a particular factual claim. The existence of evidence, credibility of that evidence, or the specific impacts already presented in the earlier speeches will often determine which side has carried the particular point. The voting issues should incorporate these key conflicts and show how your side has emerged victorious.

In practice, this means signposting the conflict, quickly reminding the audience of the arguments made by both sides, and weighing the two sides to show that your side has prevailed. Depending on the source of the conflict, weighing may simply compare the quality of the support or may actually compare the quantifiable arguments made by both teams. If it is the latter, an example of weighing would be to explain that there are more benefits than costs associated with the policy position you are supporting. For example, if your opponent claims that privatizing space exploration will place hundreds of lives at risk of crashes, your response might be that even though hundreds of lives might be at some slight risk of an accident, the increased exploration will lead to a cure for multiple chronic diseases meaning tens of thousands of lives will be saved! Debaters who properly weigh the conflict do not always have to argue there are no risks associated with her position, but that the benefits far outweigh the risks introduced by the opposing side. Just as policy debaters weigh the advantages and disadvantages (see pages 133 and 155), your voting issues should compare and contrast the impacts of both the pro and con teams to show that your side has emerged victorious.

3. Impact

As with every argument, the strongest claim and warrant cannot persuade the audience without answering the "so what?" question every audience member, and certainly every opponent, will ask. While the importance of impacts to a complete argument at any point in the round cannot be overstated, impacts are especially important in the final focus. A judge who is still asking herself "so what?" when she is thinking about your voting issues will probably cast her vote for your opponent. Your impact should be succinct and explain that because you have won a particular argument, the judge should cast a ballot in your team's favor.

The impact should explain why winning the voting issue should result in a ballot in your favor. Does this argument settle the defining debate in the round? Did you just win the argument on which your opponent based his entire case? Did your opponent concede that if you could prove this particular point you should triumph? For example, if your opponent suggests that the side of the resolution which protects the most lives should win the round, showing that private space exploration will cure diseases for thousands more than will be at risk of harm should not only push the audience to support private space exploration, but should prompt the audience to vote for your team. In these situations, the impact is that everyone agrees this argument will determine the winner. But even if the argument is not one everyone concedes should determine the round's winner, you can elevate your voting issues to a similar level. If you show that the most important argument your opponent made has a smaller impact than your argument, you give the audience a reason to vote for your team. For example, responding to the voting issue that two hundred lives will be saved if private spaceflight is not permitted with the dual impacts that private space exploration will both improve medical technology and save governments money that can be spent on medical research to save thousands of lives shows that saving lives is the more likely outcome in voting for your side, not your opponent's side. By comparing your opponents' impacts with your impacts you can show that your voting issue outweighs the main voting issue of your opponent.

No matter what voting issues you choose, they are only as strong as your ability to present impacts that tie the voting issues to the judge's ballot. Do not be afraid to explicitly say that you have won an argument and ask for the judge's vote. If the audience disagrees, they are going to vote against you anyway. You must appear confident that your voting issues have won the round. One way to show this confidence is to clearly articulate that the voting issues you have chosen are the most important points in the round. And because you have won these voting issues, the balance of the round should swing in your favor.

The final focus offers the second pro and con speakers one more chance to take the podium and convince the audience. While the earlier speeches form an important foundation on which the final focus must be built, this last speech cannot be overlooked. Identifying the important issues in the debate round, consolidating those issues into voting issues, and presenting two to three voting issues with clear impacts should be your goals in the final focus speech. Do not forget to ask for the judge's vote before you sit down, but be sure you have given him good reasons to vote for you. Debate rounds are not won solely by what is said in the final speech because both partners are indispensable to the team's success. However, a poor final speech can certainly turn the table against you in a close round. By the same token, a strong final focus can shift the judge to your side when the two teams are both strong. Focusing on the key voting issues and ignoring the petty issues of the round will go a long way toward helping the judge know both which way to vote and on what basis this decision ought to rest.

Contention 3: Introduction to Policy Debate

Observation 18: Policy Debate Rounds

"Truth springs from argument amongst friends."
-David Hume-

Formal policy debating takes place in a debate round which lasts approximately 80 minutes. This longer debate round gives both teams ample opportunity to present their arguments. The affirmative team is attempting to uphold the resolution in every argument while the negative team is focused on rejecting the resolution. Each team has four speeches and two cross-examinations. Each debater gives two speeches, cross-examines one opponent, and is cross-examined by the other opponent. Now let's take a closer look at each portion of the debate round.

> The speakers are commonly referred to as: 1A (first Affirmative speaker), 1N (first Negative speaker), 2A (second Affirmative speaker) and 2N (second Negative speaker).

Figure 15: Policy Debate Speaker Abbreviations

A. First Affirmative Constructive [1AC – 8 Minutes]

The first affirmative speaker presents the affirmative team's case in an eight-minute speech called the first affirmative constructive (1AC). Unlike all other speeches in a policy debate round, this one is completely pre-written (see page 115). The affirmative must present a **prima facie** case in this speech meaning the case must justify replacing the status quo. The 1AC sets up the boundaries and organizes the round. Most arguments introduced in the debate round by both teams will follow the same or a very similar order as this speech. Without a strong 1AC speech, the affirmative case will be easily defeated.

B. Cross-Examination of the 1A by the 2N [3 Minutes]

This cross-examination has two purposes. The first is to clarify any questions the second negative speaker or his partner might have about the affirmative case. (Some debaters request a copy of the 1AC during this cross-examination.) The second purpose is to attempt to trap the 1A or to lead him to admit problems with his case. This second purpose should only be attempted after all clarification questions have been asked. Use all cross-examinations wisely. Do not be overbearing or aggressive. Be polite as you derive logical conclusions about the affirmative case for the judge.

C. First Negative Constructive [1NC – 8 Minutes]

The first negative constructive (1NC) is used to refute the affirmative case and establish the main points of contention between the teams. All topicality violations (see page 139) and counterplans (see page 149) should be introduced here because it is unfair or "abusive" to the affirmative team to introduce these prepared arguments at any later time. The first negative speaker should try to refute any parts of the affirmative case and continue any arguments from the cross-examination. Evidence against the affirmative case should be presented in this speech as well. This is your chance to steer the debate toward your strong issues by giving a persuasive eight-minute speech about the strengths of the current system or "status quo" as well as the harmful effects of the affirmative team's plan.

D. Cross-Examination of the 1N by the 1A [3 Minutes]

The purposes of this affirmative cross-examination are for clarification of the negative arguments and for strengthening the affirmative case by leading the negative to agree with affirmative positions. Just as the negative team must use the cross-examination wisely, so too must the affirmative team. Do not be overbearing or aggressive. Be polite as you present logical conclusions about the round for the judge.

E. Second Affirmative Constructive [2AC – 8 Minutes]

This speech is the affirmative's first chance to defend their case against the arguments presented in the previous speech. Although the affirmative team may reinforce their arguments from their first speech later in the round, they cannot ignore an issue brought up in the 1NC. If the negative team points out that an argument was not addressed (a dropped argument), the negative automatically wins that issue. The negative has 13 consecutive minutes of arguments without an affirmative speech immediately following this one (the 2NC and 1NR discussed below). If the second affirmative does not address all of the arguments presented in the 1NC, her partner will be overburdened in the rebuttals and forced to concede issues that may help the negative team. Be concise. Also, give the judge a good reason to reject the status quo and enact your plan!

F. Cross-Examination of the 2A by the 1N [3 Minutes]

This cross-examination is important for both teams. If the affirmative answers a question to help her team, she can gain an advantage for her team. Likewise, if the negative team traps the affirmative in a contradiction, the judge may be so persuaded by the block of negative speeches which follow that the affirmative's final two speeches may have little chance of changing the judge's mind.

G. Second Negative Constructive [2NC – 8 Minutes]

This is the first speech of the negative block, the thirteen minute stretch of negative speeches with no affirmative speeches in between (see page 128). The affirmative team only has a cross-examination in between the two speeches of the negative block. Topicality should not be a new issue in this speech. The second negative constructive is often used to address disadvantages to the affirmative's proposal (see page 133). Finally, this is the last speech to introduce any other issues the negative team wishes to argue because they cannot do so later. After this speech, all either team is allowed to do is expand previous arguments. Be sure to give a compelling second negative constructive speech which gives the judge good reasons to vote against the affirmative case and for the current system.

H. Cross-Examination of the 2N by the 2A [3 Minutes]

This may be the most important cross-examination for the affirmative team. It is their only chance to slow the momentum of the negative block. As the negative speaker, you must hold your ground. Carefully think through your answers before you respond. Otherwise, you might give the affirmative a great advantage by allowing your negative block to be disrupted. No matter which side you are on, this final cross-examination is important. Remember, as with all cross-examinations, be polite as you prod or answer questions to maintain your persuasive powers for the remainder of the round.

I. First Negative Rebuttal [1NR – 5 Minutes]

This speech forms the second half of the negative block. In this speech, the negative team should reinforce its constructive arguments, not by repeating them, but by giving them more depth. Provide new analysis; do not just repeat the argument. The 1NR is an opportunity to strengthen arguments by supplying more evidence and expanding upon previous strong arguments while refuting the affirmative's arguments. Finally, there is no need to repeat anything your partner just said in the second negative constructive. Because the affirmative has not been able to respond to those arguments, the arguments are still alive in the round. The affirmative must address them regardless of whether you repeat them. When combined with the second negative constructive, this speech can bury the affirmative in multiple arguments and sway the entire round in favor of the negative team.

J. First Affirmative Rebuttal [1AR – 5 Minutes]

In this short five-minute speech the first affirmative speaker must respond to the arguments presented in the thirteen minute negative block. He must briefly cover every point the negative made in the negative block. Any arguments not covered in this speech are dropped or conceded arguments meaning the negative team wins them. Here, the 1A must solidify any arguments needed to help win the round. Speak quickly but clearly so that the judge understands everything. Keep moving from point to point; do not get stuck on one issue. By making arguments which encompass other arguments in the round, or "grouping arguments," the 1A can better refute the arguments leveled against his team's case. If the 1AR is weak, the affirmative will usually lose the round. However, a strong 1AR which refutes the negative arguments while also strengthening the affirmative case will give the affirmative a significant edge to win the round.

K. Second Negative Rebuttal [2NR – 5 Minutes]

In the final negative speech the 2N should try to give the judge a few clear reasons to vote against the affirmative team, against the resolution, for the status quo, and for the negative team. Although you may want to cover most of the round's arguments, your primary job in this speech is to convince the judge that **your team** should win the round. This is done by giving the judge voting issues (see page 156). It is best to select a few strong issues that motivate the judge to vote negative and promote these issues in your final speech. If possible, tell a story in this speech that the judge will remember when she makes her decision. To produce a negative ballot, you must show how problematic the affirmative team's proposed change would be if it were enacted and how wonderful the status quo is. This is your last chance to speak, so make it count.

L. Second Affirmative Rebuttal [2AR – 5 Minutes]

This is the final speech of the round. In this speech the 2A must refute the negative arguments, strengthen the affirmative arguments, and finally convince the judge to vote for the resolution. This speech should focus on the voting issues of the debate round (see page 156). Explain how your team has won each one. Do not forget, as the affirmative, you must also win all four **stock issues** (see page 109). Explain how the stock issues were won and give the judge three to five additional voting issues or reasons your team should win the round. Conclude your speech by giving a brief yet persuasive argument that the judge will remember. Staying within your time constraints is most important in this speech. Wisely use this speech to produce an affirmative ballot.

M. Preparation Time [5 Minutes Per Team, Per Round]

Many debaters find it necessary to talk with their partners during the round. Often an opponent will make an argument that can be refuted with a specific piece of evidence. In the moment, it seems important to pass this information along to your partner. However, it is not advisable to whisper during your opponent's speeches. Instead, write any comments down and pass the note to your partner during the speech. This allows you both to remain attentive to the speaker, flow, and simultaneously communicate without appearing rude. Save your comments which you must voice to your partner for preparation time, commonly called "prep time." This assures that you do not miss arguments and keeps you from being viewed as disrespectful to the speaker.

Preparation time is given to each team at the beginning of the round. Each team begins the round with five minutes to divide any way they want throughout the round before their own speeches. The affirmative does not use any prep time before the 1AC and prep time cannot be used before cross-examinations. Prep time gives partners a chance to solidify their debate "roadmap" for the round (see page 52). It allows teams time to formulate a cohesive strategy for attacking the other team's arguments or for defending their own. Prep time is used to form strategy, collect evidence, and ensure strong organization when the speaker rises to present. Be careful to manage your prep time wisely to maximize your effectiveness.

Prep time may be used at many times throughout the round, but some times are more advantageous than others. Good debaters maximize their use of prep. Because the affirmative cannot prepare for what will be argued, it is better strategy for the negative to use prep time prior to the 1NC. This gives an advantage to the negative because the affirmative will have to use prep later. The affirmative should use just a short amount of prep time before the 2AC. The negative may use prep time before the 2NC, but they should try to avoid using any prep before the 1NR because it is in the middle of the negative block. The best time for the affirmative team to use their prep time is before the 1AR to ensure no arguments from the thirteen minute negative block are ignored. Both teams should also use prep time before their final speeches. Because of cross-examination, there are three minutes stretches of non-speech time which should also be utilized in preparing speeches. If this time is effectively used, the majority of prep time will be available for strategic use.

After the round, thank your judges, congratulate the other team and put away your supplies. Use this time to prepare for future rounds and to note things to improve. Identify arguments you thought were effective and the points you could have made clearer. With the right attitude, you will develop into a stronger debater with each and every round.

> First Affirmative Constructive (1AC)
> > Cross-Examination of 1A by 2N
> First Negative Constructive (1NC)
> > Cross-Examination of 1N by 1A
> Second Affirmative Constructive (2AC)
> > Cross-Examination of 2A by 1N
> Second Negative Constructive (2NC)
> > Cross-Examination of 2N by 2A
> First Negative Rebuttal (1NR)
> First Affirmative Rebuttal (1AR)
> Second Negative Rebuttal (2NR)
> Second Affirmative Rebuttal (2AR)

Figure 16: Policy Debate Speeches and Abbreviations

Observation 19: Stock Issues

*"It is better to debate a question without settling it
than to settle a question without debating it."*
-Joseph Joubert-

Every policy debate case will encompass stock issues. Stock issues are four key questions applied to an affirmative case. These four questions ensure the affirmative follows the resolution, presents important problems, and provides a means to fix the problems. The four main stock issues in a policy debate are: *Topicality*, *Significance*, *Inherency*, and *Solvency*. Because the affirmative team's responsibility in the debate round is to uphold the resolution, the affirmative should present a complete, prima facie case and win all four stock issues in order to win the debate round.

A. The Four Stock Issues
1. Topicality
Topicality means the affirmative case is inside the bounds of the resolution. Topicality asks: (1) "Does the affirmative case do what the resolution says?"; (2) "Does the affirmative case support affirming the resolution as the affirmative team defined it?"; and (3) "Do the definitions presented by the affirmative team define the resolution as it was intended to be defined?"

The first question is relatively straightforward. If the resolution talks about human travel to outer space and the affirmative case discusses underwater fish exploration, the affirmative team is clearly not doing what the resolution says and is thus not topical. The second question asks if the affirmative has worked within the boundaries they set for themselves at the outset of the round. The affirmative team defines key words in the resolution to ensure all the debaters begin the round with the same understanding of the round's focus. These definitions further narrow the boundaries of the resolution by clarifying what exactly the resolution means by its particular words. If the affirmative team defines outer space as only the moon and Mars and the case deals with exploring Saturn, the affirmative has not met its own definitions of the resolution and is thus not topical even though the affirmative case could be topical under the resolution if the definitions were different. For example, human space exploration could certainly encompass a proposal to send humans to Saturn, but if the affirmative defines space more narrowly, Saturn falls outside the boundaries of the resolution and is thus no longer topical.

The third question is the most complicated and subject to debate because it centers on the intent of the resolution. If the resolution talks about farming and a clever affirmative manages to find a definition defining selling mortgages on Wall Street as "farming," a topicality question would arise because of the resolution's intent. A clever definition does not undermine the fact the resolution's words show a clear intent to have one topic discussed. Even a clever definition which might construe "farming" to include financial trading could violate the resolution's intent which was to discuss agriculture.[18] The negative team should point out any of these violations to the judge as reasons to reject the affirmative case. In order to do this, topicality arguments need to be properly structured to explain to the judge the importance of voting against a non-topical affirmative. The structure and method of the topicality argument are discussed on page 142.

---

[18] Because topicality based on the intent of the resolution is often not clear and is itself subject to debate, such topicality arguments should be carefully developed and ought not be relied upon to win a round.

The affirmative team has the privilege of defining the terms of the resolution; however these definitions must remain within the boundaries intended by the resolution. The entire affirmative case must uphold the resolution as defined. If the affirmative team's case (harms, plan, or advantages) does not fall within the affirmative's definition of the resolution, the affirmative team is not topical and the negative team should win on topicality alone. The negative team can also win on topicality if the negative team presents alternative definitions which show that the affirmative team's case is outside the resolution. Alternative definitions must be more credible definitions than the affirmative team's definitions and must alter the boundaries of the resolution to show that the affirmative team's case is not within a reasonable interpretation of the resolution.

For example, if the resolution requires a change in energy policy, the affirmative definitions might include the taxes paid for each mile a car drives. The negative team may have a definition from a more credible source (i.e. the Department of Energy v. *Webster's Dictionary*) which says that fees for automobiles are transportation policy and energy policy is limited to rules and fees surrounding only fuels. If the judge believes the negative's definition is a more appropriate reading of the resolution, the affirmative may be found non-topical. Such debates obviously require significant discussion of the merits of various definitions and authority for defining terminology.

Topicality is an absolute voting issue in a debate round. Due to the importance of topicality, a non-topical case should have very little chance of winning because judges are willing and encouraged to neglect the other issues in the debate and vote on topicality. (Topicality is called an "**a priori** voting issue" meaning it is the first issue the judge should consider in the debate round.) The importance of topicality to the debate may be analogized to the rules of basketball. If the out of bounds line is crossed, possession of the ball is lost. In the same way, an affirmative case outside the boundaries of the resolution should also lose possession of the round, in this case, losing the judge's vote. Developing a case which stays within the boundaries set forth in the resolution will allow the debate to focus on the policy rather than stagnating on definitions.

If topicality is an issue, it should be brought up in the first negative constructive speech. In this speech, a proper topicality structure should be utilized. Instead of stating, "The affirmative is not topical" you need to use a structured argument and lay out reasons the judge should consider your argument. Also, if you do not have a strong topicality contention, it may be in your best interest to concede topicality and refute the other portions of the case. For further discussion of topicality, see page 139.

Figure 17: Topicality Note to Negative Teams

2. Significance

Significance means the problems the affirmative team has identified within the status quo are important enough to justify changing the current system. Some debaters simply refer to this stock issue as "harms." Significance deals with two main questions: "are bad things happening now?" and "how bad are the bad things?" If bad things are not happening now, there is no reason to consider a new course of action. If the bad things are not very bad at all, there is, again, no reason to alter our current policy. A good debate case will communicate that very bad things are happening.

Significance may be measured in two ways: quantitative and qualitative. Quantitative significance is a number. A large quantity of people harmed or a large amount of money lost are examples of quantitative significance. Qualitative significance does not rely on raw numbers. Instead, the quality, or value lost, is observed. Thus, even if the quantity of problems is small, a problem may be significant because of the quality lost by those impacted. For example, if pollution in a river is killing only one child per day, the raw number may not seem significant, but the quality lost (human life) is quite substantial and could certainly warrant a change.

Great cases will attempt to prove both quantitative and qualitative significance. While there are other types of significance, quantitative and qualitative significance are the most prevalent in a debate round. Unless the harms have a significant impact, there is little justification for eliminating them with the affirmative team's plan. If we assume any change has some cost (a very safe assumption), there must be a significant enough problem to justify making the change. Without significant harms the affirmative will likely lose the round.

Significance tells an audience why they should care about the problems presented and justify making changes in the status quo. A debater who fails to convince the audience there are significant problems will be unable to convince that same audience it is worthwhile to change policies. The harms will be your best method for motivating the judge or any audience member to spend the next eight minutes listening to your proposals for fixing these problems.

Note: Some case structures (see page 115) present the stock issue of significance under the advantages. For example, in a comparative advantage case, there are no "harms" to discuss. Rather, there are advantages the status quo does not reach because the affirmative team's plan is not in place. The advantages begin by showing how the lack of the affirmative team's plan creates significant shortfalls in obtaining the goals of the current system and how the benefits of a change will be significant improvements (comparative advantages) over the status quo.

Warning! Many resolutions contain the term "significant" or a synonym. Do not confuse the stock issue of significance and the definition of significance under topicality.

For example, if your resolution asks you to significantly change United States military involvement in Afghanistan, you have not fulfilled the resolution by identifying a substantial problem, nor have you satisfied the stock issue of significance by simply making a big change. The significance stock issue may be met where a big problem exists and can be solved with only a minor change. On the other hand, a change big enough to "significantly change" a policy may not be intended to address a big problem, but could be perfectly acceptable to fulfill the requirements of the resolution.

Figure 18: Significance v. Significant

3. Inherency

Inherency means the significant problems exist and are linked to the current system the resolution requires the affirmative team to change. Inherency is typically considered when examining the cause of the problem. Inherency asks: "does the status quo cause the harms the affirmative claims?" or "does the harm exist because the resolution has not been adopted?" There are three types of inherency usually employed in policy debate: existential inherency, structural inherency, and attitudinal inherency. Each category is a more convincing link between the problem and the status quo.

First, there is *existential inherency*. Existential inherency means that the plan does not exist in the status quo and that the existence of the problem in the current system is the result of the status quo's policies or lack thereof. For example, if the resolution calls for changing the policies of the National Football League, the affirmative team says there are too few games in the National Football League season, and the plan proposes adding two games to the season, existential inherency is the number of games in the current season.

Second, there is *structural inherency*. Structural inherency claims the status quo has no capacity (no structure) to solve the harms. This lack of capacity is proven by showing a barrier to the plan (laws, rules, etc.) or by showing that the status quo lacks the necessary structure to solve the harm. If the number of football games remains the problem, structural inherency would point out that the current contract between the players and the teams explicitly limits the number of games in a season. Thus number of games is structurally inherent due to the player contracts and the collective bargaining agreement.

Finally, there is *attitudinal inherency*. Attitudinal inherency shows that the plan proposed by the affirmative, or any plan to remedy the harms, will not be implemented because of attitudes against it in the status quo that prevent the plan from being enacted. Because of these beliefs and attitudes, the current system cannot solve the identified harms. Again, if we are seeking to change the number of games in the football season, attitudes that might prevent such a change include those seeking to compare statistics who might argue any such adjustment to the length of the season will harm the integrity of historical comparison even if the length of the season has been changed before. If enough people are concerned about historical comparison, and if these same people are parties in the negotiations over lengthening the season, these attitudes might directly prevent lengthening the season.

If the affirmative states that the harm in the status quo is causing massive unemployment, they must prove this. All the negative team has to do is read evidence saying unemployment is currently low or that unemployment is caused by issues outside of the resolution or beyond the affirmative case in order to remove inherency and eliminate justification for change.

Figure 19: Inherency Example

Occasionally something other than the status quo causes a harm. When this occurs, the negative team argues "alternate causality" that there is another cause to the problem. When the negative team argues alternate causality they argue that the problems are caused by something outside the resolution and thus cannot be solved by affirming the resolution. Because the harms must stem particularly from the status quo under the resolution, the affirmative must be certain that the harms claimed do not have an alternate cause. Understanding the use of this argument is important for negative teams.

Inherency shows a need to act now with the affirmative's case to solve the problems rather than wait for the existing system to do so. If the harms can be solved with only minor repairs to the status quo, or if the status quo is already solving these harms, there is no justification for adopting the affirmative's plan. Inherency does not mean that there is no available <u>method</u> to solve the problem, however. For example, a claim that the Constitution is violated by the current system does not undermine the inherency of a harm even though <u>someone could</u> bring a case to court and the court could strike down the current law. Until the court case has been decided by at least a United States Court of Appeals, if not by the Supreme Court, inherency still exists. In the same way, just because Congress could pass a law fixing the problem does not jeopardize inherency. The negative must show that Congress has passed a law fixing the problem to undermine the harm's inherency.

4. Solvency

Solvency means the enacted plan would solve the harms in the current policy. The affirmative team must solve all the harms claimed within their case in order to be fully solvent.[19]   Solvency asks three questions: (1) "Will the problem be eliminated by the affirmative case?"; (2) "Is the affirmative's plan feasible?"; and (3) "Are the advantages of eliminating the harms desirable?" Each of these questions should be answered "yes" to prove the affirmative case solvent.   In other words, if the affirmative plan greatly reduces or eliminates the harms and will produce benefits, the affirmative team is solvent.

The advantages gained by enacting the affirmative case should first and foremost be the elimination of the problems exposed in the harms. After showing the harms are solved, the affirmative often presents additional advantages. Each advantage needs to come from the case presented, not from some outside policy change. If the advantages could be gained through other means, there is little justification for adopting the affirmative case. Also, the affirmative team can only claim advantages gained from the topical portions of the case. See page 139.

Solvency is important to the debate. The proposed plan must work to solve for the harms. Arguments against the plan which show that the plan will not be properly funded, enforced, or even implemented are all arguments which an affirmative case must withstand. However, a debate over whether or not the plan will pass is not allowed in a debate round. The affirmative team has been given the power of **fiat** in order to keep the debate focused on the need for change and the impacts of such change. Fiat means that, for purposes of the debate round, we assume that the affirmative team's case will be passed by the appropriate agent if the judge votes affirmative. Fiat power prevents the debate from centering on how a majority of Congress would vote. This allows the debate to focus on the rest of the case rather than on the politics of the present time.[20] While there may be a legitimate question over whether the political makeup of the government would actually enact the affirmative's case, for the sake of the hypothetical world of debate, debaters agree to assume that the proposed plan would pass Congress or any other agent of change the affirmative team's case specifies. In fact, arguing that politicians will refuse to pass the affirmative's case only helps show that there is attitudinal inherency on the side of the affirmative case.

Solvency is an important issue for the affirmative team. If the negative team can prove the plan will fail to actually produce advantages over the status quo, there is no reason to enact the affirmative case. Developing solvency which compels the judge to cast an affirmative ballot is an important part of constructing a winning case.

B. Summary & Critique of Stock Issues

Stock issues give debaters questions to ask about any case. While some cases may clearly utilize the stock issues, others may do so more subtly. In any case the stock issues will be present in some form or another. Although stock issues are an important means for evaluating the round, they are not the only means. Debaters should ensure their own cases fulfill each stock issue and should be sure to press any opponent who neglects to address a stock issue question in his case. Using stock issues in this fashion provides strength to the arguments regardless of the paradigm a judge uses to evaluate the round.

As the negative, you only have to win one of the four stock issues to win the round. Each stock issue is crucial to a complete affirmative case. Therefore, addressing all the stock issue

---

[19] Complete solvency is not required to win the stock issue of solvency, however. For example, if a team presents 2 significant and inherent harms, a plan to fix both of them, and ends up solving only one harm, they can win the stock issue of solvency because there is a complete case (significant, inherent, and solvent) on that particular harm.

[20] Fiat does not prevent teams from arguing about the political and social fallout from a particular policy. For example, a policy which causes a particular Senator or Congressperson to lose reelection can be challenged on the basis of that politician's assistance to particular political interests. For more details, see the *Great Debate Teacher's Edition* discussion of Politics Disadvantages.

questions and forcing the affirmative to prove each stock issue is vital to your success. If you can cast doubt on a few stock issues by the end of the round, you are well on your way to moving the judge in your direction.

Although the stock issues are important, most judges must be convinced to vote on other issues. The affirmative has to present a case in their first speech that is topical, has inherent and significant harms, and solves those harms. This is called presenting a "prima facie" case. The affirmative case is prima facie if it would persuade an individual without any preconceptions. The standard is low, but requires the affirmative's first speech to offer a complete picture of the positions being advocated. In theory, if the affirmative presents a prima facie case, proves the stock issues, and the negative never responds, the affirmative should win.

The affirmative should win all four stock issues in at least one complete section of their case. For example, an affirmative case with two harms and two advantages could win if one significant, inherent harm is solved by the plan without producing disadvantages which outweigh the advantage of solving one harm. Even if the other harm were entirely lost along with its advantage, the affirmative could still win the round.

Lastly, while stock issues may be an accurate basis for a decision, they are not always the determining factor for a judge. Stock issues judging is one of many "judging paradigms" by which judges make their decisions. If the judge has little or no experience, she may focus on who appears more confident when speaking and the stock issues may not even be a factor in her decision. More experienced judges will focus on the stock issues, but often base their decisions on the weighing of net benefits between the advantages and disadvantages. Thus, you must also persuade the judge of your position even without the use of the stock issues. The best method for persuading the judge is through the use of voting issues. For more discussion of voting issues, see page 155.

Although stock issues are a good basis for arguments, they are not the only points of argumentation which should be addressed in a debate. They are a necessary feature of every affirmative case, but not sufficient to win the debate round. For example, disadvantages (see page 133) are not covered under the stock issues listed above. While some debaters attempt to group disadvantages with solvency, this is a stretch. Also, critiques, burdens, **criteria**, values, and underlying premises are not included in the list of the stock issues. While these are important aspects of the debate, the stock issues ignore them. Because the stock issues are not comprehensive, they should never be viewed as the only paradigm from which to judge or argue a round. Debaters should answer the questions of the stock issues and then move on to additional arguments. The stock issues questions are important, but debaters who rely exclusively on the stock issues will find themselves missing many amazing arguments.

Stock issues provide all debaters a simple framework from which to debate. As debate experience grows, debaters begin to venture away from strict stock issues debating by incorporating the stock issues in their broader arguments. Assuring that the questions of the stock issues are answered will benefit both teams in providing a simple structure for the debaters and the judge.

Observation 20: Policy Case Structures

"Speak properly, and in as few words as you can, but always plainly;
for the end of speech is not ostentation, but to be understood."
-William Penn-

A debate case offers the affirmative team the opportunity to tell its story. As with any speech, the case should begin with an "attention step" which draws the audience into the story. One time-tested method of grabbing the audience's attention is to identify real-world problems your plan will solve using a quotation, story, or compelling statistic. The case proceeds to clarify the resolution and focus the round on the issues pertinent to the particular case. This means quoting the resolution, defining any terms that will clarify the meaning of the resolution, and outlining any particular methods you want the judge to use in evaluating the arguments in the round. Regardless of structure, the debate case outlines problems with the current system, proposes steps to fix these problems, and emphasizes the benefits of adopting the policy: solving the harms or problems. The goal in crafting your case is to highlight the need for the judge to cast an affirmative ballot — in other words, to vote to uphold the resolution.

There are many methods of presenting a policy debate case. Some commonly used structures include: Plan-Meets-Needs, Comparative Advantage, Criteria Analysis, Alternative Justification Analysis, and Stock Issues. While these are common structures, the possibilities are endless. Depending on your case and your experience, different structures are better than others. Regardless of the type of case you present, you must be prepared to debate against any case structure.

Debaters are not limited to the structures discussed below. While these are some of the most common structures used in debate rounds, an affirmative team may choose to employ a different case structure just as they may select a case from one of thousands of possibilities — even those you have never heard. Do your best to understand the structure an affirmative team is utilizing and debate the round on the issues, not the technicalities or supposed "rules." Choose the structure that best suits you and your case. Then work to perfect the case. In some situations you may find it valuable to alter the organization of a common case structure. Customize your case structure to your case to maximize clarity and strength of presentation as you work to uphold the resolution.

A. Case Structures

Let's examine the different case structures. A quick reference outline of the various case types may be found in Appendix 1 and examples of many of these structures are available in Appendix 3.

1. Plan-Meets-Needs

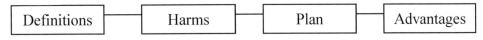

Figure 20: Plan-Meets-Needs Structure

The plan-meets-needs case structure is the most common case structure. These cases are usually clear and easy to understand. The affirmative identifies harms in the status quo (usually two or three), propose a plan to solve the harms, and finally shows that enacting the plan will solve the harms and bring about advantages. This structure uses a basic problem-cause-solution format which is comprehensible to everyone. While other structures have their advantages, using this familiar format may go a long way in helping a judge understand (and vote for) your case. (See page 185 for an example plan-meets-needs case.)

The plan-meets-needs structure requires careful wording to avoid the assumption that the harm is completely solved. Rather than trying to claim complete solvency (i.e. the harm is fully eliminated), many debaters choose to explain that the harm is mitigated or reduced. Carefully word advantages to avoid this problem. For example, the claim that terrorism is solved is most likely impossible to prove because it does not seem logically possible to anyone. Instead, wording the advantage "terrorism reduced" enables you to argue that your plan simply minimizes the harm instead of completely solving it. The plan-meets-needs structure is not only the building block of all cases, it is also an excellent structure for all levels of experience.

2. Criteria Analysis

Figure 21: Criteria Analysis Structure

Criteria Analysis cases are popular because they are simple and easy to understand. The affirmative team identifies criteria (or a criterion) for the resolution and shows how the affirmative case, unlike the current system, meets these criteria, or at least meets them better than the status quo. Under the criteria analysis case, the debate round centers on three questions to determine whether the resolution should be affirmed: (1) Is the criteria a good way to measure the pros and cons of a policy change?; (2) Do the affirmative advantages move the world closer to the criteria than the status quo?; and (3) Do the disadvantages move the world further away from the criteria than the status quo? For example, if the resolution calls for government funding for space exploration and the affirmative team proposes a criterion of safety to go along with its proposal to increase the government's role in space exploration, the affirmative will focus on the risks associated with spaceflight and argue that the government is best able to mitigate and minimize these risks. The negative will argue either that the safety concerns in private space exploration are overblown or that the government is not better than private companies at protecting safety. However, unless the negative rejects the safety criterion, disadvantages and arguments that spending government money on space exploration will result in fewer college graduates are irrelevant to the criterion and the judge's decision in the round. In other words, the criteria become the measuring stick to decide which team should win the round.

The criteria analysis structure changes the focus of the debate compared with a plan-meets-needs structured case. Instead of focusing on harms and advantages, the affirmative team must focus on how the criteria are valid and how the affirmative plan will better meet the criteria when compared with the status quo. By connecting all arguments to the criteria, the affirmative team gives the judge a reason to accept the case when he accepts your criteria. The harms of a criteria analysis case will not necessarily be inherently wrong; rather they will expose the failures of the status quo to meet the criteria. The advantages will highlight the benefits of meeting the criteria; they must prove the affirmative plan will be beneficial. (See page 188 for an example criteria analysis case.)

Some criterion are built around values including justice, life, liberty, equality, freedom, or around specific documents such as the Constitution, the Declaration of Independence, or around more measurable ideas such as health, safety, security. While judges often agree with your criteria, if the status quo meets it, you are doomed to failure. If, for example, your criterion is human health and the current policy keeps the public healthier than your policy would, your plan is not necessary.

Some affirmative teams choose criteria the negative will agree with, at least in theory, but this is not a requirement. If the negative team agrees with the criteria, the entire round will hinge on whether the plan or the status quo is better able to reach the bar set by the criteria. However, if the negative team can prove the criteria are not the best way to measure a good policy, the affirmative case will generally lose. For example, suppose the safety criterion is being used. The negative team may explain that safety is only possible when the economy is strong and so the economy is a preferable measuring stick for the debate round. By presenting disadvantages that explain how spending government money on space exploration will harm the overall economy, the affirmative's safety advantages become much less important. Note, however, that unless the negative team rejects the criterion, the economic disadvantage would not matter. When the two teams disagree about the usefulness of the specific criterion to evaluate the round, significant portions of the debate speeches are often dedicated to arguing the merits of the criteria before actually addressing the plan's ability to meet them.

Another benefit of criteria analysis cases is that the criteria may actually bring the negative team to the point of agreeing with the affirmative case. If the affirmative establishes criteria and the negative accepts them, the affirmative may be able to turn acceptance of the criteria into acceptance of the affirmative policy. For example, if the criterion is *health* and the negative accepts this as a criterion for a good policy, all the affirmative needs to do is show an increase in health in order to win the round.

Acceptance of the criteria can take many forms. The first form is explicit acceptance. If the negative team states, "We accept the affirmative's criteria" in a speech, the criteria are accepted. Another form of acceptance is silence. If the negative does not mention the criteria in their first speech, the affirmative should ask in cross-examination if the criteria have been accepted. The final form of acceptance is when the negative presents counter criteria. If, after argumentation over the criteria, the affirmative criteria are shown to be superior in this instance, the negative is forced to accept the affirmative's criteria.

The debate will hinge on whether the affirmative's proposal or status quo is better able to uphold the criterion. If the criterion is a stronger economy and the affirmative's case will increase Gross Domestic Product (GDP), but also increase unemployment, the debate will hinge on which measure of the economy is more important. If, on the other hand, the negative can present disadvantages to show that even though the affirmative case will slightly improve the economy in the short-term, the long-term harms to the economy will undermine any short-term gains, the negative team can win based on the criterion of a stronger economy. But if the negative team's disadvantages focus on how the policy will harm some endangered species and provides no link that ties the harm to the species to the economy, the affirmative team should win because the only criterion is economic strength.

Although the criteria analysis case's underlying focus on a central theme is similar to the comparative advantage case, the two case structures should not be confused.

3. Comparative Advantage

Comparative advantage cases, often called "comp-ad cases" require improvement rather than full solvency in order to gain the advantage. This case structure is used when an affirmative team wants to claim that enacting their plan will result in a "net benefit" over the status quo by showing some kind of improvement over the current system, not an elimination of a harm. The affirmative team claims that its advantages are better than the status quo when the two worlds are compared. The underlying premise of comp-ad cases is that some of the goals of the status quo could be better met with a policy change. While the status quo may already be working toward these goals, the affirmative team argues that these goals could be reached to a greater extent, faster, in a better manner, or with less corresponding harm through the affirmative case.

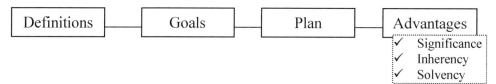

Figure 22: Comparative Advantage Structure

In a comp-ad case the affirmative begins by outlining the goals of the status quo. These are goals that the current system has already agreed upon and is working toward. A plan to better accomplish these goals is then presented. The advantages follow and show how the goals will be better met after the plan is put into action. Advantages stemming from the affirmative team's plan are compared to the pros and cons of the status quo, hence the name "comparative advantage." When comparing the advantages to the benefits of the present system, debaters divide each advantage into a three-part substructure which (1) shows where the status quo is deficient (either the status quo does not meet the goal at all, or it just barely meets the goal), (2) proves that the problem is inherent within the status quo, and (3) reveals the benefit of moving the world closer to the goal or goals as a result of enacting the affirmative team's plan. (See page 190 for an example comparative advantage case).

When deciding which team has won the debate round, an improved policy is justification for a change so long as the improvement relates to the goal. Debaters can choose this structure when they want the judge to vote for change on the basis of simple improvement. However, if your comparative advantage is small, most teams will be able to argue that there are disadvantages which outweigh the small benefit. And unlike the criteria analysis case, the disadvantages are not limited to areas affecting the goals, but may deal with any possible downside to the proposed plan. Thus, the strong comparative advantage case will find areas where the status quo is substantially lacking in reaching the stated goal and will make considerable strides toward reaching that goal.

A correctly developed comparative advantage case does not always point out devastating problems of the status quo. Rather, it shows the failure of the status quo to meet its own stated goals. The only "harms" may be the fact that the status quo does not reach the potential advantages of the affirmative plan. In other words, there really is not any harm in the current system, but if the affirmative plan were adopted, more benefits would occur. When developed, practiced, and perfected, this case structure can be very useful for many cases.

One word of warning: Comparative advantage cases provide an opportunity to examine the shortcomings of the present system compared to its own stated objectives and ideals. However, they do not allow the debate to reach areas where the entire focus of the government should be changed. Instead, a debater presenting a comparative advantage case is arguing that the government has already articulated an ideal worth advancing, but simply has poorly executed its policy to achieve those goals. By presenting an alternative path to reach what is arguably the same goal, a comparative advantage case offers debaters the chance to discuss the pros and cons of various methods in reaching good objectives.

4. Alternative Justification Analysis

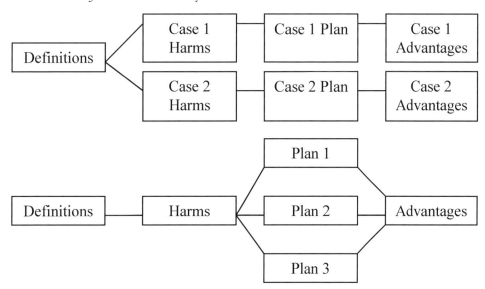

Figure 23: Two Types of Alternative Justification Analysis Structures

Alternative Justification Analysis Cases (AJACs) are complex case structures that contain many simple components. AJACs have either multiple miniature cases or multiple plans presented in the 1AC. While a unique case style, the alternative justification analysis case can be difficult to run correctly and may be confusing to both opponents and judges. Thus, AJACs should only be used after careful consideration by the team and full explanation to the audience in the round.

The AJACs structure relies on the basic debate theory that the affirmative's duty is to affirm the resolution, not to advocate for any particular case. As such, the affirmative offers the judge alternative methods of affirming the resolution which can be independently evaluated. If the judge believes the resolution has been justified on one of the plans or cases, she can cast an affirmative ballot.

    a. Mini-Cases Alternative Justification Analysis Case

The most common AJACs case presents two independent cases. If the affirmative can win with one of the cases, they win the round. For example, the affirmative team can argue that education policy should be changed by first presenting a plan to require year-round schooling and second presenting a plan to require mandatory standardized tests to graduate high school. Even though both plans address education policy, they offer their own unique harms, plans, and advantages. At the conclusion of the round, the judge can cast an affirmative ballot if he supports only the standardized test proposal, only the year-round school proposal, or both proposals. This point of debate theory is still being developed and debated so the affirmative team may spend time arguing for the validity of this structure.[21]

Alternative Justification Analysis Cases may be built using any of the other case structures for the two independent "mini-cases." They may also use different structures for each "mini-case." The greatest benefit of AJAC's cases is that the affirmative team can run two

---

[21] The justification for allowing a team to run two independent cases is identical to allowing a team to win only one of the harm-plan-advantage strings in a plan-meets-need case. Because the resolution has been justified by the affirmative team on at least one basis, a judge may cast a ballot in favor of the affirmative team (assuming the advantage(s) outweigh any disadvantages).

"independent" cases at the same time. Even if a judge dislikes one of the two plans, the judge may still vote affirmative if he likes the other plan. The ability to run two independent plans is also, however, the AJAC's greatest disadvantage. Although the negative team has to argue against two cases, the affirmative also has to defend two in the same amount of time. The negative team can present multiple disadvantages against both cases and leave the affirmative without enough time to support even one of the two cases at the conclusion of the round.

b. Multi-Plan Alternative Justification Analysis Case

Another type of AJACs case proposes three <u>plans</u> (plans, not cases) to solve the same group of harms and obtain the same advantages. For example, suppose the harm is that students graduate high school lacking basic skills in reading and mathematics. Three possible solutions might be longer school days, longer school years, and mandatory advancement exams. Rather than proposing just one of these, a multi-plan AJACs case could propose to lengthen the school day, lengthen the school year, or require a final comprehensive graduating exam. The affirmative case would argue that any of the three proposed plans would improve math and reading skills and thus warrants an affirmative vote. In this instance, the affirmative shows one or two harms and proposes two, three, or even four alternative plans to solve the harm(s). Again, the premise is that the affirmative must only win one plan (along with the harm and advantage) to win the round. Even if the judge disagrees with longer school days and standardized tests, he can vote affirmative for a plan proposing a longer school year. The benefits and shortcomings of this structure are similar to the mini-case AJACs case.

c. General Considerations for Alternative Justification Analysis Cases

Time management is the greatest hurdle in winning with an AJACs structure. Because there are two cases or three plans to defend, the 1AR is quite difficult. Grouping arguments and highlighting a central theme is much more difficult when there are so many pieces in the round. A good negative team remembers that it only needs to win one stock issue from each case to win the round and focuses its attention on attacking each case on its weakest prong. Thus, negative teams who effectively attack each case will leave the affirmative with more arguments than are feasible to rebut following the negative block. Because of this hurdle, an affirmative must be prepared to use clear, concise arguments to counter the negative's attacks.

Also note that since this structure is unfamiliar to many judges, the structure and its underlying theory must be explained early in the round. Taking time to explain the structure of a case uses time which would otherwise be used to support and advocate on behalf of the case as well as defend against the weak spots the negative exposes. Rather than pointing out the benefits of enacting the affirmative case, you waste precious time telling the judge the theoretical basis for your case.

Alternative Justification Analysis cases may be a good tool if you have two different policies you wish to propose or if there are multiple ways to solve a specific problem in the status quo. While there are some shortcomings, a good team may be able to take their case beyond these shortcomings and develop a case which is difficult to defeat. If, after careful consideration of the negative aspects to the AJAC's case a team chooses to use this structure, the obstacles may be overcome with precision and practice. It can be a very successful case structure if used and debated properly.

5. Stock Issues Structure

The stock issues case structure has a simple structure that follows the stock issues. In content, the stock issues case may seem very similar to a plan-meets-need structure. If you were to group inherency and significance, call them harms, and change solvency to advantages, you would have a plan-meets-need case. The main difference between the two case types is in presentation. Often, in the plan-meets-needs case, the stock issue of inherency is allowed to fall through the cracks, allowing the negative team to more easily win it. In a stock issues case structure, the "Inherency" section of the case points out either the structural or attitudinal barriers to the implementation of your team's plan. In essence, you want to explain why the status quo is inherently flawed and cannot fix itself.

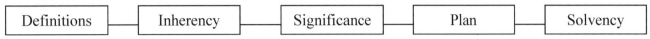

Figure 24: Stock Issues Structure

The stock issue of significance is self-explanatory. This issue is your opportunity to prove that the problems in the current system are actually big enough to warrant change. Solvency, while somewhat similar to advantages, shows how your case will solve for the stated problems. You never explicitly state advantages; rather, you show that the benefit of your case is solving the problems outlined in inherency and significance. Often, the solvency point will consist of pilot project examples or plan advocates. (See page 193 for an example stock issues case.)

Because of its simplicity and straight-forward nature, the stock issues case is an easy case to run. If you believe your judges will follow the stock issues very closely when casting a ballot, this structure will set up each argument to help the judge see the round through the stock issues. When separate advantages are difficult to find, the stock issues case is a perfect choice because your advantage is solving the problem of the status quo.

6. Whole Resolution Case

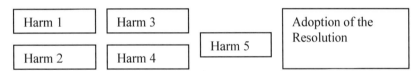

Figure 25: Whole Resolution Case Structure

Although uncommon, the whole resolution case has had times of prominence in many debate leagues. The whole resolution case asks a different question than the other case structures. Instead of asking the judge to vote for or against a specific policy, the whole resolution case asks the judge to vote for or against the resolution as a whole, hence the name whole resolution case. The whole resolution case asks a question of fact: "Should we adopt the resolution?" rather than a question of policy: "Should the policy proposed by the affirmative team be adopted?" (See page 195 for an example whole resolution case.)

The whole resolution case format is different from other more common structures because the affirmative team does not propose any specific policy change. This case structure is best discussed in the context of a resolution. For example, under the resolution, "Resolved, that the United States should significantly change its trade policy within one or both of the following areas: the Middle East and Africa," a whole resolution case tries to convince the judge that the United States should change its trade policy within the Middle East or Africa. It does not, however, propose any particular change for the judge to consider. The ultimate focus of the affirmative team will be to convince the judge that the status quo should be changed. The affirmative team presents several harms within the status quo, namely trade policy; it is imperative that these harms be inherent within trade policy itself. At least 4 or 5 harms should be presented from different areas of trade policy to show that the current trade policy is flawed. Then the affirmative simply states the status quo has many problems, and therefore it should be changed.

Each harm is a separate example of trade policy problems. One harm might be about arms trade, the next about commodities made with slave labor, another about U.S. trade policy in regards to AIDS vaccines in Africa. By giving many examples of a faulty trade policy the affirmative proves its assertion that trade policy should be changed. The goal throughout the round is to get the judge to agree with the resolution: that trade policy should be changed.

The negative's job is very different when debating against a whole resolution case. Because you are not arguing a specific policy, you can address the resolution as a whole in addition to refuting the harms. The negative team should present counter-warrants. Counter-warrants are negative assertions showing that the status quo is good. Within trade policy, the negative team can present counter-warrants by showing how the status quo is enacting more beneficial trade policies. They can be very specific, pointing out improvements in trade policy the affirmative has not addressed. Counter-warrants do not have to refute any specific point, they must refute only the resolution as a whole, proving that trade policy should not be changed. A disadvantage is another form of counter-warrant and is highly effective against whole resolution cases. If the affirmative team is arguing that the resolution needs to be adopted, the negative team has the option of identifying the harms which could occur when the resolution is adopted. Because the affirmative is not advocating a particular change, the negative team may present disadvantages of a variety of changes which would be possible under the resolution.

Whole resolution cases can be a fun way to run a different case and try out new debate theory. Since the affirmative team must only run harms, their burden is much lighter; however, because the negative team can run counter-warrants on any subject within the resolution, they have a good chance of catching the affirmative team unprepared. Because the whole resolution case requires an understanding of advanced debate theory in order to win, it is recommended only for more advanced debaters.

Case structure is an important part of debate. Learn the various case structure types in order to be prepared to debate against them. If you do not prepare for different case structures, you may be confused in debate rounds with foreign structures.

Figure 26: Why Learn Case Structures?

B. Case Building Blocks

1. Definitions

Definitions allow debaters to clarify the meaning of the resolution. Many words do not need to be defined, but definitions are helpful in outlining the nuances of some key phrases. For example, the term "income tax" may seem to have a straight-forward meaning, but tax policy experts have argued for years whether a consumption tax (such as a national sales tax) is a tax on income.[22] Thus, if the resolution required a debater to eliminate all income taxes, the definition of "income tax" could be vital to establishing the boundaries of the resolution. Debaters typically define terms that are unclear or are vital to setting clear boundaries for the scope of the resolution.

---

[22] The argument it is an income tax is that an individual would simply pay a tax based on their total income reduced by any increase in savings or investment in a year. Thus, the tax is based on an individual's income, even though the tax is actually based on the amount consumed in a given year.

A quick note about definitions in the 1AC: as debate has developed, many new tactics have been attempted. One of these new ideas is the elimination of definitions in the 1AC. Depending on the type of case, this elimination may be very appropriate. Definitions provide a standard for which to argue topicality in a debate round. If the affirmative team has doubts about whether or not their case is topical, definitions should be used to strengthen their position. By using loose definitions, they provide a foundation to prove the affirmative plan topical. However, providing this foundation does not come at a small cost, often teams will use a minute or more in the 1AC reading definitions for a case, which is obviously topical under the resolution. If you feel your case is topical, definitions could be eliminated. A mere statement of "all definitions are operational" should be sufficient. If the negative team does challenge topicality, then the affirmative team can always read definitions in the 2AC. However, more than likely, the negative team will not challenge topicality against an obviously topical case. By skipping definitions in the 1AC, you gain about thirty seconds to a minute in the 1AC that can be used to bolster your case.

2. Fiat

As initially introduced on page 113, fiat provides a means for the affirmative to implement the proposed policy. Without fiat power, the affirmative team would have to prove both that the law would be passed and that the law would be beneficial. Instead, fiat allows the round to focus on the need for change, the impacts of change, and justification for the resolution. For example, negative teams are not permitted to argue that because the National Rifle Association is a powerful lobbying force, a plan to require gun registration could not be enacted. Instead, the negative must focus on the plan to require gun registration. This provides much more clash in the round.

Fiat allows the round to focus on the hypothetical world of policy in the debate. Obviously, the outcome of a debate round has no real impact on the policy being debated. Because debates occur in an artificial environment, there is no reason to spend the debate arguing about politicians' potential votes. Rather, the debate focuses on a policy and the ramifications of policy change. By giving the affirmative team the right to enact the policy they propose, the round becomes more educational for all participants.

3. Introduction

Some debaters choose to jump right into their case by saying "We stand Resolved:" followed by the resolution. While this allows the debater to immediately begin presenting the meat of their case, such a process ignores the persuasive power of the first word in a debate round. The affirmative team has the opportunity to set up the round in a manner which benefits their arguments from the very first speech. Debaters should strongly consider this opportunity when deciding how they want to make a first impression.

A good debate case will not only present technically sound arguments, but it will also provide a persuasive argument that attracts the judge's attention and begins the process of persuading the audience members. To do this, a debater starts by telling a brief story of the problems caused by the failures of the current policy or by citing some statistic to illustrate the scope of the problems due to the current policy's failures. When writing a debate case, it is wise to consider how to briefly persuade an audience member who does not have significant debate experience or technical training. Think of the introduction as the opportunity to begin persuading the lay judge.

4. The Plan

The plan portion of the case is often overlooked, but is ultimately the most important aspect of nearly every case. The plan is the particular course of action the affirmative team is advocating to uphold the resolution and create advantages worthy of a judge's vote. A plan needs an actor, usually Congress and the President; a particular type of action or mandate, a new law such as changing the voting age from 18 to 21; a method of enforcement, fining anyone who permits an underage person to vote; and funding, money allocated to the state agencies to implement and enforce the new law. Some plans are very technical and explain many details of what the policy change will entail (some debaters call these details "planks").

For example, a case expanding space exploration investment could propose a 5-planked plan to increase the budget for a new launch vehicle by 10%, expand the budget for training new astronauts by 12%, expand the budget for NASA administration by 6%, build a new rocket each year, and hire two new scientists each month for the next three years. On the other hand, a less detailed plan is also acceptable. The case may simply state that the budgets will be expanded as needed to permit a launch every year and that Congress will make its own determination regarding the amount of funding necessary.

Obviously each point of the plan needs to be defended by the affirmative team, but minor technical arguments about the various aspects of the plan itself are unlikely to be persuasive to the judge. As the affirmative, be sure you are familiar with every detail of your plan so you can answer questions about them. However, do not spend speaking time in the round getting bogged down in the technical details of your policy proposal. Instead, save time to persuade your audience about the benefits of your case. As the negative team, it may be useful to point out logical inconsistencies within the details of the affirmative team's plan, but your stronger arguments will center on other areas, especially a plan's disadvantages.

C. Conclusion

After you write your case and begin working to perfect it, you may realize that it should be structured differently. Do Not Fear! This knowledge is part of strengthening your case. The structure you use to build your case may the difference between a good case and a great case. For example, if you constantly find yourself arguing that the status quo just needs to be improved in your plan-meets-needs case, you may be better off re-structuring your case as a comparative advantage case. In the same sense, if you argue that the value of life ought to be the central focus of any policy change and that the current policy does not protect human life, you may be better off arguing with a criteria analysis case. Altering the structure of your case allows you to focus on the arguments you actually want to make while presenting the same case ideas. No case structure is best. Every plan is unique and may (even should) be run in a unique manner.

Finally, make sure your judge and opponents know how your case is structured. If they do not understand it, you may spend the entire round explaining the structure to them instead of debating the issues. Clarity through organization is imperative when structuring your case. Do not be afraid to try different structures, but do not try them simply to use a unique structure. This strategy may backfire if the structure does not actually enhance your arguments. Find one that strengthens your case and run with it!

Observation 21: General Strategies

"The art of communication lies not in speaking or writing to be understood, but rather in speaking or writing so as not to be misunderstood!"
-Leo Richard Turner-

Policy debates offer numerous opportunities to make strategic decisions and square off against your debate opponents. While many of the strategies discussed earlier apply to all debate styles (see page 51), policy debate offers unique strategic opportunities. Remember, the most important priority is to persuade your judge. So, do not use a strategy if you do not believe it will persuade him to vote for you.

A. Affirmative Strategy

As the affirmative, you want to write a case that is complex, yet simple to comprehend. It should be complex enough to challenge the negative team by introducing some issues that they will drop or concede. At the same time your case must be simple enough that even a casual observer, with no prior debate experience or knowledge about the subject, can understand it. This delicate balance produces abundant clash on the issues in a comprehensible fashion for all parties.

1. Resolutional Analysis

The **resolutional analysis** is an important piece in the puzzle of creating an affirmative case resilient against attack. You can and should use the resolutional analysis to intentionally direct the round in your favor. This means that the resolutional analysis should be used to reinforce your case so that it is much more difficult to topple. The resolutional analysis may contain any number of important items to help present a cogent argument for the resolution. Some typical parts of a resolutional analysis may include: an introduction to the case, the resolution itself, history of the resolution, definitions of the resolution, burdens of the affirmative team, and a value criterion. (See case outlines in Appendix 1)

The introduction to the case often paints a picture of just how troublesome the status quo is. This helps to justify the resolution by showing the great injustice being done in the present system. Introductions sometimes quote a famous individual whose words apply to the round or an expert on the topic with a relevant statistic or fact. The resolution comes next. Using an introduction leads nicely into the resolution by saying, "That is why my partner and I stand, 'Resolved...'." Often teams help the judge see the importance of change by examining the history of the policy being debated. This portion of the resolutional analysis helps the judge identify the problems the affirmative will address and ties the resolution into a broader picture of the world. Next, the terms of the resolution may be defined within the resolutional analysis. While definitions are not required, they help to set the parameters of the debate round and are useful if there is a topicality challenge.

After defining the resolution, the affirmative team may present burdens. Burdens are duties the affirmative has agreed to fulfill in the round. The affirmative team argues that these burdens ought to be the standard by which the round is weighed. If the affirmative team sets up a burden for itself and cannot meet it, even if the case won the stock issues and the advantages outweigh the disadvantages, the affirmative is asking the judge to cast a negative ballot. By the same token, if the negative team accepts or fails to address the burdens, the burdens are accepted and the team which better fulfills the burdens at the end of the round wins even if the burden is not the only point of discussion in the round. For example, suppose both team accept the affirmative's burden, "In this round, the winner should be the side of the resolution which spends less money on electricity." Just as the criteria analysis case (see page 116) focuses the round on the criterion, the burden centers the round on the burden. The teams are asking the judge to ignore advantages and disadvantages that do not deal with the amount of money spent on electricity.

Burdens take many forms. Here are a few examples: "In this round, the affirmative must prove that the policy's benefits outweigh the benefits of the status quo." "In this round, the affirmative must show that the advantages of changing the status quo outweigh the disadvantages of changing." "In this round, the policy that best protects the country ought to receive your vote." Often the affirmative uses a cost-benefit analysis as a weighing mechanism for the round. If the net-benefits of the proposed change outweigh the problems of change, an affirmative ballot is warranted. There are no set limits to the particular burdens the affirmative can propose to help the judge weigh which team wins the round. However, debaters should be careful to ensure any burdens they present will make it more likely the judge will cast a ballot for the affirmative rather than confusing the round. Using burdens can tilt the round in your team's favor.

Criteria are a class of burden often presented in the resolutional analysis. Criteria are the measuring stick against which the round should be evaluated. For example, an affirmative team may propose that the judge vote for the case which best promotes economic growth. If this criterion is used, advantages and disadvantages will only matter to the extent they affect economic growth. An advantage that America will be successful in a major military endeavor is an interesting consequence from enacting the affirmative team's plan but does not actually matter if economic growth is the sole criterion against which the round is judged. Another option is to base the criterion on some particular value, like justice or freedom. The value criterion shows the underlying value the affirmative wishes to build upon in developing a defense of the resolution. By utilizing a value criterion, the affirmative can take the debate into philosophical realms and show the benefits of the value in relationship to the present system. The affirmative case uses a criterion to focus the round on issues that will attract the judge's attention and make it harder for the negative team to win the round.

2. Spikes

Spikes attempt to cut off an argument against the case before it is introduced in the round by presenting the counter-argument in the 1AC. If your case is constantly attacked on a particular ground, a spike can present evidence to show that a negative claim is unfounded before the negative team has a chance to present their argument. Not only will this give you an edge if a negative team attempts to address this issue, but it may also force the negative team to ignore it.

The basic structure of a spike would be an argument in modified three-point refutation format which directly acknowledges and refutes the opposing argument. For example, if your opponent is likely to argue that your plan will encourage employers to fire employees, a spike would identify and neutralize this argument: "Some might allege raising the minimum wage will encourage employers to lay off their employees. However, Professor Smith, [an expert economist] recently published a multi-year study which demonstrates that employers do not lay off employees as a result of an increase in the minimum wage. Therefore, there is no basis for the assertion employees will be laid off under our plan." The spike makes any argument about increasing unemployment from your minimum wage hike less potent and makes your judge more willing to ignore that argument if the negative makes it.

Use spikes sparingly. One or two in a round is sufficient. Proper use of a spike can give you an edge in defending your case as well as forces the negative team to decide whether to continue a particular line of attack. A strategic spike may discourage your opponent from attacking an issue you find to be particularly troublesome.

B. Negative

The negative team may employ numerous strategies in a debate round. These include: negative philosophy, presenting criteria, dividing the negative block, and presenting critiques. Presenting disadvantages (page 133), arguing topicality (page 142), and using a counterplan (page 149) are additional strategies for the negative to employ. They receive more detailed discussion in their own chapters. Using one or more strategies can provide the judge multiple reasons to reject the resolution and the affirmative's case.

1. Negative Philosophy

A negative philosophy is an overarching idea pressed throughout the round. For example, "Our negative philosophy is that any major change to the current policy will upset the delicate balance within the status quo and result in civil unrest."; "We believe that the current system is working fine and only needs minor changes."; "It is our negative philosophy that an elimination of _____ would cause more harm than good." A good negative philosophy gives the judge a central unifying theme for the negative team that constantly repeats throughout the round. Much like an affirmative's criterion, a negative philosophy may be based on something that everyone would agree with (the Constitution should be respected) so that the affirmative cannot argue against your philosophy's premise, but rather against the link between the premise (uphold the Constitution) and their case (any change upsets federalism!). Philosophies may also be based on evidence or theories catered to particular cases. Negative philosophies allow a negative team to focus their arguments on a central theme which will crystallize the argument for the judge. Proper use of a negative philosophy is very effective when developed throughout the round.

In the first negative speech, a negative philosophy is presented. This shows the problem inherent in changing the status quo. This philosophy is then woven throughout each negative speech. By presenting this philosophy in different ways throughout the round, the negative team is better able to argue for the benefits of the status quo while also showing how harmful the affirmative case would be.

2. Criteria

Just as criteria may be part of a good affirmative strategy, the negative team also may employ a criterion to prevent the affirmative team from focusing the debate on the stronger affirmative points in the round. This may be a good way to defeat an affirmative case. As discussed earlier, a criterion is a weighing mechanism for the judge to use in casting her vote. A criterion focuses the arguments in the round on stronger points for your team. If the affirmative proposes criteria, the negative team needs to either accept the proposed criteria and focus its arguments on explaining how the status quo best upholds the proposed criteria or explain why the particular criteria are not a good way to evaluate the round.

There are multiple ways to reject the affirmative's criteria. Negative teams can explain that the criteria are not related to the resolution or that other criteria are more important. For example, if the resolution calls for a change in agriculture policy and the affirmative's criterion is protecting jobs, the negative team might allege that agriculture policy is not about jobs, but about farming and producing food and thus the judge should not make his decision solely on the basis of whether more jobs are created. This does not mean jobs should play no role in the judge's decision, but the judge should also consider advantages and disadvantages unrelated to jobs when making his decision. The negative team could argue that an alternative criterion, the safety of the food supply, is the lens through which policy proposals ought to be evaluated and thus propose a counter-criterion of food supply safety.

If the affirmative does not propose criteria, the negative may still propose one for the round. You may present criteria, or standards for any good policy. Like a negative philosophy, these criteria can be something everyone could agree with such as justice, peace, life, etc., or they may be separate criteria supported by evidence such as that which experts in the field agree upon. You then show:

- The affirmative does not meet the standards of the criteria,
- The status quo does meet the criteria,
- Your counter-plan meets the criteria, or
- A combination of the first and second, or the first and third.

If the affirmative does not address your new criteria, they are considered to have accepted it and therefore their own case must fulfill the criteria. However, in order to win, you must prove that they cannot fulfill it. A negative criterion is a great way to focus the debate on the issues you, as the negative, feel are strongest for your team. Criteria force the affirmative to meet a higher standard while still upholding their plan. As the negative, this is very beneficial.

3. Negative Block

As we discussed in the chapter regarding policy debate rounds (see page 106), the negative team has a thirteen minute "block" of time to argue against the affirmative with only a three minute cross-examination period in between. Prior to the block, the affirmative team is often winning the round. However, the negative block is generally the best time for the negative team to take control of the round and position itself for victory. If this time is used effectively, the negative can force the affirmative to drop arguments giving the negative team an advantage. By dividing the labor of the negative case, sometimes called "splitting the block," a negative team is able to turn the thirteen minute block into one speech for the short 1AR to address.

The effective allocation of arguments by the negative includes different responsibilities for each speaker in each speech. The 1NC covers the negative philosophy, topicality (if it is an issue), criteria/goals, harms, and advantages. The 1NC may cover a simple plan argument or disadvantages as well. The 2NC then covers the remaining portions of the affirmative case. This includes briefly expanding on the negative philosophy and topicality arguments from the 1NC followed by extensive argumentation regarding the plan and additional disadvantages. Following the cross-examination, the 1NR responds to the affirmative team's arguments from the 2AC, backing up the philosophy, goal, harm, and advantage arguments made in the 1NC. Basically, the first negative speaker is only strengthening her original arguments. This leaves the 1AR to cover all thirteen minutes of arguments in only five minutes. Rather than having two speeches which essentially repeat themselves, dividing the labor of the negative team during the block allows the negative team to fully test the affirmative team's arguments to give the negative team a better chance to win the round.

4. Critiques

Critiques are effective methods of defeating your opponent's arguments. A critique, sometimes spelled "kritik" is a way to discredit certain sources of evidence and certain behaviors in a round. It may be used by both the affirmative and negative teams against a case, a source, or the resolution itself. A source critique should point out misinformation, major bias, or lack of a source's qualifications. By giving a reason to reject a source, you also give reason to reject an argument supported by that source. If a critique is successful, it will cause a judge to disregard certain arguments. However, do not simply attack sources. You must replace the argument with another one. Biased evidence is still better than no evidence at all. Critiques should be used only when you have both good evidence against the source and good evidence to fill the void created by rejecting that source.

Behavior critiques call into question the actions of a debate team. If a team is using inappropriate language, the opposing team may argue that this is justification for voting against that team. The premise behind a behavior critique is that debate rounds do not actually change policy in the real world. A vote for the affirmative team does not actually enact the resolution or proposed policy. The critique's creators argue that the judge's only influence is to reward or punish the behavior of the debaters. If debaters exhibit behavior which is antithetical to professional and educational standards, a judge can be compelled to vote against them. For example, if a debater is using a strategy of speed debate in a debate league which is supposed to foster communication, the opponent could critique the other speaker and claim that the judge should vote against the fast speaker to encourage future debaters to act in a manner which fosters communication in the debate round. An alternative example is critiquing biased language. If an opponent keeps using derogatory language to refer to a particular ethnicity or social class, asking the judge to reprimand that behavior by voting against such a debater can help influence future behavior. Critiques, when used fairly and effectively, can go a long way in winning a round.

Critique theory has developed a great deal since it was introduced in 1991. While critiques are mainly used by more advanced debaters, every debater should understand the basic premise and recognize opportunities to employ a critique. If you wish to run a critique in a round, spend some time reading about the theoretical foundation on which the critique was built and identify the most common critique platforms being used in your respective debate league.[23]

---

[23] A good foundational article is William Bennet's 1996 article "Introduction to the Kritik" published in the *Rostrum*. It is available at http://debate.uvm.edu/NFL/rostrumlib/cxkbennett0496.pdf.

Observation 22: Cross-Examination

"If you go in for argument, take care of your temper.
Your logic, if you have any, will take care of itself."
-Joseph Farrell-

Cross-examination is a very important part of the debate round. It offers the judge an unfiltered perspective of both teams' arguments under scrutiny. It also gives the judge a glimpse of how strongly both sides believe the arguments they are making. Both the examiner and the examinee must recognize the importance of cross-examination while keeping in mind that information in cross-examination is only important if the debaters connect the statements made in cross-examination to a ballot for or against the resolution in a future speech. Cross-examination gives judges the opportunity to evaluate your credibility based on how you behave during cross-examination. Be assertive, relaxed, and calm during cross-examination. Stand strong and speak in a tone which displays confidence when you are being cross-examined or cross-examining. Do not stand behind your opponent if you are cross-examining and do not concede the podium when you are being cross-examined.

A. Cross-Examining Your Opponent

As the cross-examiner, you should begin by clarifying any questions you have about your opponent's arguments that you are planning to address. Your first priority is to make sure you know what positions your opponent is advocating so that your other questions and future arguments will be relevant. For example, asking "Is it your contention that a 10% excise tax on gasoline will reduce demand for gasoline?" makes certain your opponent is really linking the excise tax and demand. Next, you should attempt to point out weaknesses in your opponent's positions. Asking questions such as: "Does your quotation from the Brookings Institution actually say demand for gasoline will fall or that people will be driven to buy more fuel efficient vehicles?" probes whether the evidence cited actually substantiates a particular argument. Questions which point out that your opponent lacks support for an argument can undermine the argument.

Finally, cross-examination provides a perfect avenue to strengthen your own arguments while you undermine your opponent's. You can trap your opponent with his own words or otherwise put him on defense by asking such questions as "Won't raising the price of gasoline make heating homes for the poor and elderly more expensive?" When your opponent is defensive, the positions he articulates appear less credible. Alternatively, you can use cross-examination to defend your positions by undermining arguments raised against your team's stances. For example, if you have argued that increasing the gasoline tax harms the poor and your opponent replied that the poor are less likely to own cars and thus only minimally harmed, you could ask a question such as "If the gasoline tax increased the price to transport food, clothing, and other necessities – products the poor obviously need – won't the higher prices for those necessities harm the poor?" Keep in mind that you are to remain in control of the cross-examination at all times. If you ask a question and receive a sufficient answer, say "thank you" and move on to your next question. Never allow your opponent to make speeches instead of answering your questions.

B. Being Cross-Examined

Following a constructive speech, it is common to say "I am now open for cross-examination." When you open the door to cross-examination be ready for the questions and prepare to use each question as a springboard to further explain to the judge why she should vote for your side in the round. Your first goal when answering a cross-examination question is to ensure your opponent and judge both fully understand your positions. If your opponent asks a question which shows he does not understand a key fact in your argument, begin your answer by clarifying that particular point. Make yourself as clear as possible so everyone knows what position you are taking. Beyond clarifying, your answers should also seek to advance your position. Every question is an attempt to undermine your arguments, but with each answer you have the chance not only to prevent your arguments from being undermined, but also to actually make your argument stronger. Every second of cross-examination you talk about the validity of your points is effectively free speech time to advance your position.

On the other hand, be careful not to make your answer long-winded for the sake of talking. When you are asked a question, answer in a concise manner, even giving a "yes" or "no" if possible. You may then expand your answer if the cross-examiner allows you to do so. Avoid rambling answers, but focus on your basic argument by returning to its main premise. If your opponent lets you give a half minute endorsement of your argument, do it, but make it short and sweet. Finally, try to find ways to connect your answers to other strong points in your case. If your opponent tries to undermine your harm, be sure to explain that the harm will be reduced with your plan which will create significant advantages. By tying every question back to your strongest arguments, you are showing the judge an easy path to casting a ballot in your favor.

Be calm when you are being cross-examined. Be careful not to get excited. Always avoid sounding rude. Do not be afraid of being cross-examined. Listen carefully to the questions in order to avoid traps. Do not be afraid to answer questions, even if the questions harm your case. If you attempt to avoid answering the questions, you will do yourself more harm than good because the judge will note your avoidance of the issue and give it additional weight in the round. Also, do not allow the opposing team to use circular reasoning or to make a speech in their cross-examination. If they begin to make a speech, interrupt and politely request a question. Never answer loaded or unfair questions that require you to make statements which negatively affect you no matter how you answer (see Figure 27). Finally, if you are unsure about the answer to a question, do not be afraid to say so. Asking a clarifying question before you answer or admitting that you are uncertain of the answer is perfectly acceptable and will help you avoid saying something you will regret. It is better not to give an answer than to give an incorrect one.

> "Have you stopped beating your dog?" Answering yes admits you have beaten your dog in the past; answering no concedes you still beat your dog. Either answer forces you to make an untrue (or at least unflattering) statement. Loaded questions should not be asked or answered.

Figure 27: A Loaded Question

C. Three Tips for Cross-Examination

Whether you are cross-examining or being cross-examined, remember three things. (1) Look at the judge. She is the person you are trying to convince. Do not look at your opponent. Keep the judge's attention to assist in your persuasion. (2) Remain poised. Be polite and do not be overly aggressive. If you are overbearing or rude, the judge will not appreciate it and may vote against your team. (3) After an answer is given, tie it back to your arguments in the speeches which follow along with clear impacts. Getting your opponent to negate his own case in cross-examination is only valuable when you address it in your next speech! Cross-examination is an enjoyable part of the round. Use it to your advantage.

Observation 23: Disadvantages

"To change and to change for the better are two different things"
-German Proverb-

Disadvantages are arguments against an affirmative case which show how the plan, if enacted, would result in negative consequences. As the affirmative team claims a vote for its plan will result in positive outcomes for society, the negative team's disadvantages assert that a vote for the affirmative plan will harm society. These negative consequences of the affirmative's plan are justifications to maintain the status quo. By presenting disadvantages, the negative team provides a tangible cost to change which the judge can weigh against the hypothetical benefits of the advantages.

Disadvantages are valuable arguments that allow the negative team to go on offense. Rather than defending the status quo, arguing about the inability of a plan to solve a problem, or pointing out the insignificance of a problem, disadvantages allow the negative team to take ownership of arguments in the round. At the end of a round without disadvantages, a judge is left with very few reasons to vote *for* the negative team. On the affirmative team's side, even small advantages are still benefits and arguments for change; on the negative team's side, there are only arguments *against* change. However, with disadvantages, the negative side is equipped with something to counter-balance the affirmative advantages. Because people prefer to vote *for* rather than *against* something, giving the judge a status quo which lacks atrocious disadvantages offers him something to vote for and often tips the scale in the negative team's favor.

A. Types of Disadvantages

There are numerous styles of disadvantages. Some are simply workability problems, others are miniature disadvantages, and still others are complete disadvantages. Workability problems identify a difficulty in actually implementing the plan that prevents the advantages from occurring. Both mini disadvantages and complete disadvantages show a negative consequence of the affirmative plan, but mini disadvantages do not utilize the structure of disadvantages that many judges have come to expect in formal debate rounds. Each disadvantage style has its own uses and benefits which must be considered when developing negative arguments.

1. Workability Problems

Workability problems are basic plan arguments which challenge the affirmative case's ability to produce the stated advantages. Unlike most disadvantages which identify problems the affirmative team is overlooking that will be caused by the affirmative team's plan, the workability problem simply identifies unforeseen problems in carrying out the affirmative team's plan. For example, if the case does not allocate any funding to increase the size of the military, then the advantages the affirmative team claims from having a larger military could not occur. Other workability arguments point to the plan's proposed agency of implementation. If an inappropriate agency (or no agency at all) is tasked with implementing a plan, the plan may not work. For example, if the Environmental Protection Agency is placed in charge of a new reading program in schools, a negative team could effectively argue that EPA's lack of expertise in literacy means the affirmative team will not be able to achieve the advantage of greater literacy.

Other workability problems include: enforcement (the wrong agency is tasked with enforcing the proposal or there is no punishment for those who violate the proposal); execution (the agency tasked with implementing the proposal does not have the skills to bring about the new policy); or jurisdiction (the agency tasked to enforce the plan does not have power over the people the plan seeks to influence. For example, if the plan calls for the United Nations to stop a human rights violation in a nation that is not a member of the United Nations, the affirmative team will be unable to achieve the advantage because the United Nations has no jurisdiction to enforce its policies in non-member nations). If any plan cannot produce advantages, the negative team may label the shortfall a workability problem. If the workability problem prevents any advantage, the negative team could win by showing that there is little or no benefit to a proposed plan.

2. Mini Disadvantages

Mini disadvantages show a problem caused by passing the affirmative plan. For example, after a law to open the borders is passed, terrorism will increase because there are no longer border checks for criminals. Mini disadvantages typically have two parts: links and impacts. The link in the border example would be that the affirmative team is opening the border without safety checks and the impact is greater terrorism. While this argument may be compelling, its lack of the full disadvantage structure may leave the mini disadvantage more vulnerable to attack. Also, many more experienced judges and debaters expect full disadvantages and may not consider these mini disadvantages to be compelling reasons to vote negative. These disadvantages may be better than full disadvantages if the judge is not familiar with the structure of full disadvantages or if the judge is willing to accept this shortened form. The benefit of mini disadvantages is that more can be presented because they take less time to develop. However, limit yourself to only as many disadvantages as the judge can digest and you can be sure to weigh against the affirmative's advantages in your final speeches.

3. Fully Structured Disadvantages

Full disadvantages show the problems associated with the affirmative team's plan. These latent dysfunctions give the judge a strong reason to cast a ballot against the affirmative team. For example, the negative team can argue that a disadvantage of an affirmative team plan to eliminate agricultural subsidies is that the plan would increase food prices, put farmers out of business, and jeopardize the food supply. Full disadvantages have four parts: *link, brink, uniqueness,* and *impact.* There may be multiple links and impacts in a disadvantage. Links simply connect the plan and the problem. In the agriculture example, the link simply noted that the affirmative eliminated subsidies to farmers. A brink shows how the current system is already near the edge of the problem. By enacting the affirmative case, we push the status quo into the disadvantage which it might otherwise have avoided. In the agriculture example, the brink explained that the current agricultural economy was extremely weak as many farmers live from subsidy check to subsidy check as their only means of income.

Uniqueness proves that a disadvantage will occur only under the affirmative's case. Unless the affirmative case is enacted, this disadvantage will not be able to occur. If a disadvantage could result from any government change or is equally likely to occur in the status quo, the disadvantage is not justification to reject the change proposed by the affirmative. But, if the affirmative plan will uniquely affect the status quo, this unique harm is a reason to reject the case. Uniqueness of the agriculture disadvantage was that the government was not planning to alter the current subsidies program. (Uniqueness is similar to the stock issue of inherency, discussed on page 111.)

Impacts expose the negative consequences of the affirmative plan. Impacts show the extent to which the disadvantage will affect society and will be harmful. The subsidy elimination disadvantage had numerous impacts. The many impacts allowed selection of the strongest few impacts for the specific round (the impacts the team believed the judge would find most persuasive). Some impacts included reduction of food supplies, increased prices for food, and decline of land values. Some impacts had sub-impacts which could also be run. For example, the impact "Farms go out of business," had further impacts that farmers would go on unemployment which would cost the government the same amount of money as the subsidies but without the production of food! Impacts give the magnitude of the disadvantage to weigh against the advantages of the affirmative case.

B. Using Disadvantages

No negative team should advocate for the status quo without identifying disadvantages affirming the resolution would create. Even a generic disadvantage identifying a benefit the current system provides which the resolution requires to be reduced or eliminated will provide a reason to vote for the status quo. Rather than simply lining up reasons to vote against the affirmative case and the resolution, the disadvantage offers the negative team a strong argument against change. In fact, even with the power of "presumption" — that unless the affirmative team can overcome their burden of proof and show that change is needed, we assume the status quo is sufficient and a negative ballot is appropriate — a disadvantage will protect against a very minor harm being resolved and create only a slight advantage for change. While presumption is certainly the friend of the negative, disadvantages help in solidifying this presumption in favor of the status quo.

Limit the number of disadvantages you present – you want the judge to believe an affirmative ballot will actually result in specific problems, not a collection of wild hypothetical worries. Only run the number of disadvantages you can actually develop, explain, and impact in the remaining speeches.

Figure 28: Carefully Choose Disadvantages

1. When to Present Disadvantages

Disadvantages should be presented in constructive speeches because those speeches build or construct the negative case against change and for the status quo. There is significant debate among debate theorists about how much information must be presented in the 1NC and how many negative attacks may be preserved until the 2NC without conceding an issue (division of labor in the negative block is discussed in greater detail on page 128). Generally, however, disadvantages may be introduced in the 2NC even though they limit the time for discussion in the debate round. If, however, you are planning to run a counterplan, and the justification for or unique advantage of your counterplan is to avoid a disadvantage created by the affirmative case, you should present those disadvantages in the 1NC (see page 149 for further discussion of counterplans).

2. Case Specific v. Generic Disadvantages

Some disadvantages will only link to an affirmative case if particular steps are taken; other disadvantages are inherent in any change to the status quo. For example, consider a resolution that calls for a change in trade policy with South America. A case specific disadvantage would identify that increasing trade with Venezuela is likely to strengthen President Hugo Chavez's hand and scare away foreign investors from Venezuela who fear Chavez's willingness to confiscate private companies' property. Obviously, if the affirmative case only increases trade or alters any other policy with Brazil, the specific disadvantages of a change in policy with Venezuela is not linked to the affirmative case. Therefore, there is no actual disadvantage. On the other hand, a generic disadvantage which argues that any increase in trade with South America will result in lost jobs in the United States' textile industry because South America produces less expensive textiles could apply to any plan under the resolution that increases trade with South America. An alternative disadvantage saying that improving trade with South America will harm relationships with Asian countries will also apply to any plan under the resolution. Whether the affirmative case proposes subsidies to encourage imports from South America or reduces protectionist trade barriers with South America, these disadvantages will link to the affirmative plan.

Case specific disadvantages are generally stronger arguments against a particular change. Audience members will be more likely to accept that negative consequences are likely if your evidence actually links to the particular plan the affirmative presents. Further, your argument sounds much more reasonable. If you argue that affirming the resolution will always result in a negative consequence, your judge may believe you are stretching the evidence beyond its intended scope or that you do not have enough strong arguments against the particular proposal up for debate. If, on the other hand, your argument is specific to the change suggested in the affirmative case, presenting the disadvantage looks less opportunistic and much more like a reasonable concern that the change will create unintended consequences.

Judges tend to be more willing to forgive affirmative teams who cannot answer every generic disadvantage than those who cannot answer every specific disadvantage. This is one more reason generic disadvantages may be weaker than case specific disadvantages. Your audience is expecting a debate on the pros and cons not only of the resolution itself, but also of the particular aspects of the affirmative plan presented to support the resolution. Generic disadvantages are much stronger against less predictable affirmative cases or as one disadvantage presented alongside more specific disadvantages.

3. Impact

As with all arguments, disadvantages are only as strong as their impacts. To affect the debate round and the ultimate ballot, the impacts of the disadvantages need to outweigh the impacts of the affirmative team's advantages. Debaters should spend time weighing the impacts of the advantages and disadvantages both after presenting disadvantages and when refuting disadvantages. If, for example, the affirmative's advantage is that two million jobs will be created and the negative's disadvantage is that ten jobs will be lost, the advantage outweighs the disadvantage and there remain significant reasons to cast an affirmative ballot. Debaters should not expect the judge to weigh the impacts. Debaters should instead present the comparison and identify which direction the balance should fall.

Debaters often neglect presenting the impact of disadvantages in a persuasive manner. The impacts should relate to something the judge cares about. For example, a case which offers one hundred needy students the opportunity to attend college might sound wonderful until the negative team presents a disadvantage showing that this college education will saddle those students with such high debt they can never afford to purchase a home. The disadvantage has two separate impacts, both of which should be identified and weighted against the advantage: high debt load and inability to become homeowners. An excellent disadvantage identifies both impacts (the high debt and inability to purchase a home) and explains how they outweigh the affirmative's case's benefits of only one hundred new college students both with respect to those students and society as a whole.

No matter what disadvantages are presented, they should be compared to the affirmative's advantages. While the earlier example of ten v. two million jobs makes for easy comparison, disadvantages and advantages are often more difficult to compare. For example, if the affirmative advantage creates two million new jobs, but the disadvantage identifies a serious illness which will befall two hundred thousand people, comparing job opportunities and health can be difficult to quantify and compare. Debaters should practice comparing impacts to one another even when they are dissimilar. Both sides will obviously contend their impact is greater. Persuasive arguments can certainly be made that it is worth losing jobs to maintain health or that jobs provide sick individuals access to health care. So it is ultimately up to the debaters to practice articulating a message which can persuade the judge that the impact of a disadvantage or advantage is greater and should sway the vote.

When running disadvantages, it is vital to remind the judge for the remainder of the round that the benefits of enacting the affirmative plan would be insufficient to overcome the serious impacts of the many disadvantages. Presented properly throughout the round, a negative disadvantage can not only neutralize the affirmative's advantages, but can also identify the strength of the status quo and persuade the judge that change is not only unnecessary, but would be harmful.

C. Affirmative Responses to Disadvantages

When an opponent presents a disadvantage, there are generally three options for the affirmative team. First, the team could attempt to de-link it from the disadvantage or show that the disadvantage will not occur under your plan. Second, the team could weigh the impacts of the disadvantage and show they are less important than the advantages of the affirmative case. Finally, the team could "turn" the disadvantage to show it is actually an advantage of the affirmative case. Each strategy has pros and cons in attacking a disadvantage. You should plan in advance which path to take long before the round begins because your first opportunity to respond is often in the 1AR. If you wait until then, you will not have enough time to waver between the different strategies.

De-linking a disadvantage is the most common response when the negative team presents a disadvantage. The affirmative team can dismiss an entire disadvantage simply by showing that the chain of events leading to the adverse impact will not occur. For example, suppose the disadvantage claims that because the affirmative case requires individuals to pay a ten dollar fee to enroll in a cell phone plan, the poor will not have access to cell phones and will be left in danger during an emergency. If the affirmative case provides a fee waiver voucher to individuals are already eligible for welfare benefits, the affirmative team simply replies that this disadvantage does not link to the affirmative case because the voucher will prevent the very disadvantage the negative team presented. De-linking is the easiest response and clearly identifies why the judge should not consider a particular disadvantage in her final analysis when casting the ballot.

Another strategy for addressing disadvantages is to simply compare and contrast the pros and cons of the advantages and disadvantages. Doing so admits there is no perfect affirmative case, but that the benefits from the affirmative case are sufficient to justify voting for the resolution even if some harms might befall society. If the affirmative case will result in numerous significant advantages and result in only minimal disadvantages, the affirmative should highlight this comparison and conclude there is still significant justification for an affirmative ballot even in the face of the disadvantages. Be very clear. Quantify exactly how much better the affirmative plan will be than the status quo and the negative disadvantages. Identify how many people will benefit; how much growth or contraction there will be in the economy; how many lives will be saved; and how much less your proposal will cost than the status quo. Then compare these benefits to the costs your opponent presents in the form of disadvantages.[24] Each comparison provides an avenue for the judge to justify casting a ballot in your favor.

Finally, some disadvantages are ripe for being turned into advantages for the affirmative team. These turns or turnarounds identify a supposed disadvantage and make it an advantage. Consider the example of weighing advantages and disadvantages in footnote 24. Rather than simply accepting that losing 100,000 textile manufacturing jobs is a disadvantage, the turnaround points out that these 100,000 individuals may actually be better off in the stronger economy so that losing their current jobs is actually an advantage for them and for the country as a whole. How do you do this? Incorporating the same arguments as the footnote, the affirmative team can present evidence that most of the 100,000 people who will lose their textile manufacturing jobs have valuable technical skills to make specialized protective clothing that are being under-utilized in the textile plant. By closing the textile plant, these technical skills in highly-specialized protective clothing for the military will be allowed to thrive. The higher-skilled work is better paid. Once the affirmative case is enacted, these individuals will be able to use their skills in the higher paying jobs. Thus, even though they will lose their jobs in the short-run, in the long-run, these same individuals will actually have better jobs. Because the negative team has already proposed and supported the conclusion the disadvantage will occur, they can only attack the turnaround by trying to show that the turnaround itself cannot happen. The negative team's only argument is that the high-tech skills needed to manufacture military clothing will not be utilized, not that the original textile plants will close. The negative team cannot try to de-link the affirmative case from this now-turned disadvantage, only the case from the new impact.

The turnaround is the strongest response to a disadvantage. De-linking is an excellent strategy, but it can be challenging when the negative team runs a specific disadvantage against your particular case. While weighing the impacts is a vital skill each debater needs to build, there are times the judge will decide your weighing method is not the same as hers. The turnaround will be difficult for the negative team to overcome and will give you an edge in the final analysis of the round.

By the end of the round, the affirmative team must firmly establish their advantages as reasons to cast an affirmative ballot. A strong negative will present disadvantages and show how these disadvantages significantly outweigh any advantages gained by the affirmative case. If the negative team shows that the advantages of the affirmative team's case are insignificant or even non-existent, while simultaneously articulating the negative consequences of change, the judge will be compelled to cast a negative ballot. The affirmative team, on the other hand, must weigh the benefits of their plan against the disadvantages the negative presents. They must also explain to the judge that either the disadvantages will not occur or that the advantages are worth taking the risk that the disadvantages may also occur. This cost-benefit-analysis should be employed by both teams to weigh the impacts of the advantages and disadvantages to explain to the judge the reasons for and against affirming the resolution. A good disadvantage gives the judge one more compelling reason to reject the affirmative case and instead preserve and protect the status quo.

---

[24] For example: The negative team asserts our plan will result in 100,000 lost jobs in textile manufacturing in the United States. Even assuming these 100,000 jobs are lost, our case produces two key advantages which outweigh that disadvantage: First, our plan will create 45,000 high-paying technology-sector jobs in the United States, all of which earn more than twice the income of the 100,000 who lost their jobs. Second, our plan will increase GDP by nearly $1 trillion per year for the next ten years which will benefit every American as their standard of living will rise. Therefore, the benefits of our plan outweigh the loss of the jobs in the context of the entire United States economy.

Observation 24: Topicality

"Give no decision till both sides thou'st heard."
-Phocylides-

Topicality is often misunderstood by debaters. Although most understand what it is — a stock issue that requires the affirmative team to stay on topic — many do not understand how topicality should be used in the debate round. Topicality is more than just another voting issue in the debate round, it is foundational. Topicality is the first obstacle the affirmative team must overcome to even have a chance to win the round. Understanding the theory of topicality, its proper use, and its application will make you a better, more credible debater.

A. Topicality in Theory

Topicality establishes the boundaries of a debate round. Much as a basketball court or soccer field establishes a field of play, topicality says what can and cannot be discussed in a debate round. And just as stepping outside the basketball court results in a loss of possession of the basketball, proposing a case outside the resolution results in a loss of the debate round. Despite the harsh reality that crossing the line will end in defeat, the boundaries also provide significant predictability and make the game — whether it be a game of soccer or debate — much more fun.

Topicality is an *a priori* issue or a primary issue in a debate round. Before anything else can be considered and debated, the case must be deemed within the bounds of the resolution. Topicality is the most important consideration for the judge at the beginning of the round because it affects the real debate and not only the hypothetical world of policies on which the debate will focus. In this sense, topicality is a pre-fiat issue: the judge votes on topicality before even asking whether the case should be adopted.[25] A non-topical affirmative case should be rejected by the judge and the judge should cast a negative ballot. (The round does not stop based on a topicality decision, but the judge votes on topicality regardless of the rest of the round.) The most important reason topicality exists is to provide clash in the round. If the negative has no idea what the affirmative will talk about, the likelihood of clash in the debate round is small.

Requiring the affirmative team to follow a set resolution allows both teams to research the topic before the round to develop greater knowledge and provide more substance in the arguments made during the round (see page 39 for research tips). The ability to learn about a topic before the round provides educational value for all participants in the debate round. Thus, topicality is an important issue to consider during the debate round as well as while constructing a case.

B. Two Types of Topicality

Topicality can be separated into two types: resolutional and definitional. Resolutional topicality means that the affirmative case is within the bounds of the resolution. Resolutional topicality does not take into consideration the definitions either team provides in the round. Instead, resolutional topicality refers to the resolution as it is written. If the resolution deals

---

[25] Post-fiat issues include the harms, plan, advantages, disadvantages, and workability. Post-fiat debates are about the pros and cons of a particular policy and most debate rounds will focus on such post-fiat issues. Topicality, on the other hand, does not ask whether a particular policy should be enacted, it asks whether the debate is focused on the topic selected before the round began.

with gun control and the case only changes textiles trade policies of the United States toward Taiwan, the resolution is not being upheld by the affirmative.

Definitional topicality refers to the definitions the affirmative team present to narrow the resolution. The affirmative team's case must not only fit within the boundaries of the resolution, but it must also fit squarely within the boundaries of the resolution as defined by the affirmative team. For example, if the resolution calls for changing immigration policy and the affirmative team defined immigration as moving to a different continent, a case dealing with people who move from Canada to the United States would be non-topical because it was not dealing with immigration as it was defined by the affirmative team. Even though immigration is generally considered moving between countries, if the affirmative team narrows the definition to only people who change continents, the affirmative case would be outside the bounds of the resolution as they defined it.

Definitional topicality frequently hinges on the definition being used. Poor definitions are often an invitation for the negative to find a reason to reject them and present new definitions which move your case outside the resolution. There are many methods of defining terms in a debate round. While there is no best way to define terms, different methods are valuable in different rounds and for different resolutions. Learning the different ways to define terms is important to building a strong case on either side of the resolution. Some methods of defining terms include dictionary definitions, examples, common usages, authority, operational definitions, definition by negation, and a combination of methods.

1. Types of Definitions

The affirmative team has the privilege of defining terms at the beginning of the round. When a topic is announced, the authors of the resolution generally have a particular idea in mind, but they do not provide a list of definitions debaters must use. Instead, debaters may turn to a variety of sources in clarifying the meaning of the resolution.

Dictionary. Dictionary definitions are often preferred by debaters because they are generally accepted as an authority on the meaning of words. Using a credible definition from a dictionary is preferred to using your own definition based on personal experience. While the dictionary provides wonderful definitions, there are times when the dictionary is inadequate for a debate case. This is especially true when the resolution uses a phrase and the dictionary only defines the words individually or when the resolution uses a technical term. Arguing that your definition is best based on its citation in a dictionary can be a useful argument.

Example. Definition by example points out a real life illustration which makes the definition more clear. For instance, the definition of "School Vouchers" can be seen in the example of the state of Ohio's law which allowed students to go to private schools using government funds. This law was upheld by the Supreme Court. This example shows all sides in the debate exactly what is meant by the term school vouchers.

Common Usage. The meaning of words can often be ascertained by simply looking to their usage in modern language. For example, "America" is a word which typically refers to "The United States of America." While "America" actually applies to the entire Western Hemisphere, it is common to say "America" and mean the USA. Because of its common usage, "America" means the United States of America. Employing the common usage for a definition is good because the judge and others in the round think of the term that way.

Authority. The experts in the particular field being debated are often the best sources of defining the terms of the debate. For example, in a debate over income taxes, an economist who is the leading authority on tax law at Harvard will be well equipped to define income taxes. While other definitions might suffice, her expertise will give additional validity to the definition. If the resolution uses a specific technical term such as "military intervention" it may be useful to find a definition from an expert on military history or policy to provide clear boundaries of the meaning of such a term.

Operational. Operational definitions define terms by their usage in the debate round. For example, debaters often define what the resolution means by an application they have incorporated in the plan within their case. If the plan is to open trade with Zimbabwe, the definition of trade policy with Africa is operationally defined as trade with the African nation of Zimbabwe.

Definition by Negation. Identifying what the term does not mean is another way to define a term. If the term being defined is "income tax," the definition might be: "All taxes other than: excise taxes, sales taxes, property taxes, tariffs, and social security taxes." By clarifying what is not an income tax, the term income tax is defined.

Combination of Methods. A term may be best defined by combining the methods already discussed. Presenting a definition from an authority such as a dictionary coupled with an example of the application makes a strong definition. Having multiple definitions which support your interpretation of the resolution is helpful to your case especially if your opponent challenges a definition.

2. Challenging Definitions

The affirmative team's definitions are not sacrosanct. If the affirmative team presents definitions that change the meaning of the resolution, the negative team is permitted to contest the definitions as part of the topicality argument. For example, assume the affirmative team defines "space exploration policy" as "exploring all spaces on the globe" and proposes a policy to expand ocean floor research. The negative team may want to challenge the definition of space exploration to argue the affirmative team's case is outside the bounds of the resolution. In other cases, the negative may present alternative definitions that place the affirmative case outside the bounds of the resolution. For example, suppose the affirmative team proposes to alter energy policy by increasing automobile fuel economy standards. The negative team might provide an alternative definition that energy policy relates the exploration and distribution of energy, not the actual consumption while transportation policy deals with the manufacturing of vehicles.

In order to present new definitions and argue topicality on the basis of these counter-definitions, the negative team needs to have reasons or "standards" to prefer a definition over the affirmative's definition. Freeley and Steinberg, authors of one of a widely circulated debate textbook, present standards of definitions which can be used to show a reason to prefer the definitions one provides in relationship to his opponent. These standards include official definitions, grammar, field context, common usage, bright line, and fair limits. Unless there is justification for a new definition, the affirmative's definition will be allowed to stand.

Official Definition. The official definition would be one mandated by the resolution. For example, if the resolution deals with United States military policies on weapons of mass destruction, the United States military's official definition of these weapons will determine what weapons fall within the resolution even if some other definition includes different weapons.

Grammar. The standard of grammar states that the context of the sentence is important and needs to be considered when defining the resolution. For example, if the resolution deals with "United States Trade Policy," defining "trade policy" as a whole rather than as separate words is a preferable.

Field Context. If the affirmative team defines a term differently than the experts, you can argue a definition from an expert in the field is preferable. For example, if "income tax" is defined by a dictionary, quoting a definition of income tax from a Harvard economist may be even better. If this definition is different than the dictionary, the dictionary should be rejected. The new definition could move the affirmative case outside of the resolution as defined.

Common Usage. Just like definition by field context, a team's definition that violates the common usage of a word can be attacked. Using a definition which better meets the standards of the common use is a reason to prefer one definition over another. For example, if the affirmative team says that the "America" means the western hemisphere, you can argue that the common usage of "America" is the United States of America and not the North and South American continents. Using such an expansive definition of "America" is a reason to reject the definition because it moves the affirmative case beyond the boundaries of the resolution.

Bright Line. The standard of a bright line argues that a definition should clearly show what is and what is not within the boundaries of the resolution. This standard attempts to rule out ambiguous and subjective definitions. For example, "significant" is defined in many dictionaries as important. While important may be a good definition, what is important can be subjective. Instead, a definition which points to a percentage is much less subjective and gives a much clearer distinction between the sides in a debate.

Fair Limits. Definitions limit the scope of the resolution. Often, definitions can define the resolution so narrowly that there is no room for the affirmative team to argue. In the same sense, a definition of the resolution which is too broad will leave the negative team with little ground to argue. The standard of fair limits points out that the new definition (or whichever one is presented by a team) gives fair ground to both teams. For example, noting that there are other cases which may fit within the resolution as defined is a means of proving that the definition provides fair limits for the debate.

C. Arguing Topicality

If your opponent proposes a case beyond the boundaries of the resolution, you have four choices: You can ignore the violation and develop your case to undermine the proposal; you can attack your opponent's non-topicality while focusing on undermining the other aspects of the case; you can focus your attack on topicality with only minimal argumentation on the remaining issues; or you can go all in on topicality and ignore every other issue in the round. Usually, extremes are ill advised. So obviously your best bet is to balance attacks on topicality with multiple attacks on the rest of your opponent's case.

1. Basics

Once you and your partner decide to attack topicality, you must structure the argument in a persuasive manner. You cannot simply say "The affirmative case is not topical." and move on to your other arguments against the case. Instead, you must make a persuasive compelling case to justify the judge casting a ballot in your favor on topicality alone. As with all arguments, you should make your claim — the affirmative case is non-topical; support your claim — explain why your opponent's case is outside the resolution; and present the impact — if your opponent's case is not topical, the quality of debate in the round will be undermined and thus the affirmative team should lose the round. Be sure to present an impact by answering the questions: "Why does it matter that we talk about the resolution and only the resolution?" and "What should the judge do if the affirmative team starts talking about something other than the resolution?" (Hint: she should vote for you!)

Topicality attacks must be made in the first negative constructive speech and further developed in the second constructive speech. It is not fair to the affirmative team to wait until any later in the round than the very first speech to begin attacking topicality because it is an *a priori* voting issue. In other words, if you are not running a topical case, you should lose, even if you propose a plan that would save the world. In the final speech, you should again emphasize the non-topicality of your opponent's case and remind the judge why voting for a non-topical case is improper. If you genuinely believe the affirmative case is not topical, topicality should be your first voting issue at the end of the round (see page 155).

2. Structure

Topicality arguments are most effective when they follow a structure including particular components judges expect as part of a complete topicality argument, sometimes called a "topicality press." Debaters may alter the terminology and order, but the three main components of a topicality argument include: *Resolution* (or *Standards*), *Violation*, and *Impact*. These components explain not only that the affirmative case has strayed outside the permissible boundaries, but also why those boundaries are immensely important and why the judge ought to ignore every other issue in the round and cast a negative ballot.

a. Resolution/Standards

A topicality press should begin with the resolution — the focus of the debate round. If you want to argue that the affirmative case is outside the boundaries of the resolution, you must explain the boundaries. The first step is to define the resolution. You can either (1) accept the definitions the affirmative team used or (2) redefine the resolution in some other manner. If you accept the affirmative team's definitions, you must allege their case does not uphold the resolution as defined. (This is a highly unlikely scenario because most teams will try to find definitions that make their own case topical.) For example, if the resolution requires the affirmative team to change education policy and the affirmative team defines "education" as the elementary and secondary school but proposes a plan to provide subsidies for college education, there is no need to re-define the resolution to begin explaining that the case violates the resolution as defined by the affirmative team. If, however, the resolution requires changing college education policy and the affirmative defines "college education" to include not only the undergraduate college, but also the entire university system in order to run a case to increase the number of medical schools, re-defining the resolution to limit college education to only undergraduate education will be the first step in the topicality challenge.

If you disagree with the affirmative team's definition of the resolution, you should present alternative definitions to clarify what the resolution ought to be. In the medical schools example, this would mean explaining that while colloquially we refer to all post-secondary education as "college," the term actually connotes education below graduate study. By explaining the negative team's definition of the resolution and providing justifications for this alternative interpretation of the terms of the resolution, the negative team begins their topicality press.

If the affirmative team has defined the term, the negative team must prove that the definition should be rejected before the judge will accept a new definition. Not only should you present new definitions, but you must also show that the negative team's definitions are better than the definitions the affirmative team has chosen. There are numerous sources of definitions. As discussed above, there are multiple ways to evaluate the quality of a definition. If you are attempting to present new definitions for the terms of the resolution, you should explain the new definition's superiority using one of these reasons to prefer. For example, the dictionary definition of "college" might include the colloquial reference to a university, but an official definition from the Department of Education which differentiates between secondary and post-secondary education would provide a more reasonable clarification of the resolution's meaning.

b. Violation

After presenting the alternative interpretation of the resolution based on a new definition and explaining the superiority of the new definition, the negative team is prepared to identify the violation — why the affirmative case is outside the boundaries of the resolution. This step can be very simple. Having set up a clear boundary for the resolution using the definition of college education, the negative team simply says, "Because college education policy deals only with undergraduate programs, the affirmative team's plan to open additional medical schools is outside the bounds of the resolution." As long as the Resolution/Standards section is properly developed, the violation should be no more than one step.

c. Impact

The most important part of an argument is the impact, even though it is most often neglected (see page 13). The impact in a topicality argument answers the question, "Why should the judge care that the affirmative team is running a non-topical case?" While saying that running a non-topical case is against the rules might be enough for some judges, most judges will want reasons to cast a ballot based on topicality. Your job is to answer this question so the judge feels compelled to cast a negative ballot.

The first impact states that because the affirmative case is outside the bounds of the resolution, it is not topical. Assuming the judge believes that the affirmative case it not topical, the next set of impacts are intended to help the judge justify casting a ballot for the negative team.

Non-topical cases make the debate round less interesting. If the negative team is prepared to discuss state and federal college subsidies and standardized tests for college graduation, but the affirmative team attempts to discuss dissertation committee assignments for Ph.D. students or the need for more doctors to treat the aging population, there will be little clash between the two teams. If the purpose of debate is to search for truth, and the goals of each debater are to develop useful skills in argumentation, speaking, and critical thinking for the real world, having a debate round in which both teams cannot actually dialog with one another will fail to reach this purpose and these goals. Many debaters make this loss of educational value argument the impact to their topicality argument. The argument to the judge is generally, "If this affirmative case were allowed to pass the test of topicality, this round would be less likely to provide the educational benefits each debater and member of the audience hopes to obtain as a part of the round."

Another argument many negative teams employ is the social contract. Debate relies on an agreement that the resolution will be the focus of the debate round. If one team decides to play the game outside those boundaries, the contract has been violated. This argument would be identical to a soccer coach telling a referee to call a forfeit against an opposing team that refused to ever bring the ball onto the field of play, but instead tried to have its own scrimmage on an adjacent soccer field. A violation of the agreement to abide by the resolution justifies a negative ballot.

A final argument is technical, relying on the theory that judges in a debate round are voting either to affirm or negate the resolution, not for the negative or affirmative team. While debaters usually request an affirmative or negative ballot, what all debaters are really requesting is a vote from the judge to affirm or reject the resolution. Because the judge is deciding whether to vote in favor of the resolution, a non-topical case cannot provide any justification for casting a ballot in favor of the topic. Even if the affirmative team's case shows a significant problem (there are too few doctors), proposes a plan to address the problem (open more medical schools), and explains how the proposal will solve the problem (the shortage of physicians will be reduced and eliminated in some number of years), the judge lacks the authority to actually vote for that plan. The ballot does not give the judge the option to vote for or against enacting the affirmative team's plan. Instead, it requires a vote for or against the resolution. Thus, debaters often argue that the judge lacks the jurisdiction or authority to vote for a case outside the resolution.

The impact is vital to a topicality press. A negative team must identify at least one impact at the conclusion of the topicality argument.[26] Certainly, more than one impact could be identified. Finally, debaters should not be afraid to mention that topicality is an *a priori* voting issue meaning that the judge must assure herself that the case is topical before she has jurisdiction to vote for the case or the resolution.

D. Extratopicality

Topicality is related to, but is not the same as extratopicality. Topicality asks whether an affirmative team has presented a case to uphold the resolution. Extratopicality means upholding the resolution and then doing something more than the resolution asks. For example, if the resolution calls for a change in college education policy, a plan that increases the number of scholarships for both undergraduates and graduate students is extratopical — such a plan does not only advocate for affirming the resolution, it advocates for more. Unlike non-topical cases in which the judge votes against the affirmative team, extratopicality simply limits the advantages an affirmative team can claim as justifications for casting an affirmative ballot.

1. Topicality Diagram

Many coaches use circle diagrams to illustrate the differences between the types of topicality. The white circle represents the resolution and the dark circle represents the affirmative case (see Figure 29). First there is non-topicality. Non-topicality may be illustrated by an empty white circle (the resolution). For example, changing trade policy with China does not fill any portion of the resolution circle for a resolution that calls for a change in trade policy with Brazil. Thus, the affirmative in this instance would lose the round for not fulfilling the resolution.

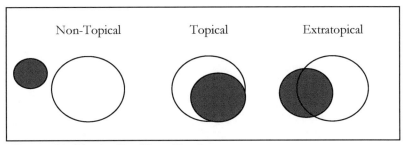

Figure 29: Topicality Visualized

The second diagram indicates topicality. A topical case is illustrated by a case circle that is completely within the resolution circle. For example, changing policy on trading ethanol with Brazil fits the Brazil trade policy resolution. Eliminating corporate taxes would also be fully

---

[26] There are multiple alternative impacts a debater might use. For example, they can argue expanding the resolution to new extremes creates an unfair research burden (an extension of the educational value argument) or that if the judge permits this interpretation of the resolution to pass muster, even more abusive and extreme interpretations will begin to creep in and the resolution will lose its power to define the boundaries of the debate round.

within a resolution circle requiring a change in tax policy. The resolution circle's outer edge is clearly defined and the changes proposed by the affirmative case are fully inside that circle.

Finally, there is extratopicality. Extratopicality is adhering to the resolution plus something else. A circle illustrating portions both within and outside the resolution circle visually indicates extratopicality. For example, changing the tariffs on ethanol imported from every nation in the world would not only change trade policy with Brazil (topical), but would also change trade policy with every other country (extratopical). Changing education policy while simultaneously altering tax policy by providing school vouchers to students in low-performing public schools and also increasing the child tax credit would be extratopical if the resolution requires a change in education policy. While the child tax credit may be in greater need of change, the resolution only allows a change in education policy. Extratopicality is fulfilling the resolution and then doing more. While the additional modifications may be beneficial, the resolution only permits a change in one area. The affirmative team's plan must remain within the bounds of the resolution.

The key difference between non-topicality and extratopicality is that non-topicality is grounds for a negative ballot while extratopicality is not. The affirmative team is required to fulfill the resolution and violates this duty in presenting a non-topical case. However, an affirmative plan with extratopical planks still fulfills the resolution. By upholding the resolution, the affirmative does not lose the round on the basis of topicality. Instead, extratopicality is a test of the claimed advantages. The affirmative team can only justify casting a ballot for the resolution if the advantages come from the topical portions of the plan. If the advantages the affirmative team claims are only achieved because ethanol tariffs on Canadian ethanol were increased, there is no justification to enact the topical portion (tariffs on Brazilian ethanol) of the affirmative case.

2. Arguing Extratopicality

Debaters typically argue extratopicality incorrectly in two ways. First, debaters argue that extratopicality implies non-topicality. This is simply incorrect. Being extratopical implies that an affirmative case has fulfilled the resolution and more. It does not mean the resolution is ignored or has not been fulfilled. Second, debaters often assume that the affirmative team may gain benefits from extratopical mandates in their plans. An extratopical mandate in a plan may be used. For example, the plan may extend beyond the geographical limits of the resolution (ethanol from countries other than Brazil), however, the advantages from such extension beyond the resolution must not be claimed.

Suppose a resolution required freer trade with Brazil. A case which extends freer trade to all of South America would be allowed, however, the advantages touted may only stem from the newly freer trade with Brazil. While there are advantages from the extension of the affirmative team's plan to regions beyond the resolution's boundaries as the affirmative would at least claim, it is illegitimate for the affirmative to claim those advantages if the action is not warranted by the resolution. While extratopical mandates may be utilized, any and all advantages must directly link to the topical portions of the plan. This rule also extends to extratopical planks in affirmative plans intended to prevent a disadvantage from occurring. The negative team should point out that these advantages (including the avoidance of a disadvantage) stem from the extratopical portions of the plan and therefore should not be weighed into the decision in favor of the affirmative team.

As the negative team, if you prove that all the affirmative team's advantages stem from the extratopical portions of the plan, you are in wonderful shape! By proving that the advantages are only possible with extratopical mandates, there remains no justification to enact the resolution. Or, if the plan will not work without an extratopical mandate, the negative team should also win. For example, an affirmative case that identifies the number of people without health insurance as the harm, proposes a plan to offer health insurance to all Americans, and claims an advantage of universal health coverage when the resolution permits only health care to be given to the poor would not actually achieve the claimed advantage without giving insurance to all. If the negative team can identify the advantages stemming from the extratopical plan sections, they should articulate to the judge that those advantages cannot be part of the justification for casting an affirmative ballot. Just as the judge does not have the jurisdiction to vote for a non-topical plan, the judge does not have the jurisdiction to consider extratopical mandates as a justification for casting an affirmative ballot.

If the distinction between the topicalities is still confusing, think of it this way. Topicality is a key voting issue if the affirmative team does not meet its test. However, once topicality is fulfilled, it becomes a non-issue in the round. Extratopicality may then become an issue. Now the advantages gained are in question. If the affirmative team gains their advantages only by going above and beyond the bounds of the resolution, they have not provided sufficient justification to affirm the resolution as is and there is no justification for enacting their plan under the resolution. Good debaters understand the distinctions between non-topicality and extratopicality. They also know when an affirmative team's case should lose (non-topical) or when the judge should disregard advantages (extratopicality). Advanced debaters recognize when to make topicality and extratopicality an issue in the round.

Observation 25: Counterplans

"The sounder your argument, the more satisfaction you get out of it."
-Edward W. Howe-

A counterplan is an alternative plan proposed by the negative team to obtain both the same advantages as the affirmative team's plan that comes with additional benefits (either more advantages or avoiding disadvantages) compared to the affirmative team's plan's advantages. Rather than defending the status quo, the negative team chooses to argue that an alternative plan is best able to meet the challenges of the present system. For example, assume the affirmative team's plan identifies the cost of college as being too high, calls for providing 100 full-tuition college scholarships for women majoring in engineering, and claims the advantage that college is more affordable. The negative team's counterplan might propose making college tuition tax deductible for every family which would not only make college more affordable for the 100 students who receive scholarships under the affirmative team's plan, but additionally, it would not limit those who benefit from the scholarships to only women who pursue engineering. By providing an additional advantage, the counterplan is arguably a better policy change for the judge to consider as opposed to the affirmative's plan.

A. Counterplan Requirements

In general, counterplans are non-topical. A non-topical counterplan means that you could not propose to enact the same policy if you were the affirmative team. If you are running a counterplan, you should be prepared to explain how your case is outside the bounds of the resolution. For example, if the resolution calls for an increase in alternative energy production, a non-topical counterplan could not boost solar energy production, but could increase the production of traditional energy production (gas and oil). For further discussion of topicality, see page 139.

Every counterplan needs to be mutually exclusive of the affirmative team's plan meaning that the plan and counterplan are contradictory and unable to coexist. The affirmative case and the counterplan must not be able to be enacted at the same time. For example, if the affirmative team's plan calls for a subsidy to build a wind farm and the counterplan offers a subsidy to manufacturers of alternative energy equipment, there is nothing to prevent the affirmative team from adopting the negative team's counterplan as part of the affirmative team's plan. If both the plan and counterplan could be simultaneously enacted (without violating topicality), the affirmative team can permute, borrow, the counterplan and add it to their plan. Thus, the affirmative team gains all the advantages of the affirmative case, the negative counterplan, and any special advantage of enacting the two policies simultaneously in order to make the affirmative plan even stronger. This would leave the negative team with nothing more to argue.

Counterplans must also be competitive, that is, the counterplan must be superior to both the plan and any possible combination of the plan and counterplan. To show your counterplan is competitive, there must be some unique advantage to the counterplan the affirmative plan cannot achieve. The advantages come in two main forms: unique advantages and avoiding disadvantages. Many counterplans claim they will create benefits the affirmative team's plan cannot achieve. These advantages may include such run-of-the-mill advantages as increasing the number of jobs, reducing crime, or saving the government money vis-à-vis the status quo. Alternatively, many negative teams choose to present disadvantages stemming from the affirmative team's plan which cannot be linked to the counterplan.

An example of both kinds of competitiveness might be helpful. If your opponent reduces the price of gasoline by permitting additional oil drilling and claims the economy is enhanced, you may choose to propose a counterplan of shifting to a renewable fuel economy. You may show the competitiveness of this counterplan by identifying a new advantage created by the counterplan or by showing that the counterplan avoids a disadvantage of the affirmative team's plan. A new advantage might be that because renewable fuels may be able to provide low-cost energy for much longer than oil, the economy will be stronger for a much longer period of time. An avoided disadvantage might be that your proposal is competitive because oil places our environment at risk from oil spills, a risk which renewable sources avoid. Competitiveness can be shown by either identifying unique advantages your counterplan provides *or* by identifying disadvantages unique to the affirmative plan which the counterplan avoids.

B. Counterplan Types

Most debaters use three major counterplan types: Plan-exclusive counterplans, Agent counterplans, and Plan-inclusive counterplans. These three types do not cover the entire universe of counterplan styles, but many counterplans fit into one of these categories. Depending on your objectives and what your research turns up, each counterplan style has its pros and cons.

1. Plan-exclusive Counterplans

A plan-exclusive counterplan proposes an entirely different plan than the one proposed by the affirmative team. For example, if the affirmative team proposes to increase spending on space exploration, the negative team's counterplan might propose to spend more money on foreign aid. Often the two plans will have more similarity, but the key factor making a counterplan plan-exclusive is that the two plans are not similar. A plan-exclusive counterplan's main strength is that there is no question it is mutually exclusive – the two plans are not compatible. The main weakness, however, is that plan-exclusive counterplans often have difficulty achieving the same advantages the affirmative proposes.

Plan-exclusive counterplans are valuable when the plan proposed by the affirmative team, or the resolution itself, will lead to disadvantages. The competitiveness of the plan-exclusive counterplan is that it avoids particular disadvantages stemming directly from the resolution. For example, if the resolution calls for increasing government-sponsored space exploration, a disadvantage that government-funded space exploration increases international hostilities might be applicable. To avoid this disadvantage, the negative counterplan might argue that the government should simply spend the money that would be used on space exploration to promote international relations instead. Doing so would avoid the disadvantage of international hostilities while simultaneously providing avenues for international cooperation in space exploration. Thus, any advantages of the advancement of knowledge and technological advances from space exploration would also be achieved without the negative consequences of international tension.

2. Agent Counterplans

Some debaters really think their opponents have stumbled upon a wonderful idea – providing subsidies to promote space travel – but think the affirmative team has chosen the wrong actor to implement the plan. Often the affirmative team has chosen such an actor because the resolution required them to do so. When this situation arises, the negative team's best option is to run an agent counterplan. Agent counterplans enact a plan eerily similar to the affirmative team's plan, but use an alternative actor. If your opponent is running a plan calling for the United States government to increase NASA funding to explore space, you might call for an international body such as the United Nations (UN) or the North Atlantic Treaty Organization (NATO) to provide the same levels of funding for the identical project. To gain unique advantages, you would argue that the United States cannot, by itself, afford space exploration, but the benefits to the NATO countries would be substantial enough that the United States, cooperating with the other nations, could now afford to spend more without undermining other necessary programs by cutting their funding. You might also argue that the alternative agent will better execute the plan, will be more effective in implementation of the plan, will do it faster, or will be less prone to corruption or failure.

The agent counterplan is useful when your opponent proposes a very strong plan. Instead of trying to defeat the plan on its merits, the negative team can propose adopting the plan with some alternative actor. The unique actor must create unique advantages that are only possible because the affirmative team's actor is no longer acting (either by itself or at all). Many teams choose to propose an agent counterplan in which a state government implements the identical plan as the affirmative team's federal government proposal. In this counterplan, the affirmative team obtains the same advantages, but avoids the potential disadvantage of wasted money when the federal government transfers money to the states before spending that money on the particular project proposed by the affirmative team.

There are two pitfalls to agent counterplans. First, you are admitting that the proposal the affirmative team is making is, at least somewhat, a good idea. It may be hard to convince the judge that if your opponent's idea is great when someone else implements the idea, the proposed agent in the affirmative case will be completely unable to achieve similar advantages. Second, many judges may think you are supporting the same plan as the affirmative team. If they decide that change is needed, they may simply vote for the resolution. If you are using an agent counterplan, you must be sure to explain how your plan is different from the affirmative plan, how the agent the affirmative team has chosen will be unsuccessful in obtaining the claimed advantages, and how the resolution itself prevents your opponent from proposing a wonderful plan such as yours.

3. Plan-inclusive Counterplans

When simply proposing the affirmative team's plan as a counterplan with an alternative agent of change is not sufficient, many negative teams choose to propose a plan-inclusive counterplan. Plan-inclusive counterplans use many of the affirmative plans' raw materials, but instead of building a foundation that supports the resolution, the negative builds a counterplan upon which the resolution is unable to stand. A plan-inclusive counterplan recognizes that the affirmative has proposed a plan the judge may be compelled to choose, but then identifies key distinctive features which differentiate the plans and make voting negative attractive.

The delay counterplan passes the affirmative plan on some future date rather than immediately. The negative counterplan can be implemented after some significant barrier is overcome. For example, if the affirmative team proposes selling AIDS drugs to sub-Saharan African nations at a very low cost, a negative team might identify that corrupt governments in some very needy nations would steal these drugs and sell them to more developed countries for a personal profit without any benefit to those in need of the treatments. A delay counterplan could propose to sell the identical drugs at the identical price the affirmative has set, but only do so after particular benchmarks are achieved such as when certain assurances are made that the people in need will actually receive the medication. Thus, the counterplan would be competitive because it avoids the disadvantage of providing financial support to corrupt leaders while obtaining all the benefits of helping children and others with AIDS. In fact, avoiding this disadvantage is itself a unique advantage since the argument was that the corrupt leaders prevent those in need from obtaining the treatment at the new lower price.

Another plan-inclusive counterplan is the exclusionary counterplan which only enacts portions of the affirmative plan. The portions of the affirmative plan the counterplan adopts are beneficial, while the remaining portions of the affirmative plan create disadvantages. The competitiveness is, again, avoiding the disadvantage or better implementation of the proposed plan. For example, suppose the affirmative team has identified obesity as the harm and wants to both impose a tax on sugar and provide a subsidy to individuals who exercise more than 30 minutes per day. An exclusionary counterplan might only select one plank of the proposal. It may propose the subsidy to those who exercise, but remove the sugar tax. If the negative team argues that a tax on sugar will only encourage people to shift their consumption to synthetic forms of sugar which have significant health-related costs to the populace, and further that sugar itself is not the cause of obesity, but rather a lack of physical activity, the negative counterplan is not subject to a significant criticism. By proposing only to subsidize exercise, and not to encourage the citizenry to try all kinds of risky alternative sweeteners, the negative counterplan will arguably obtain the unique advantages of actually reducing obesity.

C. Affirmative Responses to Counterplans

If your opponent decides to run a counterplan, you generally have three options. First, you can test the mutual exclusivity of the two plans by permutation, proposing that both the plan and counterplan be enacted simultaneously. Second, you may attack the counterplan by identifying disadvantages from the counterplan to show the counterplan is not competitive. Finally, like a policy analyst, you may simply compare and contrast the pros and cons of the two competing plans to show the counterplan is not competitive with the affirmative team's plan. Each strategy effectively attacks a counterplan. You and your partner should identify which strategic path to take before the 2AC.

Affirmative teams can protect the resolution by identifying counterplans that could be enacted under the resolution. An affirmative debater will *permute* the negative team's counterplan in the 2AC by specifically identifying how the plan and counterplan could be enacted together. If the affirmative can permute the counterplan, the counterplan is suddenly further justification to vote for the resolution which the negative team has spent an entire speech advocating. Permutations test the exclusivity of the counterplan by hypothesizing the world in which the plan and counterplan are both enacted. If this world is possible, there is no reason to prefer the counterplan. Remember, by proposing a counterplan, the negative team has given up the advantage of presumption that the status quo is sufficient and does not need to be changed. Thus, if the negative team's counterplan is permuted, the negative team will lose the round.

As noted earlier in the discussion of disadvantages on page 133, disadvantages provide a justification for maintaining the status quo rather than risking the new plan. Just as negative teams present disadvantages of changing from the status quo to a new policy, an affirmative team faced with a counterplan may present disadvantages to identify serious flaws in the negative team's counterplan. If the affirmative team shows that enacting the counterplan will produce unintended negative consequences, the judge will be very unlikely to cast a ballot for the counterplan. As with all counterplans, the key is to weigh the issues for the judge at the end of the round and identify how the costs of the counterplan outweigh any potential benefits.

A final strategy for addressing counterplans is to simply compare and contrast the pros and cons of the two plans. If there are special disadvantages or unique critiques that only apply to the counterplan and not your plan, you should provide those as sources of comparison. Clearly contrast how much better the affirmative advantages are compared to the negative counterplan's advantages. Show that there are more disadvantages to the counterplan than the affirmative plan. Quantify everything to make it easier for the judge to follow your comparisons and recognize that the plan is superior to the counterplan.

D. Counterplan Strategy

Counterplans are often difficult to sell to your judge. Rather than providing support for the status quo, you are arguing that change is needed – just not the kind of change the affirmative team supports. Even though this all makes perfect sense in theory, unless you are very clear in your arguments during the round, you may still confuse your judge. With that in mind, debaters should ensure their counterplans are very clear. The simpler the plan, the easier it is for your judge to understand and vote for it. If you need more than one minute to explain your particular alternative policy proposal before you even begin to explain its unique advantages, you are probably going to confuse the judge and lose her vote. Make one or two clear proposals in a concise manner so your judge will be able to follow along.

After you propose your counterplan, make very clear the unique advantages you will obtain. If these advantages are the same as the affirmative's advantages but to a greater extent or degree, make sure you can quantify the differences. If you can produce additional unique advantages, be sure you contrast those with the advantages the affirmative team is already claiming. Finally, disadvantages are the best way to compare the two plans. Your plan must produce every advantage the affirmative team has claimed while simultaneously avoiding the major pitfall(s) of the affirmative team's plan. If the counterplan does this, you will be able to make a solid case to your judge that while change is in fact very necessary, the change proposed by the affirmative team to affirm the resolution is not as beneficial or worthy of a vote as the change you propose. By providing your audience a clear contrast in the benefits of the two plans, you make your counterplan shine!

Observation 26: Issues

"The difficult part in an argument is not to defend one's
opinion, but rather to know it."
-André Maurois-

By the end of the debate round, a judge will be left with multiple arguments, substantial quantities of evidence, and many refuted contentions. Synthesizing these points to make a clear appeal for your side of the debate will require quick analysis of the many arguments currently under discussion. A good debater will assist the judge in identifying the important points of the round and focus his attention on the reasons to cast a ballot for or against the resolution.

A. Tier of Issues

Debate rounds are filled with many arguments covering a plethora of issues. Each issue has different relevance for a round. Deciding which issues to cover is an essential aspect of becoming a stronger debater. In considering the issues you address, it is important to be able to identify what type of issue you are dealing with. A tier of issues assists in this process. The tier identifies three different categories of issues in a debate: *potential issues*, *contested issues*, and *ultimate issues*. Each category is more focused than the one before it and gives debaters the ability to hone in on the most important arguments to make in a round. This section will discuss the tier of issues and will then examine *ultimate* issues more closely by investigating *voting issues*.

Potential issues encompass any arguments that could arise in a debate. The negative team prepares arguments to reply to dozens of cases which might be argued in a round. The affirmative team tries to anticipate the arguments which will be made in response to their case and readies refutation arguments to support the case in each area. Potential issues include anything that may possibly be argued. Debaters can prepare themselves to debate potential issues by thoroughly researching the topic, gathering an extensive amount of evidence, and learning to identify the issues being addressed. If debaters prepare for the potential issues, they can focus on strengthening the arguments they already have crafted.

Contested issues are the arguments actually raised in the debate round. The majority of the debate will focus on these issues. Each contested issue will have arguments made on both sides and will provide the majority of the clash throughout the round. Being prepared to argue your position on the contested issues is important to winning the arguments. Learning to identify issues which are contested in the round, arguing those issues, and ignoring the uncontested potential issues is important to the success of your argumentation.

The debate round will focus on numerous issues as it moves from speech to speech. By the end of the round, there will be many contested issues on the table. In the final two rebuttal speeches debaters need to start narrowing the arguments presented to a few key issues in the round. Much like voting issues, these final issues are the most important points on which the round hinges. This category of issues is known as ultimate issues. Ultimate issues influence the judge and members of the audience to vote in one direction or another. The ability to weed out the ultimate issues from among the several contested issues is an important skill for debaters to learn.

The tier of issues is a method for debaters to categorize the arguments in a debate round. Preparing for potential issues will give the debater confidence to argue any presented point in a debate round. Selecting the issues to contest from among the potential issues allows for clash in the round. Narrowing the arguments to only the ultimate issues at the end of the round clarifies all the argumentation in the round and gives the judge cause to vote for a position. The use of the tier of issues helps debaters effectively hone in on their best arguments and press these arguments throughout a debate round.

B. Voting Issues

In the debate round, the judge must assimilate, synthesize, and decipher numerous arguments. Both teams present various arguments, back up their arguments with evidence, and refute opposing arguments. By the end of the round, a judge's flow sheet (see page 47), not to mention her mind, will be full, often to the point of overload. While arguments may be "won on the flow," there may still be confusion in the judge's mind as to who the clear winner should be. This brings the importance of voting issues, or "voters," to light. Voting issues may be considered criteria for judging the debate round. The judge should vote for whichever voting issue is shown to be most pressing. Voting issues give the judge clear reasons to cast a ballot for one team or another while also boiling down the key points of the round so that they will be clearly understood.

Voting issues are broad, all-inclusive reasons to cast a ballot in a team's favor. Voting issues are not simply another name for the stock issues (see page 109). While the stock issues may be included, the stock issues are simply one of the voting issues you and your partner may bring into the round. Voting issues are also not simply rehashing the debate round to repeat the arguments your side has won. For example, a voting issue should not sound like this, "When looking to our first harm, our significance was that one million dollars are wasted every year. Since the evidence has shown this and the negative team has conceded this issue, we have proven that there is a one million dollar cost." Instead, voting issues strategically remind the judge of the best justification for casting a ballot in your favor.

Voting issues are your team's opportunity to give the judge clear, concise, and compelling reasons which show that you have won the round. Good voting issues are important enough that they could claim to be independent justification for a vote in your team's favor. A voting issue of magnitude will go a long way in persuading the judge. Voting issues should be able to succinctly label and persuade the judge of your position. Often, strong voting issues summarize many arguments from the round. Labeling a group of arguments such as the "disadvantages" of the affirmative plan helps the judge to identify and focus on the argument being made. Voting issues are unique to each round. While there may be some voters which will arise in nearly every round (advantages on the affirmative side, disadvantages on the negative), most voting issues are based on the specific argumentation in the round.

What do voting issues look like in a debate round? Typically, in the 2NR, the speaker will cover a few arguments and then address between two and ten voting issues. Some teams use the "five fatal flaws" on negative, while other teams prefer focusing on such areas as stock issues, disadvantages, workability, benefits of the status quo, the negative philosophy, cost-benefit analysis, criteria, advantages vs. disadvantages, or no reason to change. Each voting issue should be labeled at the beginning of the speech and then addressed by the speaker. For example, "In this speech I will be giving you 3 reasons to cast a negative ballot: disadvantages, topicality, and failure to meet the criteria." The speech then proceeds in that order: disadvantages, topicality, and criteria.

Be sure to address all the issues you say you will be covering. By telling the judge there are six reasons to vote negative and then proceeding to present only five, you lose persuasive power because mismanaging your time and missing a point could reduce your credibility. Sticking to your arguments is important to the successful use of the voting issues. Be sure to use all the voting issues you present and impact each one to votes by giving the judge a reason this issue warrants a ballot in your favor.

In the 2AR, the speaker will rise and reply to any negative voters which need a response and then proceed to present his own voters. (If the negative team's voting issues can be refuted while presenting affirmative voting issues, it is recommended that the 2AR speaker do so.) Telling the judge there are key reasons to cast an affirmative ballot and then presenting each reason with an impact to her vote is the most effective means of presenting the voting issues of a debate round.

Voting issues synthesize information. For example, if the first and second harm have been the major issues debated in the round, your voting issues may include each of these. The proper use of a voting issue takes your stance, labels it as a voting issue, and shows, once and for all, that your position has emerged victorious. Once you have persuaded the judge of your position and called it a voting issue, never forget to point out that the voting issue is independent justification for casting a ballot in your team's favor.

The greatest benefits of using voting issues include focusing the debate round, strengthening your issues, and giving the final speeches a logical flow. Rather than the final speech moving straight down the flow, beginning with topicality and then addressing each advantage, the final speech should focus on only the issues which the judge needs to keep in mind as she votes. The debate is no longer hundreds of arguments thrown onto the table, but is instead a synthesized group of arguments which all can be easily examined by the judge. Utilizing voting issues allows you to focus on the key issues of your case. Rather than simply answering the arguments of the opposition, using voting issues turns the focus to the arguments you have won and provides the judge with clear and compelling reasons to vote in your favor. By presenting voting issues in your final speech, the judge will look at the issues you highlight which, if used correctly, leave the judge focusing on your strongest winning arguments. Finally, using voters helps to keep your final speech on track. Rather than guessing how long it will take to reach the end of the flow, voting issues can be evenly spaced throughout the final speech. This makes time management much easier because there are a set number of issues to cover in your final speech. This also allows time to provide a strong conclusion which crystallizes your team's arguments into a marketable package. Utilizing voting issues will enhance your ability to make a final speech with an impact.

In Conclusion

"People generally quarrel because they cannot argue."

-Gilbert Keith Chesterton-

You now have the basics you need to start debating. Although all this information may seem overwhelming, with some practice and experience you will be ready to debate in a clear and convincing manner before any audience. Prepare for your debate as soon as possible, practice as often as feasible, and research to learn as much about the topic as you are able. If you work hard and accept criticism and feedback from your coach, teammates, judges, and parents, you can develop excellent debate skills. Remember, the more you practice to debate correctly, the better you will debate. Keep improving on what you have learned. Pass this knowledge on to others and get out there and debate!

The gift of communication, like many other gifts, may be used for many purposes. Some debaters use communication selfishly, others employ the skills to speak for those unable to speak for themselves, and still others communicate a message they believe should be shared with the world around them. Successful communication often results in glory to the speaker, but personal glory cannot be our main objective in learning the skills of communication. Once we cross the line by communicating only to win accolades for ourselves we lose the power our communication can give. While overcoming the fear of public speaking and becoming effective communicators are goals of all forensics programs, competitive debate will give you the tools to deliver any message you feel called to share and support that message even if it comes under attack. Never forget, the trophies are going to fade away, but the lives you touch will live forever! Train yourself in the skills of communication, practice these skills to become excellent, and utilize these skills to deliver the message you have been given. If you keep the right perspective, your communication will be a success and you will have the opportunity to participate in many great debates.

Glossary & Definitions

"How many a dispute could have been deflated into a single paragraph if the disputants had dared to define their terms."
-Aristotle-

Debates often hinge on the meaning of a word or phrase. If debaters cannot understand each other they will be as two ships passing in the night. The judge and audience will be disappointed because there will be no true clash. Clear definitions set up a high quality debate. Just as a debate round needs clear definitions, a debate textbook may be easier to understand with clarification of key terms.

➤ A Priori: *A Priori* is a Latin term meaning "what is before." The phrase is used in debate to describe issues a judge should consider before asking whether a team has supported the resolution. For example, if an affirmative or pro team does not present a topical case (one that advocates upholding the resolution), even if that team makes excellent arguments in favor of the position the judge should vote against the non-topical case. Debaters must be sure they are winning all *a priori* issues as well as the other arguments in the debate round.

➤ Advantage: Advantages are the beneficial results the affirmative team in a policy debate claims their plan will create. The advantages show that the world will be improved if the affirmative team's plan is put into place. The affirmative team will tell the judge that the advantages justify casting a ballot in favor of the resolution.

➤ Affirmative team: The affirmative generally refers to the affirmative team in a policy or Lincoln-Douglas debate. The affirmative team is required to affirm or uphold the resolution which means that the affirmative team must support the resolution. The affirmative team wins the debate by showing that the resolution ought to be adopted. This is usually done by presenting a case to alter the current system in a particular manner consistent with the resolution.

➤ Attention step: The attention step grabs the audience's attention and draws them into the first speech of a debate round. Rather than assuming the audience cares about the resolution, the attention step shows the audience respect by making the debate topic relevant to the members of the audience.

➤ Ballot: At the end of the debate round the judge will make a decision for or against the resolution. The judge casts her vote on a ballot that indicates which team wins the debate round. The ballot also provides feedback for the debaters and a reason for the judge's decision (RFD). The ballot is a useful tool to help debaters improve and should be read carefully by debaters and their coaches. For more information see page 63.

➤ Brief: A brief is a method of compiling evidence by specific topics to be used in a debate round. By organizing evidence topically, debaters prepare the evidence they find in their research to use in a debate round. Most briefs include evidence that may be used to support one particular argument.

➢ Burden: Burdens are the requirements a team must fulfill to win the debate round. An affirmative team has some burdens in every round (they must support the resolution and present a prima facie case); both teams have burdens to prove what they say and burdens to rebut/refute what the other team says. Finally, both teams may establish burdens they must meet to win. For example, both teams may establish a burden that the winning case will produce greater economic growth in the United States, and provide this criterion against which any policy should be evaluated. If the teams accept new burdens in the debate round, the judge will make his or her decision based, at least in part, on which team fulfilled these burdens.

➢ Case: Debate teams use their first speech to present a case which lays out specific contentions that either support or oppose the resolution. The case narrows the resolution and provides a rough outline for the specific aspects of the topic the debaters hope to discuss in the debate round. Cases should be pre-written and offer the judge a clear justification to vote for or against the resolution.

➢ Clash: Clash is a direct conflict of arguments in a debate round. Clash is a term used by debaters to refer to refutation and argumentation moving through each of an opponent's arguments and disputing them. In other words, clash is debate ping-pong. Good debate rounds provide abundant clashing of ideas which result in enjoyment for the debaters.

➢ Club: A debate club is a group of teams who meet together to learn and practice debate. They may share information, evidence, and expertise. Clubs are usually comprised of students from the same school, town, or region, but some students even have national "clubs" that work together online. A club often has one or more coaches who teach classes and give direction to the debaters. A club provides the opportunity to share the workload of research, writing, and practice in a community to hone their skills.

➢ Con team: Con refers to the public forum debate team arguing against the resolution. It is public forum debate's version of policy debate's negative team. The con team attempts to articulate reasons the judge should reject the resolution. Con teams generally attack the pro case and present their own contentions to argue against the truth of the resolution.

➢ Constructive speech: The first four speeches in a public forum debate round or policy debate round are called "constructive speeches." The purpose of a constructive speech is to build the arguments both teams believe will support their side of the resolution. After the constructive speeches are delivered, neither team may present a new argument, but must summarize and weigh the arguments already made to argue that the judge should cast a ballot in their team's favor.

➢ Counterplan: A counterplan is a plan presented by the negative team in a policy debate to change the status quo using a different method than the affirmative has proposed (usually outside the resolution). Rather than saying the affirmative's objectives are incorrect, the counterplan argues that the affirmative team's method for reaching those objectives is inferior to the negative team's method embodied in the counterplan. Most negative teams choose to attack the affirmative case using methods other than a counterplan. See page 149 for more discussion of counterplans.

➤ Criteria: Criteria are a measuring stick or standard affirmative teams often introduce as a burden they want the judge to use in weighing arguments in the round. For example, a team may set the criterion for the round as a safer country. Under such a criterion, the affirmative is asking the judge to vote for the side of the resolution that gives the most safety to the country. If the negative team proves the status quo is safest, the judge should vote negative, and if the affirmative team proves their case creates a safer world, the judge should vote affirmative. A criterion is one burden debate teams take upon themselves and can agree to use as a measuring stick against which the judge should measure the positions of the teams.

➤ Crossfire: Crossfire is a three-minute period after every pair of speeches in a public forum debate round where both debaters stand up and ask and answer questions from one another. It has similar purposes to cross-examination, but requires more concise questions and answers as both teams must share the limited time. The third and final crossfire in the round is called the grand crossfire because all four debaters will ask and answer questions during the crossfire. See page 89 for further discussion.

➤ Cross-examination: Cross-examination is often referred to as: *cross*, *CrossX*, and *CX*. Cross-examination is a three-minute period after each constructive speech in policy debate and Lincoln-Douglas debate in which opponents question the previous speaker. This period of questioning is used to enhance understanding of arguments, to gain additional information from the other team, to test the arguments of the opposition, and to set up the questioner's own attacks. See page 131 for more cross-examination details.

➤ Debate: Debate is the practice of comparing and contrasting ideas. The goal of true debate is to search for truth. Arguing is not quarrelling or bickering. Quarreling never leads to a solution, but only drives both sides further apart. A good debate presents contentions on each side of an issue with the hope that the truth or best answer will prevail. Formal academic debate provides a structured means for students to learn the skills of critical thinking, argumentation, and communication. When truth is the goal, debate is very valuable.

➤ Disadvantage: Disadvantages are negative results of the change proposed by the affirmative team. The negative team presents disadvantages as reasons to reject an affirmative ballot. A disadvantage is an independent reason to reject the resolution, even if the affirmative case produces benefits. Disadvantages are commonly referred to as "disads" and abbreviated as DAs. See page 133 for further discussion of disadvantages.

➤ Dropped Arguments: A dropped argument refers to an argument brought up in a round which the opposing team does not address. All dropped arguments, according to debate theory, are conceded issues by the dropping team. This means if the other team points out this error, they win that argument in the round. A dropped argument does not mean the other team wins the round, but only that particular argument. Note, however, not all judges are strict about this rule and others do not always accept it. So, just ensure YOU do not drop or ignore arguments unless you are willing to concede that particular point.

➤ Evidence: Debate evidence is an excerpt of any publically available published work used to support a claim made in the round. Books, magazines, professional journals, newspapers, pamphlets, Internet articles, television or radio broadcasts, and other published materials are just some of the sources debaters will quote in support of their arguments. Debaters often organize their evidence into "blocks" or "briefs" with multiple quotations in support of a particular argument on one page for easy reference during the debate round.

➢ Fallacy: A fallacy is a false argument that appears to be true. Fallacies misuse logic to reach a conclusion even though further scrutiny would show the argument does not support the alleged conclusion. See page 24.

➢ Fiat: Fiat is the authority of an affirmative team to enact their case for purposes of academic debate. Fiat assumes that the case the affirmative presents will pass Congress and be signed by the President (or any other actor the resolution specifies). Rather than focusing the debate on the question of whether the government will pass the law being proposed in the affirmative team's plan, fiat allows the debate to focus on the resolution's merits as well as the pros and cons of the specific plan outlined by the affirmative.

➢ Final Focus: The final focus is the last two speeches in a public forum debate round. These short speeches provide one last opportunity to synthesize the arguments already presented and explain to the judge why she should vote for or against the resolution. Most debaters present voting issues in these speeches.

➢ Flowing: Flowing is a special method of note taking used in debate. Flowing allows debaters to make sure they address each argument made by the opponent in the round, and keep track of the evidence read and arguments conceded by both teams. See page 47 for more information about flowing.

➢ Forensics: Forensics is a term used to describe all competitive public speaking events (such as debate). The American Heritage Dictionary defines forensics as, "The art or study of formal debate; argumentation." Despite a dictionary definition referring mainly to debate, *forensics* has been adopted as a general term for all competitive speaking events.

➢ Forensics League: Forensics leagues coordinate tournaments and provide resources to competitors, clubs, and coaches. Most leagues set the resolutions teams will debate. Many states and localities have their own forensics leagues in addition to the many national leagues. Some of the major national high school forensics leagues include:
  ➢ NAUDL[27] is the National Association for Urban Debate Leagues. NAUDL is a high school debate league for students in many major city centers. It conducts competitions in cities across the country and hosts a national championship each year.
  ➢ NCFCA[28] is the National Christian Forensics and Communications Association. NCFCA is a forensics league for home educated students. It facilitates tournaments in competitive forensics across the country and hosts an annual national tournament.
  ➢ NCFL[29] is the National Catholic Forensics League. NCFL is a major high school speech and debate league which conducts its own national tournament as well as facilitating tournaments nationwide for Parochial and other schools. NCFL membership, despite the league's name, is not limited to Catholics. Many public

---

[27] See www.urbandebate.org for more information.
[28] See www.ncfca.org for more information.
[29] See www.ncfl.org for more information.

schools, non-Catholic religious schools, and other debate clubs are members of NCFL in addition to many Catholic institutions.

  ➢ NFL[30] is the National Forensics League. NFL is a major governing body of high school speech and debate and facilitates an annual national tournament. Many debate leagues across the country rely on the NFL for training, support, resolutions, and competition rulemaking. For example, the NFL debate resolutions are typically used by competitors in NAUDL, NCFL, and NFL.[31]

  ➢ STOA[32] is a forensics league for Christian home educated students. It hosts the annual Christian home school National Tournament of Champions and events across the country.

➢ Grand Crossfire: The grand crossfire is the final crossfire in a public forum debate round. All four debaters ask each other questions and answer one another's questions. This is the final opportunity to question the opponent before the final focus speeches.

➢ Impact: Impacts provide an answer to the important question, "so what?" An impact explains why an argument matters and why the audience should care about the particular argument. Many impacts weigh and compare arguments made by the two teams in the round.

➢ Judge: The judge is the decision maker in a formal debate round. Judges do not have to have any particular training or experience before they judge a round, but most judges are coaches, teachers, parents, and members of the community. The judge takes notes and watches a debate round. After the round, the judge fills out the ballot to cast his vote for one team.

➢ Negative team: The negative team is the team opposing the resolution in a policy or Lincoln-Douglas debate. The negative team is required to reject the resolution. This usually means opposing the resolution embodied in the affirmative's case. Thus, a negative team would contend that the particular change the affirmative supports is unnecessary, will be unsuccessful, or will create unintended harmful consequences, any of which may be reasons to prefer the status quo/current system.

➢ Negative Block: The negative block is a thirteen-minute period divided between two speeches in which the negative team gives back-to-back speeches in a policy debate round. The only period dividing the two speeches is a three minute cross-examination by the affirmative team. Because there is no opportunity for the affirmative to give a speech or respond to the arguments made during the block until the conclusion of the block, these speeches are often treated like one speech by the negative team. The partners are not required to repeat any arguments made by one another during the block. See page 128 for further discussion of strategies for the negative block.

➢ Paradigm: A paradigm is the worldview or perspective from which anyone views the world. Debate judges have different perspectives on what is important in a debate round and what kinds of arguments they find most persuasive. Identifying the paradigm of anyone you are trying to persuade enables you to cater your arguments to be most persuasive.

---

[30] See www.nflonline.org for more information.
[31] The National Federation of State High School Associations Speech, Debate & Theatre Association convenes a committee to select the topic used by these leagues, but the topic is generally considered the "NFL topic."
[32] See www.stoausa.org for more information.

➤ Plan: A plan is the course of action the policy debate affirmative team proposes to uphold the resolution. The term is also colloquially used to define an entire affirmative team's case.

➤ Presumption: Presumption is the underlying belief that the resolution does not need to be adopted. In practice, presumption requires the team arguing in favor of the resolution to overcome this "presumption" against the resolution. Unless the team supporting the resolution can show there is a justification to vote for the resolution, the negative or con team should win the debate round. The same is true in real life. Unless you can show that there is a problem, it will be difficult to persuade anyone that change is needed.

➤ Prima Facie: (Pronounced: *prima-fasha* or *prima-fashee*) *Prima facie* is Latin for "on the first face." This means that any case, in a vacuum, would stand on its own after its first reading. In other words, any reasonable person, without refutation of the case or previous bias, would see reasons to enact the case after the first speech. If the resolution is "We should go play soccer" and the first speech does not address playing soccer, the affirmative has obviously failed to show any reason to go play soccer. This case is not prima facie. Failing to present a prima facie case does NOT mean leaving some questions unanswered or proving the case "beyond a doubt." A prima facie case simply means someone could reasonably believe the resolution should be affirmed based on the case as it was read in the first speech. An affirmative team that fails to present a prima facie case in its first speech should lose the debate round.

➤ Pro team: The pro team is public forum debate's version of the affirmative. Rather than presenting a case to alter the current system, the pro team presents a case with contentions to argue for the truth of the resolution.

➤ Rebuttal: The last four speeches in a policy debate round are rebuttal speeches. These speeches summarize the arguments from the constructive speeches and provide the judge clear voting issues. Rebuttals offer a final opportunity to persuade the judge to vote for or against the resolution.

➤ Refutation: Refutation is responding to an opposing argument by rejecting the argument while at the same time strengthening your own argument on that same point. A debate is full of arguments, refutation of opponent's arguments, and strengthening arguments refuted by opponents. See page 15 for further discussion of refutation.

➤ Resolution: The resolution is the focus of a debate. One side (the affirmative team in policy debate and the pro team in public forum debate) must support this resolution. A policy debate resolution usually calls for a change in the current state of the world or status quo. Debate leagues typically change policy debate resolutions annually. Public forum debate resolutions ask debaters to compare two states of the world or evaluate whether a particular policy change would be beneficial. These resolutions usually change monthly.

> ➤ Policy resolution examples: "Resolved: The United States federal government should substantially increase its public health assistance to Sub-Saharan Africa." "Resolved: That the United States should substantially change the rules governing campaign finance." "Resolved: That the United States should significantly change its immigration policy." "Resolved: That the United States should substantially change its federal agricultural policy." "Resolved: That the United States federal government should establish a foreign

policy substantially increasing its support of United Nations peacekeeping operations."

> Public Forum resolution examples: "Resolved: The United States federal government should permit the use of financial incentives to encourage organ donation." "Resolved: NATO presence improves the lives of Afghan citizens." "Resolved: The costs of a college education outweigh the benefits." "Resolved: Private sector investment in human space exploration is preferable to public sector investment."

> Resolutional Analysis: The resolutional analysis provides a framework from which the debate round can proceed. While completely optional, it presents the definition of the resolution, burdens of the affirmative team in the round, criteria for the round, and any other preliminary information necessary to the debate. The resolutional analysis helps focus the debate round onto the strongest points of the affirmative team. See page 125.

> Roadmap: Roadmaps are basic outlines presented before a debate speech to let the audience know what to expect. When a debater gives a speech, she can make it easier for the audience to follow along by providing a brief outline of the main points before diving into the speech. The outline of the entire speech or even the list of arguments or responses helps the judge to flow and the audience to follow all the arguments. Roadmaps also ensure the judge flows arguments in the particular place where the debaters want them.

> Round: A debate round is the formal debate session offering both teams multiple opportunities to present their arguments and counter the arguments of the opposition. In policy debate, a debate round lasts approximately eighty minutes. In public forum debate, a round lasts approximately forty-five minutes. For more information, see page 75 for public forum and page 105 for policy debate.

> Signpost: Signposts are short statements made during debate speeches to help the audience keep track of the organization of the speech. Signposts identify which argument is being made to ensure the judge knows where to flow an argument. While a roadmap provides a preview of the speech's path, the signposts flesh out the more specific contours of the arguments within each segment of the speech.

> Status Quo: *Status Quo* is Latin for "the way things are." In debate, the status quo is the current system, method, or laws which are being changed by the affirmative case. If there are currently 435 members of Congress, a 435 member United States Congress is the status quo.

> Stock Issues: Stock issues are questions which may be applied to an affirmative case to see if the case fulfills its burdens. The affirmative has a burden to prove a need for the resolution. There are four major stock issues in a policy debate round: Topicality, Inherency, Significance, and Solvency. Topicality means the case discusses the resolution. Inherency means the problem is connected to the status quo. Significance means the problems are meaningful enough to warrant concern. Solvency means the problem is solved by enacting the affirmative case. According to the *stock issues paradigm* for judging, the affirmative team should win all four stock issues in order to win the debate round. Stock issues are sometimes referred to as "voting issues." While voting issues may include the stock issues, voting issues extend beyond simply the stock issues. See page 109 for further discussion of the stock issues.

➤ Team: A debate team argues for one side in a debate round. "Teams" consists of one or two people (one in Lincoln-Douglas and two in Policy, Public Forum, and Parliamentary Debate).

➤ Topicality: Topicality is the requirement that the affirmative or pro team must argue in favor of the resolution. While there are many different arguments the affirmative or pro team may make to support the resolution, these arguments must support the resolution. Topicality ensures that the resolution remains the focus of the debate round. See page 139 for more information about topicality in policy debate.

➤ Tournament: A debate tournament consists of several rounds of debating against various teams. Most tournaments consist of six or eight preliminary rounds after which the top teams "break" to *outrounds* (elimination rounds). Debaters compete on both sides of the resolution during a tournament.

➤ Voting Issues: Voting issues or "voters" are the ultimate reasons debaters present justifying a vote for their team in the debate round. In the final speech for each side, debaters argue that the voting issues support a ballot in their team's favor. See page 97 for more discussion of voting issues in public forum and page 156 for a fuller explanation of voting issues in policy debate.

Appendix 1: Outlines for Debate

"The superior man is modest in his speech, but exceeds in his actions."
-Confucius-

This appendix includes:
- Case Structures
- Resolutional Analysis Structure
- Brief Structure
- Counterplan Structure
- Disadvantage Structure
- Topicality Violation Structure

Plan-Meets-Needs Case

Observation 1, Definitions
- Definition 1
- Definition 2

Observation 2, Harms

    Harm A.
1. Significance
2. Inherency
3. Impact

    Harm B.
1. Significance
2. Inherency
3. Impact

Observation 3, Plan

    Agent: (Congress and President)

    Mandates:
1.
2.
3.

    Funding:

    Agency: (Enforcement)

Observation 4, Advantages:

    Advantage A.

    Advantage B.

Comparative Advantage Case

Observation 1, Definitions
- Definition 1
- Definition 2

Observation 2, Goals

    Goal A

    Goal B

Observation 3, Plan

    Agent: (Congress and President)

    Mandates:
1.
2.

    Funding:

    Agency: (Enforcement)

Observation 4, Advantages: (goals better upheld)

    Advantage A.

        Significance:

        Inherency:

        Solvency:

    Advantage B.

        Significance:

        Inherency:

        Solvency:

Criteria Analysis Case

Observation 1, Definitions
- Definition 1
- Definition 2

Observation 2, Criteria

Observation 3, Harms

    Harm A.
1. Significance
2. Inherency
3. Impact

    Harm B.
1. Significance
2. Inherency
3. Impact

Observation 4, Plan

    Agent: (Congress and President)

    Mandates:
1.
2.
3.

    Funding:

    Agency: (Enforcement)

Observation 4, Advantages:

    Advantage A.

    Advantage B.

Stock Issues Case.

Observation 1, Definitions
- Definition 1
- Definition 2

Observation 2, Inherency

    Inherency A.

    Inherency B.

Observation 3, Significance

    Significance A.
1.
2.

    Significance B.
1.
2.

Observation 4, Plan/Solvency

    Agent: (Congress and the President)

    Mandates:
1.
2.
3.

    Funding:

    Agency: (Enforcement)

Observation 5, Solvency

    Solvency A.

    Solvency B.

Alternative Justification Analysis Case
(2 mini-cases).
Definitions
  - ➤ Definition 1
  - ➤ Definition 2
Case 1:
  Observation 1, Harm(s)
      Significance
      Inherency
      Impact
  Observation 2, Plan
      Agent: (Congress and President)

      Mandates:
      1.
      2.
      Funding:
      Agency: (Enforcement)
  Observation 3, Advantage(s)
      Advantage
Case 2:
  Observation 1, Goal
      Goal stated
  Observation 2, Plan
      Agency: (Congress and President)
      Mandates:
      1.
      2.
      Funding:
      Agent: (Enforcement)
  Observation 3, Advantage
          Significance:
          Inherency:
          Solvency:

Alternative Justification Analysis Case.
(3 plans).
Observation 1, Definitions
  - ➤ Definition 1
  - ➤ Definition 2
Observation 2, Harm(s)
      Significance
      Inherency
      Impact
Observation 3, Plans
Plan 1:
      Agent: (Congress and the President)
      Mandates:
          1.
          2.
      Funding:
      Agency: (Enforcement)
Plan 2:
Agent: (Congress and the President)
      Mandates:
          1.
      Funding:
      Agency: (Enforcement)
Plan 3:
Agent: (Congress and the President)
      Mandates:
          1.
          2.
      Funding:
      Agency: (Enforcement)
Observation 4, Advantage(s)

Whole Resolution Case
Observation 1, Definitions
  - ➤ Definition 1
  - ➤ Definition 2
Observation 2, Harms
      Harm 1
      Harm 2
      Harm 3
      Harm 4
      Harm 5
Observation 3, Plan/Solvency
      Agent: (Congress and the President)
      Mandate: The government will follow the resolution
      Funding: Normal budgetary means
      Agency: (Enforcement)
Observation 4, Solvency
      All harms can be solved through the resolution and an
      affirmative ballot enacts a plan to solve these harms.

Resolutional Analysis

Introduction:
Resolution:
History:
Definitions:
Burdens:
      Cost-benefit analysis
      Net-benefits
      Superior to the status quo
      Solve the problems outlined
      Prove the necessity of resolution
Value Criteria(on):

Brief

Tag. (A few words describing the quotation)

Title: (of article)
Date:
Author:
Publication: (Magazine, newspaper, website, etc.)
Page:
Website:

Quotation: (Underline sections of quotation to be read)

Also, see the example block in Appendix 2.

Counterplan

Non-Topical:
    ➤ Definition 1
    ➤ Definition 2
Plan
      Agent: (Congress and President)
      Mandates:
          1.
          2.
          3.
      Funding:
      Agency: (Enforcement)
Advantages: Benefits above affirmative's advantages.

Unique
(Not like the affirmative plan);
(May not be run simultaneously with the affirmative plan);
(May not be permuted).

Disadvantage (fully structured)

Link(s):
    1.
    (2.)
    (3.)
Brink:

Uniqueness:

Impact(s):
    1.
    (2.)
    (3.)
    (4.)

Topicality Violation

1. Definition(s) [or counter-definition(s)]
2. Violation

    Does not meet own/new definition or resolution.
3. Standards – Reasons to prefer (select one or more)

    Field Contextuality: Definition from a more qualified individual in the same field as the resolution.

    Limits are Best: Too broad a resolution (including everything under the sun) does not foster good debate.

    Official definitions: The official definition is better than others.

    Common Usage: Because this term is commonly used in one sense, it is better to define it in that way.

    Grammar: The context of the words and the grammar surrounding it promote this definition over the previous.

    Reasonability: This definition allows both teams equal grounds.

    Dictionary Definitions are best: A definition from a non-dictionary source may not be as credible in this situation.

    Bright Line: Rule out ambiguity/subjectivity

    Fair Limits: There are topical cases under these definitions.

    Show that the affirmative's definition fails to meet the standard and ought to be rejected when compared to your definition.
4. Voting Issue/Impact

    Topicality is an a priori issue.

    Topicality is a voting issue.

    Non-Topicality is independent justification for a negative ballot.

Stock Issues and Case Structures

♦ Plan-Meets-Needs: Definitions (Topicality), Harms (Significance and Inherency), Advantages (Solvency).

♦ Criteria Analysis: Definitions (Topicality), Harms (Significance, and Inherency), Advantages (Solvency).

♦ Comparative Advantage: Definitions (Topicality), Advantages (Significance, Inherency, and Solvency).

♦ Alternative Justification Analysis: Definitions (Topicality). Other stock issues vary depending on the case structure used within AJAC's.

♦ Stock Issues: Definitions, Inherency, Significance, Solvency

♦ Whole Resolution: Harms; overall problems with the status quo, adoption of the resolution

Appendix 2: Additional Resources

"There's nothing I like less than bad arguments for a view that I hold dear."
-Rose Kennedy-

This appendix includes:

- Web Links
- Flowsheet
- Sample ballots designed by Jonathan Wolfson
- Suggested Reading
- Sample Evidence Block

Debate Web Links

<u>High School Speech and Debate</u>

The Great Debate website:	www.greatdebate.net
Lifelong Communicators:	www.lifelongcommunicators.org
NAUDL:	www.urbandebate.org
NCFCA:	www.ncfca.org
NFL:	www.nflonline.org
NCFL:	www.ncfl.org
STOA:	www.stoausa.org
Summer Debate Institute:	www.summerdebateinstitute.com

<u>Collegiate Forensics</u>

American Parliamentary Debate Assoc.	www.apdaweb.org
National Parliamentary Debate Assoc.	www.parlidebate.org
Cross Examination Debate Assoc.	www.cedadebate.org
American Forensics Assoc.	www.americanforensics.org
National Forensics Assoc.	www.nationalforensics.org

<u>Government</u>

Congress:	http://www.house.gov
Congressional Record:	http://thomas.loc.gov
Senate:	http://www.senate.gov
United States Code:	www4.law.cornell.edu/uscode
White House:	http://www.whitehouse.gov
United Nations:	http://www.un.org

<u>Think Tanks</u>

Brookings Institute:	www.brook.edu
Cato Institute:	www.cato.org
Heritage Foundation:	www.heritage.org
National Center for Policy Analysis:	www.ncpa.org
Urban Institute:	www.urban.org

<u>Search Engines</u>
Google.com
Northernlight.com
Yahoo.com

Resolution specific and other debate links, including all of the above, plus many more, will be posted on "The Great Debate" website www.greatdebate.net and on Twitter @mygreatdebate.

Flowsheet for policy debate

1AC	1NC	2AC	2NC	1NR	1AR	2NR	2AR

Flowsheet for public forum debate

1PC	1CC	2PC	2CC	PS	CS	PFF	CFF

Sample Debate Ballot

AFFIRMATIVE/PRO	NEGATIVE/CON
First Affirmative Speaker:	**First Negative Speaker:**
Speaker Points (1-5 for each category) • Persuasiveness _____ • Organization _____ • Delivery _____ • Evidence _____ • Cross-Examination _____ • Refutation _____ Total:	Speaker Points (1-5 for each category) • Persuasiveness _____ • Organization _____ • Delivery _____ • Evidence _____ • Cross-Examination _____ • Refutation _____ Total:
Speaker Comments:	Speaker Comments:
Second Affirmative Speaker:	**Second Negative Speaker:**
Speaker Points (1-5 for each category) • Persuasiveness _____ • Organization _____ • Delivery _____ • Evidence _____ • Cross-Examination _____ • Refutation _____ Total:	Speaker Points (1-5 for each category) • Persuasiveness _____ • Organization _____ • Delivery _____ • Evidence _____ • Cross-Examination _____ • Refutation _____ Total:
Speaker Comments:	Speaker Comments:

I voted for (circle one):   Affirmative/Pro   Negative/Con

Reason for Decision:

Suggested Additional Reading

Freeley, Austin J., and David L. Steinberg. <u>Argumentation and Debate. Critical Thinking for Reasoned Decision Making</u>. 10th ed. Belmont, CA: Wadsworth, 2000.

National Forensics Association. <u>NFA Lincoln-Douglas Rules</u>. <http://www.bethel.edu/Majors/Communication/nfa/ldrules.html>.

National Parliamentary Debate Association. <u>Rules of Debating</u>. < http://www.bethel.edu/Majors/Communication/npda/npdarules.html>.

The Great Debate Website: www.greatdebate.net

Sample Evidence Block

This is a sample of an evidence block which is explained on page 36. This block was built against a slave labor in the Ivory Coast case run under the African and Middle Eastern trade policy resolution. The block is created to attack specific points of a case. Cutting evidence into this format is helpful in preparing to argue against a case you know is going to be presented.

TOPIC: **Cocoa Labor-MAIN**

> ➤ **AFF Harm #1) Slave/Child Labor in Cocoa Fields**

1) The US already has a 'no-slavery' trade policy
The International Labor Rights Fund, May 30, 2002
On May 30, 2002, ILRF submitted a formal complaint to the US Customs Service, based on its failure to initiate an investigation and enforcement action under section 307 of the Tariff Act of 1930, 19 U.S.C. § 1307. The act, passed into law in 1997, prohibits the importation of products made with "forced or indentured child labor." ILRF provided ample evidence from ground research to add to already existing evidence to initiate a case for barring the entry of cocoa beans into the United States.

2) Action is already being taken
Slavery will be ended in Ivory Coast by 2005
San Jose Mercury News | October 1, 2001
The government of Ivory Coast, which supplies 43 percent of U.S. cocoa, and anti-slavery organizations, have endorsed the chocolate industry's plan. The plan calls for eliminating child slavery, monitoring working conditions on farms, and, by 2005, certifying that no 'worst forms of child labor' — including slavery — were used to produce chocolate and cocoa."

3) A New 'International Foundation' has been formed
UN office for the coordination of Humanitarian Affairs | 4 Jul 2002
Chocolate-manufacturing companies, NGOs and other stakeholders have set up an international foundation to eliminate child labor in West Africa's cocoa industry.

4) Children Traditionally Work in the fields
The International Institute of Tropical Agriculture | July 2002
In West Africa, children in rural areas have traditionally worked in agriculture as part of the family unit.

5) Harm is not quantified
Larry Graham, President of the National Confectioners Association and the Chocolate Manufacturers Association | May 2, 2002
No one knows how extensive this problem is; we don't know if it's four farms, 400 farms, 4,000 farms.

> ### Plan #1) Stop Importing Cocoa from Nations that Use Slavery

1) Not the Right Strategy
Kevin Bales, consultant to the UN on slavery and trafficking, May 31, 2002
Cutting off imports is a strategy. We don't think it's the right one for this situation. The economy of the country is absolutely dependent on cocoa.

2) Free Trade is the solution

Harry Anthony Patrinos, of the Human Capital Development and Operations Policy
Free trade is part of the solution to eradicating child labor. This is because a free trade regime promotes development worldwide. And as countries develop, the incidence of child labor decreases substantially.

3) We Aren't Justified in Restricting Trade

Harry Anthony Patrinos, of the Human Capital Development and Operations Policy
Threatening trade restrictions based on labor standards is not justified. The problem with such a stance is that (i) not all forms of child labor are exploitive or cruel; (ii) the age deemed "child" labor is not clear; (iii) poor countries cannot necessarily afford such measures; (iv) levels poverty would increase; and (v) school attendance would decline.

> ### DA #1) Entire Cocoa Industry Punished

It's Impossible to trace the roots of the cocoa
Canada NewsWire, Domestic News | February 13, 2002
While some farms probably do use legitimate labor, once cocoa beans are mixed together for export, it is impossible to know which beans that are bought and turned into chocolate, have been made with child slave labor.

> ### Source Qualifications:

Kevin Bales is the world's leading expert on contemporary slavery. A professor of sociology at the University of Surrey, Roehampton in London and consultant to the UN on slavery and trafficking, Kevin has spent 8 years researching slavery, traveling to 5 continents.

The International Labor Rights Fund is an advocacy organization dedicated to achieving just and humane treatment for workers worldwide. ILRF serves a unique role among human rights organizations as advocates for and with working poor around the world.

Appendix 3: Sample Cases

"Speak clearly, if you speak at all; carve every word before you let it fall."
-Oliver Wendell Holmes-

• Please note:

> The authors of these cases have been gracious enough to allow publication of their work to assist you. Please do not use these cases for any purpose other than learning about writing cases. Thank you.

Also, these cases have been only slightly modified in style. This allows you to observe different stylistic forms different debaters use.

Public Forum Sample Case

This case follows the basic 3-point format discussed on page 83 and discusses the topic debated in April 2011 in the National Forensics League.

According to the Department of Health and Human Services, "18 people die each day waiting for transplants that can't take place because of the shortage of donated organs." [Womenshealth.gov Organ Donation and Transplantation Fact Sheet Feb. 17, 2010 (http://www.womenshealth.gov/publications/our-publications/fact-sheet/organ-donation.cfm)]

The American Medical Association News reported: "It is a wait that could be drastically shortened or even eliminated if a market for live and cadaveric organs were allowed to operate, according to a paper co-authored by Nobel Prize-winning economist Gary S. Becker" [Amednews "Economists' study says paying for organs would cut wait lists" Jan. 28, 2008. (http://www.ama-assn.org/amednews/2008/01/28/prsb0128.htm)]

Because many of these deaths are preventable by incentives for organ donation, my partner and I support the resolution: Resolved: The United States federal government should permit the use of financial incentives to encourage organ donation.

We will show the need for financial incentives through three contentions: (1) the organ shortage is growing worse (2) financial incentives help the poor and (3) financial incentives will increase organ donations.

1. The organ shortage is growing worse

Organ donation needs far exceed demand and people are dying waiting for organs which will never arrive. Economists Beard, Jackson, and Kaserman note: "Because the waiting list has grown every year for which data are available, it is obvious that the altruistic organ procurement system has never once cleared the market during this period. That is, the demand for transplantable organs has exceeded the supply every year since at least 1988."

They published a study in 2007 projecting lives lost from the organ shortage: "Even more tragically, over the entire period of both actual and predicted values, a cumulative total of 196,310 patients are conservatively expected to die by 2015 as a consequence of the ongoing shortage" [Beard, T. Randolph; Jackson, John D.; Kaserman, David L. (2007, December 22). "The Failure of U.S. Organ Procurement Policy: how many deaths will it take 'til we know that too many people have died?" *The Free Library*. (2007). (http://www.thefreelibrary.com/The Failure of U.S. Organ Procurement Policy: "how many deaths will...-a0173923141)] Clearly the status quo is not able to provide the life-saving organs so many people need and this problem will only get worse in the future.

2. Financial incentives help the poor

Some argue offering financial incentives for organ donation will exploit the poor, but providing a financial reward will offer significant benefit to those of very minimal means. Richard Epstein explained: "Given the general diminishing marginal utility of wealth, on balance we would expect that the largest gain from increased income would go to those who are the poorest off financially, not those who are well endowed." [Richard A. Epstein, The Human and Economic Dimensions of Altruism: The Case of Organ Transplantation, January 2008, The Chicago Working Paper Series, 03/06/11, http://www.law.uchicago.edu/files/files/385.pdf]

A regulated market which sets prices for organs can offer a large payment to poor individuals who can use this money to significantly improve their position in life, not only their own, but that of their entire family.

3. Financial Incentives will increase organ donations

When financial incentives for organ donation are permitted, donation rates could triple. Michael Lusaght and Jaclyn Mason noted: "Estimates of the number of "lost" cadaveric donors vary, but most experts believe that existing donation rates could certainly be tripled, from about 20 per million population to 60 per million population." [Michael J. Lysaght, and Jaclyn Mason. "The Case for Financial Incentives to Encourage Organ Donation." ASAIO Journal 46.3 (2000): 253-256. Web. 3 Mar 2011.] Permitting financial incentives will save countless lives by tripling the number of available organs for those in need.

The present system leaves tens of thousands of individuals to die waiting for organs which never come. Permitting financial incentives will not only reduce this shortage and offer the opportunity of life to the thousands waiting for organ donations, but will improve the lives of the poor in our society. For these reasons my partner and I urge a pro ballot.

Plan-Meets-Needs Sample Case

     This case, in plan-meets-needs format, was run by David Shaw and Jonathan Wolfson at the beginning of the 2000-2001 season. This case was dropped in January of 2001 after the INS (Immigration and Naturalization Service) began addressing the harms.

     The basic contentions of this case are that <u>real</u> refugees are turned away and that INS detainees are mistreated in the jails. To solve these problems, those seeking refugee status were allowed to have their day in court and detentions required court orders to reduce their quantity and duration.

     The plan-meets-needs structure is explained on page 115.

Human Rights First Affirmative. David Shaw and Jonathan Wolfson. Revised November 9, 2000
     Resolved: That the United States should significantly change its immigration policy.
Observation I: Boundaries A. Resolutional Analysis
U.S. immigration policy should reflect the nation's historical commitment to liberty and justice. This commitment should be particularly be evident in policy toward refugees and asylum-seekers.
     Lawyers Committee for Human Rights, *Is This America? The Denial of Due Process to Asylum Seekers in the United States,* (October 2000): 4.
"Since the refugee Pilgrims first landed almost 400 years ago, the United States has served as a refuge for those fleeing persecution and oppression. . . . [After World War II] the United States led the effort to establish universally recognized human rights, including 'the right to seek and enjoy in other countries asylum from persecution.' "
B. Definitions
  Definition 1. Significantly – adverb. in a significant manner, so as to convey some meaning; expressively, meaningly (*Oxford English Dictionary*, Second Ed.).
  Definition 2. U.S. immigration policy is defined by Deborah A. Cobb-Clark, of the Department of Economics, Research School of Sciences, the Australian National University, Canberra, Australia, as, "How to select those individuals allowed to immigrate." ["Incorporating U.S. Policy into a Model of the Immigration Decision." Sept. 1996. Page 3.]
All other terms are defined operationally.
Observation II: Harms
Harm A: Expedited removal unjustly deprives asylum-seekers of real due process.
1. Significance (a) Expedited removal is fundamentally flawed.
     Lawyers Committee for Human Rights, *Is This America? The Denial of Due Process to Asylum Seekers in the United States,* (October 2000): 4-5.
"<u>Changes to American immigration law passed by Congress in 1996 have severely undermined the ability of genuine refugees to seek asylum here and have led to the mistaken return of refugees facing persecution in their home countries.</u> Before these changes, American law largely honored its obligation to give refugees a fair opportunity to present asylum claim and its obligation not to return legitimate refugees back to their persecutors. But <u>under the system of 'expedited removal,' a uniformed enforcement officer of the Immigration and Naturalization Service (INS)</u> – as opposed to a specially trained immigration judge – <u>can turn a refugee back at the airport or border crossing without due process and without meaningful review.</u> The proceedings are conducted so swiftly th[ese] mistakes are inevitable, and those who are removed are barred from re-entering the United States for five years. Furthermore, secondary inspection – the stage of the process during which erroneous decisions are most likely to be made – is conducted behind closed doors, with virtually no meaningful scrutiny by independent observers."
(b) Expedited removal is conducted without accountability.
     Lawyers Committee for Human Rights, *Is This America? The Denial of Due Process to Asylum Seekers in the United States,* (October 2000): 5.
"The impact of expedited removal has been enormous. In fiscal year 1997 through fiscal year 1999, 99% of all [89,035] persons subjected to expedited removal were turned away from the United States on the spot at secondary inspection, without any further review to determine whether they had a credible fear of persecution and might be entitled to asylum or had a claim of lawful immigration status."
2. Inherency
(a) Current law mandates expedited removal.
     Human Rights Watch, "Locked Away: Immigration Detainees in Jail in the United States," *Human Rights Watch Report,* www.hrw.org/reports98/us-immig/, (September, 1998): 2.
"IIRIRA also created a new deportation process, called 'expedited removal,' the intent of which is to process and deport individuals who enter the United States without valid documents as quickly as possible."
(b) Broad, constitutionally granted federal authority over immigration bars a judicial remedy.

Zadvydas v. *Underdown* 97-31345, Fifth Circuit Court. Filed August 11, 1999, page 6.

"The power of the national government to act in the immigration sphere is thus essentially plenary."

(c) Public opinion is likely to block a congressional remedy

Amnesty International, *United States of America: Lost in the Labyrinth: Detention of Asylum-Seekers*, (September 1999): 15.

"In recent years, however, the US public and politicians have expressed increased concern about undocumented migrants *per se*, failing to distinguish between asylum-seekers and those who migrate for economic reasons.

"In March, 1993, the popular US news program *60 Minutes* broadcast a segment called 'How Did He Get Here?' This program, seen by millions of people in the USA, suggested that any foreign national could enter and pass through airports into US communities by saying the 'magic words: political asylum.' . . . The impression given was that people posing a danger to the US could pass by immigration official who were seemingly helpless to stop them."

3. Impact

(a) Denial of due process and judicial review undermines the rule of law.

Anthony Lewis, (Two time Pulitzer Prize winning veteran journalist and weekly columnist for *The New York Times*) "The Rest Is Silence," *The New York Times*, (November 11, 1996): A15.

"That is why it is important to have independent courts review administrative decisions, Judge Kozinski said – especially decisions of this kind, [an asylum case,] which 'can mean the difference between freedom and oppression and, quite possibly, life and death.'

"Judge Kozinski's point about the importance of judicial review drew a further opinion from Judge Reinhardt and the third member of the panel, Judge Michael D. Hawkins. 'We wholeheartedly agree,' they wrote. Without that check, 'grave injustices could take place.'

"The assurance that official orders are subject to review by independent courts is central to the American vision of 'a government of laws, and not of men.' "

(b) It further ensures the unjust return of many legitimate asylum-seekers.

Lawyers Committee for Human Rights, *Is This America? The Denial of Due Process to Asylum Seekers in the United States*, (October 2000): 6.

"An ethnic Albanian student from Kosovo, who had been beaten and imprisoned by Serbian police because of his ethnicity, arrived at a California airport on January 20, 1999. Although he spoke only Albanian, INS inspectors at the airport provided him with a Serbian interpreter, with whom he could not communicate. Despite his attempts to explain his ethnic origin in broken English, the INS inspectors ordered him deported and put him on a plane back to Mexico City where his flight had originated."

Harm B: The INS is abusive toward immigrant detainees.

1. Significance

(a) The INS holds administrative detention immigrants in jails with convicted criminals.

Human Rights Watch, "Human Rights Watch Condemns Detention Practices of INS," www.hrw.org/reports98/us-immig, (September 9, 1998): 1.

"INS detainees are in administrative detention; that is, they are not serving a criminal sentence or awaiting trial on criminal charges. But since the INS has decided to contract with local jails and has refused to insist on separate, special treatment of immigration detainees who are held in these jails, an INS detainee's experience in a local jail is no different from that of a local inmate."

(b) INS detainees in jails account for 60% of total INS administrative detainees.

Human Rights Watch, "Human Rights Watch Condemns Detention Practices of INS,"

"The U.S. Immigration and Naturalization Service (INS) is currently housing more than 60 percent of its 15,000 detainees in local jails throughout the country."

(c) Immigrants seeking asylum from oppressive regimes among those jailed.

Human Rights Watch, "Human Rights Watch Condemns Detention Practices of INS,"

"INS detainees-including asylum seekers-are being held in jails entirely inappropriate to their non-criminal status where they may be mixed with accused and convicted criminal inmates, and where they are sometimes subjected to physical mistreatment and grossly inadequate conditions of confinement. . . .

"Asylum seekers, in particular, are protected by international refugee law and deserving of special treatment. Asylum seekers should never be held in local jails. In fact, international standards urge governments to detain asylum seekers only in exceptional cases. Nevertheless, the INS does not differentiate between asylum seekers and other immigration detainees, and they are sent to jails around the country without regard to their particular legal and psychological needs."

2. Inherency: The INS lacks infrastructure to house administrative detainees in separate facilities.

Human Rights Watch, "Human Rights Watch Condemns Detention Practices of INS,"

"Faced with an overwhelming, immediate demand for detention space, the agency has handed over control of its detainees to local sheriffs and other jail officials without ensuring that basic international and national standards requiring humane treatment and adequate conditions are met."

3. Impact: Immigrants are mistreated in U.S. jails.

> Human Rights Watch, "Human Rights Watch Condemns Detention Practices of INS,"

"Many INS detainees interviewed by Human Rights Watch who were held at local jails have been subjected to physical mistreatment at the hands of correctional officers. In a dramatic case now unfolding, INS detainees held in Jackson County Jail in Florida alleged that jail officials administered electric shocks on shackled detainees in July 1998. Nine guards pleaded guilty or were convicted in 1998 for physically abusing INS detainees held in Union County Jail in New Jersey. INS detainees in local jails in California, Louisiana, New Hampshire, and elsewhere have held hunger strikes during the past year following incidents of alleged mistreatment and to protest poor conditions."

Observation III: Plan

A. Agent: U.S. Congress & President B. Mandates: 1. Repeal portions of the Illegal Immigration Reform and Immigrant Responsibility Act pertaining to: (a) Expedited removal and (b) Mandatory detention. 2. Enact legislation requiring all deportations to be ordered by a judge in Immigration Court and subject to quick appeal and judicial review. 3. Enact legislation requiring a court order to detain aliens subject to timely deportation proceedings. 4. Enact legislation requiring the supervised release of all asylum seekers waiting judicial, refugee status determination proceeding. C. Enforcement: INS and federal judiciary D. Funding: Present and normal budgetary means and process

Observation IV: Advantages

<u>Advantage A</u>: Due process and judicial review will be restored.

(1) Solvency: Past precedent demonstrate that judicial review will restore due process.

> Anthony Lewis, (Two time Pulitzer Prize winning veteran journalist and weekly columnist for *The New York Times*) "The Rest Is Silence," *The New York Times*, (November 11, 1996): A15.

"Because his plea was heard by independent judges, Francisco Rodriguez-Roman[, a Cuban refugee,] will not be sent back to tyranny. Others will not be so fortunate in the future. For Congress, in the immigration bill just enacted, made the decisions of immigration judges in asylum cases final. There will be not review by an independent court."

(2) Significance: The restoration of due process of law and judicial review will ensure that the U.S. remains committed to the rule of law, and not of men.

<u>Advantage B</u>: Asylum-seekers will be appropriately treated. A supervised release program is workable.

> Arthur C. Helton, (Senior fellow, Council on Foreign Affairs), Letter to INS Commissioner Gene McNary, September 9, 1991, as quoted in Amnesty International's *United States of America: Lost in the Labyrinth: Detention of Asylum-Seekers*, (September 1999): 13.

"[A] well conceived and carefully administered release program that works closely with the community can address the government's interests in preventing absconding while targeting for attention those who pose danger to the community as well as avoiding the unnecessary detention of refugees" (internal quotation marks omitted).

Criteria Analysis Sample Case

This is a criteria analysis case. (Value is used instead of criteria in the case, but the value is really another name for criteria.) This case was written and run by Eric Wallace and Courtney Winther from Modesto, California.

The basic claim is that limited government should be valued in agricultural policy. This value/criteria is being violated in three ways: rich farmers receive money from taxpayers, tax revenue is wasted, and poor farmers are hurt by helping larger farms. To solve these harms, elimination of agricultural subsidies and their corresponding taxes is proposed. As with a plan-meets-needs case, the advantages are the direct results of the elimination of the harm(s).

Also note, although most cases cite the resolution, this transcript does not. However, it is highly recommended that you quote the resolution in full in your first speech.

Criteria Analysis cases are discussed on page 116.

During the founding era of our republic, it was assumed that the powers of the federal government should be few and enumerated. To achieve this goal, our founders wanted strict limits on the law-making authority of Congress. Nowhere was Congress or the federal government given the power to take from one citizen solely for the purpose giving to another. This practice, known to economists and political scientists as the "redistribution of wealth" was promoted by Karl Marx, but never by our founding fathers.

It was Thomas Jefferson who wrote that: "[The] policy [of my country] is, to leave their citizens free, neither restraining nor aiding them in their pursuits. Though the interposition of government, in matters of intervention, has its use, yet it is in practice so inseparable from abuse, that they think it better not to meddle with it." While it is permissible for government to tax its citizens for the purpose of purchasing the goods and services it needs to perform its legitimate functions, it is an abuse of law-making to tax for the express purpose of redistribution. Agricultural subsidy programs have brought redistribution of wealth to agriculture and are themselves an icon to limitless law-making. Because of this grievous situation, we will be discussing agricultural subsidies in today's debate. Webster's 1964 dictionary defines agriculture as "The science and art of farming; work of cultivating the soil, producing crops, and raising livestock." Morgan Rose tells us that subsidies are "payments from a government for which it receives no goods or services in return. They are usually provided under the auspices of support for a specific group of people or industry that is seen to be in need of assistance." Throughout this debate, we will uphold the value of limited law-making. Under sub-point one, we find the purpose of government. People create a government when they come together as a common group to defend their life, liberty, and property. The purpose of the government is to use force to defend the people's rights. Frederic Bastiat explains that defense is the only justified use of force both for individuals and the common group, as in government. "Thus, since an individual cannot lawfully use force against the person, liberty, or property of another individual, then the common force—for the same reason--cannot lawfully be used to destroy the person, liberty, or property of individuals or groups." James Madison echoed these boundaries of government in The Federalist, number 54. "Government is instituted no less for the protection of the property, than of the persons of individuals." Under sub-point two, we see that subsidies violate the purpose of government. The familiar refrain "From each according to his ability, to each according to his need" is a perfect characterization of the ideas behind the agricultural subsidy system in America. The idea of taking money from taxpayers for the express purpose of handing it to farmers is a fundamental violation of the purpose of government and an invasion upon the taxpayer's property rights. Morgan Rose, in 2002, explains this violation when he says that giving money to struggling farmers . . . "Seems like a generous thing for the government to do, doesn't it? The problem, of course, is that it is easy to be generous with someone else's money, and all that any government has is someone else's money." The agricultural subsidies in America are a violation of property rights and a redistribution of wealth that is foreign to the principles of limited government on which America was founded. We can see the consequences of this flawed policy in the harms.

Harm 1: Welfare for the Rich

While our stance is that subsidies are an inherent violation of the purpose of government, we can see that subsidies fail at accomplishing even what they were created to do. Agricultural subsidies were instituted for the purpose of giving aid to the needy American farmer. However subsidies have gone to the large and very wealthy individuals and corporations--and even the government itself.

John Kelly reported on September 10, 2001 for the *Associated Press*, that:
"At least 20 Fortune 500 companies and more than 1,200 universities and governmentfarms, including state prisons, received checks from federal programs touted by politicians as a way to prop up needy farmers."

The San Francisco Chronicle said in their editorial on December 20, 2001, "The congressional debate inevitably tends to revolve around the plight of 'family farmers,' but half of all federal payments go to the largest

8 percent of farms." Subsidies are nothing more than money the government pays to itself or those who already have plenty, rather than going to those in want.

Harm 2: Taxdollars Wasted

The cost of subsidy programs has skyrocketed, requiring even more tax dollars every year. The American agricultural subsidies have been built on the back of the American taxpayer.

Chris Edwards and Tad Dehaven from fiscal policy studies at the Cato Institute wrote on October 18, 2001, "Total direct subsidy payments to farmers have soared to more than $20 billion per year the past three years, up from an average of $9 billion per year in the early 1990s. Congress has passed huge supplemental farm bills every year since 1998; the most recent bill, passed in July, has a taxpayer price tag of $5.5 billion." Not only does this simply waste taxpayer's dollars, the effect upon the rest of the economy is dramatic. When the government takes money from taxpayers to support subsidies, the taxpayers can no longer use their money to support other areas of the economy.

Harm 3: Small Farms Destroyed

By giving subsidies to large farms and corporations, they are further empowered to buy-out the smaller competitors-- the small family farms that subsidies were supposed to help. Brian Riedl at the Heritage Foundation wrote on February 5, 2002: "Because the largest, most profitable farms and agribusinesses also receive the lion's share of subsidies, they are able to use their funding to buy out smaller farms. . . . Far from saving the family farms, the current farm subsidy system is destroying them."

Because the weight of these harms demands a solution, we propose the following plan:

Our mandate is to eliminate all federal agricultural subsidies and the corresponding tax dollars taken to support these subsidies. Because our policy calls for the elimination of control, no funding or enforcement will be needed. Our agency is Congress and the President.

Through the adoption of our policy, a number of advantages will result.

Advantage 1: Eliminate Welfare for the Rich

No longer will the government be taking taxpayer money and giving it to the rich. Chris Edwards and Tad Dehaven at the Cato Institute wrote in 2001 "As Congress works to reauthorize farm programs, it threatens to move further away from reform by institutionalizing high levels of farm welfare. Instead, Congress should push the farm sector back into the market economy by repealing federal farm subsidies."

Advantage 2: Elimination of Tax Dollar Waste

By adopting our policy, the wasting of taxpayers' money through agricultural subsidies will be stopped. Chris Edwards and Tad Dehaven wrote "It is not a good deal for U.S. agricultural production to be distorted by such large subsidies, and it is certainly not good deal for U.S. taxpayers who foot the bill. After six decades of government intervention and rising subsidies, it is time for Congress to phase out the farm welfare state."

Advantage 3: Small Farms Preserved

Subsidies empowered the large farms and corporations to take over and destroy small farms. By eliminating subsidies, this power is eliminated as well.

Adam Smith summarized how a just government should operate in a free society when he said: "Every man, as long as he does not violate the laws of justice, is left perfectly free to pursue his own interest his own way, and to bring both his industry and capital into competition with those of any other man…"

While our government has violated our chance as Americans to pursue our own interest, we can restore this opportunity by eliminating the subsidies that our government has placed on agriculture.

Thank you. I am now open for cross-examination.

Comparative Advantage Sample Case

This is a comparative advantage case regarding wetlands. Benjamin and Jonathan Wolfson ran this case for the entire season of 2001-2002.

As you can see, the goals set forth are twofold: reasonable guidelines for wetland regulation and upholding the constitutional standards of property rights. To better achieve these goals, wetlands would be classified by their ecological value, regulations would be reduced on "low-value" wetlands, and compensation, consistent with the 5th Amendment of the Constitution, would be given to owners of wetlands still regulated. This plan claimed two comparative advantages: that wetland regulation would be reasonable and scientific and that constitutional rights to property would be better upheld.

Comparative Advantage cases are discussed on page 117.

In Muncie, Indiana, an 80-year-old farmer who had farmed his entire life on the same farm as his father and grandfather before him, inadvertently broke a water pipe flooding the field. Federal agents arrived and told him he was no longer allowed to farm his farm because it was a "wetland." [CLEAN WATER AMENDMENTS OF 1995 (House of Representatives - May 10, 1995) Representative Shuster of PA.]

A Pennsylvania family was prevented from selling their 127-acre ancestral farm, valued at $190,000, after it was labeled a wetland. The Federal Government offered the family no compensation.

These are only a few [of the many] examples of how honest hard-working Americans can run afoul of our wetlands law.[**HON. JACK FIELDS in the House of Representatives** *TUESDAY, MARCH 16, 1993]*

The current wetland policy applies arbitrary guidelines to all lands regardless of their value to the environment.

This forces farmers, even those with a mere wet spot, to give up the use of their land, which is often their only potential for income.

To make matters even worse, the constitutional rights of landowners, guaranteed by the 5th Amendment, are violated when they lose the right to use their land and they receive no compensation for it.

➤ That is why we stand firmly

> *"Resolved: That the United States should substantially change its federal agricultural policy"*

Before we examine the issue of wetlands, let's define some key terms in

Observation 1, Definitions.

> Substantially is defined by *The American Heritage Dictionary* of the *English Language, Fourth Edition 2000 as:*
> > Considerable in importance, value, degree, amount, or extent: *won by a substantial margin*
> Secretary of Agriculture, Ann Veneman, stated "Contemporary agricultural policy extends well beyond simply price and income support programs. It includes trade, conservation, agricultural research, animal and plant health, food safety and human health and other programs."

Now that the resolution has been clearly defined, let's examine the goals of wetland policy in

Observation 2, Goals

Any good wetland policy must:

1. Provide reasonable guidelines for the purpose of wetland regulation.
2. Uphold Constitutional standards of property rights.

Because these goals are not currently being met, we present

Observation 3, The Plan.

> Congress and the President will enact a law with three mandates which:
1. Classifies wetlands by ecological value for regulation.
2. Requires just compensation at fair market value for all "takings" of private lands for wetland protection. "Takings" are: The transfer of possession or control.
3. Permits the acquisition and full regulation of lands through "takings" only on "class A" wetlands.

Any necessary funding will come from the current United States Department of Agriculture (USDA), Environmental Protection Agency (EPA) and the Army Corps of Engineers budgets for wetland regulation.

> Compensation will cost less than $30 million per year.

The USDA, EPA and the Army Corps will enforce this plan.

> The Heritage Foundation explains:

Wetlands would be divided into classes, such as "A," "B," "C," etc. Government would be authorized to acquire only those with the highest ecological value (class "A"), which would merit the highest degree of protection. Lower categories or classes could be given lesser degrees of protection. (Congressman James Hayes' bill, H.R.1330, would put just such a system into place by dividing wetlands into three categories and requiring payment to affected

landowners in Class "A" wetlands.) This would avoid the inherent waste of spending scarce economic resources on relatively unimportant low-value wetlands and enable the country to target its efforts toward protection of more valuable ecosystems. Moreover, since the government would be obligated to purchase only the highest-valued wetland property, its intrusion into the personal affairs of middle-class Americans would be kept to a minimum.
{The Heritage Foundation. *A Guide to Wetlands Policy and Reauthorization of the Clean Water Act.* By John Shanahan, June 22, 1994. Heritage.org}

We reserve the right to further explain this plan as needed throughout this round.

Once this plan is enacted, the goals of providing reasonable wetland guidelines and upholding constitutional property rights will be more completely upheld.

Observation 4, Advantages explains

Our first advantage is Reasonable Scientific Guidelines.

The guidelines for wetland regulation will be based on scientific ecological value rather then wetness.

Significance Arbitrary Guidelines

Arbitrary guidelines label wetlands illogically

Senator Bennet Johnston explained in 1995:

First, this legislation will require that Federal jurisdictional wetlands be classified into three categories: high-, medium-, and low-valued wetlands , based on the relative wetlands functions present. Today, the section 404 program regulates all wetlands equally rigidly, whether the wetland is a pristine, high-value wetland or a wet spot in a field. This treatment of wetlands defies logic and common sense.
[STATEMENTS ON INTRODUCED BILLS AND JOINT RESOLUTIONS (Senate - October 05, 1994) THE WETLANDS REGULATORY REFORM ACT OF 1995. SENATOR J. BENNET JOHNSTON. Senate 2506]

Inherency No Classification

This problem is inherent in the current wetland policy because wetlands are not classified according to their scientific ecological value, but rather by their wetness.

In 1995, Senator John Breaux stated:

We do not have a wetlands classification system in current law. To be fair and to strike balance and reason in wetlands regulation we must identify and regulate according to the very real differences in wetlands value and function.
[THE WETLANDS REGULATORY REFORM ACT OF 1995 STATEMENTS ON INTRODUCED BILLS AND JOINT RESOLUTIONS (Senate - May 25, 1995) . SENATOR JOHN BREAUX.]

Solvency Reasonable Scientific Guidelines

Reasonable scientific guidelines will both preserve pristine wetlands and allow farmers to use their land.

In 1993, Representative Don Young agreed:

This legislation is a complete overhaul of the 404 program. It starts by expanding the activities that require permits, while protecting traditional exemptions such as farming, ranching, and silviculture. It also recognizes that all wetlands are not of equal value and should not be treated the same. It divides wetlands into three classifications, with varying requirements based on the habitat, water quality characteristics, and flood control qualities of each wetland. This will overcome a significant shortcoming in the existing program by allowing greater protections for those high value wetlands while still allowing for economic growth in this Nation. [HON. DON YOUNG in the House THURSDAY, MARCH 11, 1993 H.R. 1330, THE COMPREHENSIVE WETLANDS CONSERVATION AND MANAGEMENT ACT OF 1993]

Our second advantage is that Constitutional rights are upheld.

Owners of wetlands will have their constitutional rights to property upheld.

Significance Constitution violated

By taking away private property use and refusing to compensate the owner, the current wetland regulation violates our constitutional right to private property.

The Competitive Enterprise Institute echoed this sentiment in 1999:

These regulations deny private landowners the productive use of their land without compensation. These regulations have bankrupted landowners and even sent Americans to jail for the "crime" of wetland modification without a federal permit.
{Competitive Enterprise Institute. Issue Brief: Wetlands. March 1999. CEI.org}

Inherency Government Refuses to compensate

The government does not want to compensate landowners for taking away the use of their land.

The Heritage Foundation explains:

The Administration is on record as opposing payments to landowners whose property is designated a wetland. Office

of Management and Budget Director Leon Panetta says it would be "an unnecessary and unwise use of taxpayer dollars" and <u>a drain on the federal budget.</u> (Speaking at a hearing before the Committee on Public Works and Transportation's Subcommittee on Water Resources and Environment, U.S. House of Representatives, May 26, 1994.) <u>Landowners counter that regulatory takings are a drain on the family budget.</u>
{The Heritage Foundation. *A Guide to Wetlands Policy and Reauthorization of the Clean Water Act.* By John Shanahan, June 22, 1994. Heritage.org}

Solvency <u>**Constitution upheld**</u>
By compensating landowners for the taking of their land when it is a true wetland in need of protection, the Constitution will be better upheld.

In 1994, The Heritage Foundation agreed:
Congress can answer the charges of unfairness by landowners who have seen their life savings destroyed by onerous wetlands regulations simply by requiring the government to pay for the value of the land it takes.
{The Heritage Foundation. *A Guide to Wetlands Policy and Reauthorization of the Clean Water Act.* By John Shanahan, June 22, 1994. Heritage.org}

Once this plan is enacted, the arbitrary guidelines used in labeling wetlands will be replaced by a reasonable scientific classification system and the private property rights guaranteed under the Constitution will be upheld.

Then people like you and I will no longer be left to wonder if property we inherit, like the family in Pennsylvania, will be declared a wetland leaving us to pay taxes on property we can neither use nor sell.

The Heritage Foundation summarized the need for change in 1994:
Although the Clean Water Act never was designed as a vehicle to protect wetlands, it has evolved into a regulatory nightmare for ordinary Americans who simply want to use their land as they intended when they took out a mortgage on their property. If Americans still believe in the basic concepts upon which this nation was built -- liberty, opportunity, and the right to reap the rewards of hard effort -- they must reverse the current wetland policy of essentially confiscating land from the nation's most productive and valuable citizens.
[The Heritage Foundation. *A Guide to Wetlands Policy and Reautorization of the Clean Water Act.* By John Shanahan, June 22, 1994. Heritage.org]

Thank you, I am now open for cross-examination.

Stock Issues Sample Case

This is a stock issues case regarding unilateral sanctions on Africa and the Middle East. Jonathan Krive and Brett Lane ran this case during the 2002-2003 season.

This case goes through the stock issues and presents arguments based on inherency, significance, and solvency using a plan to eliminate unilateral sanctions. Rather than addressing harms and incorporating the stock issues within these harms, this case alters the outline and independently examines each stock issue question.

Stock issues cases are discussed on page 120.

In 432 B.C., the Athenian leader Pericles imposed the first recorded trade sanctions. As a result, Megara, the sanctioned country, appealed to Sparta for aid, resulting in the Peloponnesian War. In 1807, President Jefferson embargoed all U.S. trade with Europe to protest British attacks on U.S. merchant ships. This effort also proved to be an economic disaster. The track record of unilateral trade sanctions only reinforces the fact, which our government has continually ignored: sanctions have failed.

The expression goes, "if at first you don't succeed try-try again." However, the United States Trade Policy has tried, and tried, and tried again, and it still has not succeeded. It is for this reason that my partner and I are firmly resolved that the United States should significantly change it's Trade Policy within one or both of the following areas: the Middle East and Africa.

Before I go any further, I would like to clarify that all terms will be operationally defined by the affirmative team throughout this debate round.

Observation 1: INHERENCY
1) Skewed Favoritism According to the Center for Strategic and International Studies, 1999

The process of formulating and implementing unilateral sanctions, both within the executive branch and the Congress, is inherently skewed in favor of imposing the sanction and, often, doing so quickly with little regard for whether or not the sanction is likely to achieve its intended result. International diplomacy is slow moving and only partially effective at best, which leads to public frustration and the desire to do something more forceful.

The people of the United States demand a trade policy that works. Congress, in order to appease this demand, enacts sanctions that have little of the desired affect. In essence, Congress is implementing a feel-good-policy.

Richard N. Haass, Director of the Foreign Policy Studies program at the Brookings Institution, June 1998

Why, then, is there such a clamor to impose sanctions on South Africa? The answer, as former secretary of defense James R. Schlesinger remarked that sanctions "appeal to Americans because they seem to be a substitute for the stiffer measures that may be required." In short, they are a way of making ourselves feel that we are doing something substantive about a serious problem without really doing anything at all.

The problem is that we are paying a heavy price for invoking this "feel good" policy over and over again.

The status quo is a system based on quick emotions rather than logical analysis of effective policies. Congress has continued the attempt to appease the populous with sanctions.

Observation 2: SIGNIFICANCE
  Point 1) Sanctions: The Foreign Policy Failure Dan Griswold, the CATO institute, May 30th 2002
As well as inflicting economic damage, sanctions have been a foreign policy flop. The Nuclear Proliferation Act of 1994 failed to deter India and Pakistan from testing nuclear weapons in May of 1998. Sanctions have utterly failed to change the nature or basic behavior of governments in Burma, Iran, Nigeria, and a number of other target countries.

  Wall Street Journal, September 11, 1985
No matter how tight the sanctions eventually become against South Africa, they are unlikely to deny that country any essential commodities. As one South African economist recently put it, "Given time, we can probably replace whatever we can't import"
Sanctions have failed time and time again. This failure is not a new phenomenon. But the important question is, "why does this matter?" Why should you judge, care about this foreign policy flop? The following explanations are three reasons why you adopt the affirmative policy.

  Point a) Sanctions Are Economically Devastating
Richard N. Haass, Director of the Foreign Policy Studies program at the Brookings Institution, June 1998

Sanctions can be expensive for American business, farmers, and workers. There is a tendency to overlook or underestimate the direct cost of sanctions, perhaps because their costs do not show up in U.S. government budget tables. Sanctions cost U.S. companies untold billions of dollars a year in lost sales and returns on investment--and costs many thousands of workers their jobs.

The sheer economic devastation caused by our trade policy is staggering. This devastation alone merits a change in our trade policy. The next problem we find is on an international level.

Point b) Hypocritical International Policy

Following the anniversary of September 11, President Bush spoke to a group of United Nations leaders. He stated that something must be done about the Iraqi violations of UN resolutions. In direct defiance of the UN resolution, Iraq was not letting weapons inspectors into the country.

However, when we look at our own trade policy, and our use of trade sanctions, we find that the United States while perhaps on a different level, is also violating UN resolutions. This breach of agreement causes to appear as hypocrites.

UN General Assembly Resolution 44/215 (Dec. 22, 1989).

Countries should refrain from threatening or applying trade and financial restrictions, blockades, embargoes, and other economic sanctions, incompatible with the provisions of the Charter of the United Nations and in violation[thereof], against... countries as a form of political and economic coercion.

The same thing that President Bush pointed out at the UN council is the very thing that the status quo is violating. This is a completely hypocritical policy that deserves notice and deserves change.

The International Economist, 1997

U.S. unilateral sanctions cause damage to foreign relations because they undermine the principles and institutions of economic freedom and international free trade, which have taken years of painstaking effort to construct.

Point c) Innocent Lives Taken Associated Press "Iraq: Sanctions—The Silence Weapon," 8/13/2002

Sanctions are the most brutal form of war because they punish an entire population, targeting helpless children, most of all. Sanctions are a weapon of mass destruction. From 1990, when sanctions were imposed on Iraq until 1995, half a million children under the age of five died of malnutrition and preventable diseases.

Sanctions promote the loss of innocent life. Some might say that the United States is not responsible for these deaths; That Saddam is starving his people.

Mr. Nafeez Ahmed, a political analyst and human rights activist based in London. He is Director of the Institute for Policy Research & Development and a Researcher at the Islamic Human Rights Commission, October 30, 2001

Recently released internal U.S. Defense Intelligence Agency (DIA) documents reveal that the United States anticipated the dire civilian health consequences of destroying Iraq's drinking water and sanitation systems in the Gulf War. The documents also illustrate U.S. awareness that sanctions would lead to the inevitable destruction of the Iraqi water system, resulting in a devastating humanitarian crisis for the Iraqi people.

We knew. The United States government knew that sanctions would be the death of hundreds of thousands of children, that it would destroy innocent lives. This kind of human slaughter must end immediately. Change must come now.

Observation 3: PLAN/SOLVENCY

Because of the three devastating consequences of sanctions, my partner and I present to you the following plan. - The use of unilateral trade sanctions will be eliminated, except in the use of arms transfers.

Agency: Congress

Enforcement: US Inspector General's Office and the Federal Trade Commission

Lastly, Observation 4: Solvency

According to The International Economist, 1997

The U.S. should resist employing the blunt weapons of economic sanctions when more refined tools exist that can achieve our ends more effectively and with less damage to our own interests.

By rejecting change, we can 'try again,' See how many more times we can fail; or we can come to the realization that sanctions have never and will never work. They will only harm American citizens and the citizens of the targeted countries. As American's we need to stop this feel-good policymaking and look at the actual repercussions of our actions, actions of hypocrisy, actions of devastation, actions that kill.

Whole Resolution Sample Case

This is a whole resolution case regarding United States trade policy with Africa and the Middle East. Jonathan Krive and Brett Lane ran this case during the 2002-2003 season.

This case is unique in comparison to many other cases. Instead of focusing on one or two specific areas to change, this case questions the truth of the resolution. The ultimate question at the end of the round is: "Is the resolution true?" The affirmative presents different examples of problems with the status quo (in this case 5) and then simply argues that a change ought to be made which would result in advantages.

Whole resolution cases are discussed on page 121.

"The increased role of international trade, much like the effects of a major new technology, presents opportunities for many people and problems for some. A confident nation should welcome this change --not passively, but by addressing the conditions that contribute to the selective problems and the major problems of our current policies."

This statement by William A. Niskanen, Chairman of the Cato Institute, explains the reason we are here today: to address the problems in our Trade Policies with the Middle East and Africa. The affirmative team stands **resolved** that the United States should significantly change its trade policy within one or both of the following areas: the Middle East and Africa.

In order to justify this resolution, we will identify a number of reasons why change is warranted. Debaters refer to this type of case as a Whole Resolutional Affirmative case. Alfred C. Snyder, Professor of Forensics at the University of Vermont says that a Whole Resolutional case is a generic debate argument which says that the resolution must be debated in a holistic manner to determine its probable truth.

In other words, this debate will center on the resolution as a whole, and at the end of the debate you the judge, will be asked to agree or disagree with the resolution as a whole.

Our current trade policy allows the following five problems:

1) Aids Atrocities

The status quo is not amiable to the current AIDS situation in Africa. Consider what Toby Kasper, an HIV treatment educator and Access Campaign Coordinator in Cape Town, South Africa said in March 1999,"Two countries have attempted to bring HIV treatments down to affordable levels via compulsory licensing, but stiff American opposition has blocked these efforts… The U.S. again imposed trade sanctions when South Africa tried to codify the principles of compulsory licensure in a revision of its national Medicines Act."

Our trade policy is not conducive to helping the African people. According to Newsweek in July 2001, "With 15,000 people contracting HIV every day, even a partially effective immunization could work wonders."

2) Failed Unilateral Sanctions

US trade policy has continued to implement unilateral sanctions despite the overwhelming evidence that unilateral sanctions fail. According to Dan Griswold, from the CATO institute, May 30th 2002, "As well as inflicting economic damage, sanctions have been a foreign policy flop. Sanctions have utterly failed to change the nature or basic behavior of governments in Burma, Iran, Nigeria, and a number of other target countries."

As Richard N. Haass, Director of the Foreign Policy Studies program at the Brookings Institution said, In short, sanctions are a way of making ourselves feel that we are doing something substantive about a serious problem without really doing anything at all.

The problem is, unilateral sanctions have not only failed, but they have also damaged the United States. Richard Haass goes on to say, "The problem is that we are paying a heavy price for invoking this "feel good" policy over and over again." Sanctions cost U.S. companies untold billions of dollars a year in lost sales and returns on investment--and costs many thousands of workers their jobs. Furthermore sanctions have also brutally damaged the target population, without hurting the repressive government.

Former U.S. Attorney General Ramsey Clark, UN Security Council | 1998
"Economic sanctions are weapons of mass destruction directed at a whole people. While the entire people is punished by their economic impact, the greatest harm is overwhelmingly on the poorest and weakest—infants, children, the chronically ill, and the elderly. There is no crueler violation of fundamental human rights than this sanctions policy."

3) Arms Transfers to Enemies

While our trade policy may have the intention of aiding nations through weapons trade, our policy has allowed trade with undemocratic regimes and human rights violators. According to William D. Hartung, the Director of the Institute's Arms Trade Resource Center, at the Center for International Policy in Feb 2001, "54% of U.S. arms transfers to the developing world went to undemocratic governments with severe human rights violations, representing total transfers of $5.8 billion to these regimes in one year."

Because of the loopholes in our Arms Transfer laws, often our own weapons come back to haunt us.

The World Policy Institute in New York reported in February 2001, "Many of the high-profile terrorist acts against U.S. facilities and U.S. citizens in recent years-including the terror bombings of the World Trade Center, the U.S. embassies in Kenya and Tanzania, and the recent attack on the USS Cole in Yemen-can be traced back to networks of Afghani "freedom fighters" who received much of their training and many of their weapons at U.S. taxpayer expense during the 1980s."

4) Supporting Slavery

I think the Global Exchange Newsletter best described our status quo in the winter of 2002, it says, "When most people bite into a candy bar, it is unlikely that they take even a moment to consider where the chocolate they enjoy comes from. If they knew, it probably wouldn't taste as sweet. In 1998, an investigation by the International Labor Organization (ILO), a UN agency, uncovered a reemergence of child slavery in the cocoa fields of the Ivory Coast, where 43 percent of the world's cocoa comes from. Two years later, a report by the US State Department concluded that in recent years approximately 15,000 children aged 9 to12 have been sold into forced labor on cotton, coffee and cocoa plantations in the north of the country. At the beginning of the 21st century, the children of West Africa are trapped in conditions that were supposed to have been eliminated in the 19th century."

The status quo allows for the support of child slavery. The New York Post summarized May 10th 2001, "Forty percent of cocoa products imported by U.S. manufacturers comes from the Ivory Coast, where agricultural slavery and child trafficking is widespread."

Not only does our trade policy support child slavery, but our current policy also supports terrorism.

5) Trade Sponsored Terrorism

While US trade policy doesn't directly support terrorism through trade, several policy loopholes allow our money to go to the very people that our nation is warring against.

The Wall Street reported on Journal Jan 24, 2002, 'Wadih el Hage, who was convicted last year of conspiracy in connection with the 1998 bombings of U.S. embassies in Kenya and Tanzania, provides the strongest documentary evidence to date of al Qaeda's involvement in the tanzanite trade."

These five problems exemplify the reasons that our policy needs to be changed. Because action must be taken, my partner and I present the following plan:

Mandate that:

The United States WILL significantly change its trade policy within one or both of the following areas: The Middle East and Africa.

Congress and the President will serve as our **agency** to pass this plan. And it will be **funded** by the General Congressional Budget or other normal means.

Solvency: All 5 of the harms we identified require a significant change to trade policy with in the Middle East or Africa. Once action is taken, each and every one of these harms can be solved.

Change is justified. The status quo is inherently flawed. I ask you to consider our proposition and bring much needed change to trade policy by agreeing with and **affirming** the resolution.

Index

Notes

Made in the USA
Monee, IL
11 September 2023

42579563R00114